African Americans Against

African Americans Against the Bomb

Nuclear Weapons, Colonialism,
and the Black Freedom Movement

Vincent J. Intondi

Stanford University Press
Stanford, California

Stanford University Press
Stanford, California

Printed in the United States of America on acid-free, archival-quality paper

Library of Congress Cataloging-in-Publication Data
Intondi, Vincent J., author.
 African Americans against the bomb : nuclear weapons, colonialism, and the Black freedom movement / Vincent J. Intondi.
     pages cm.— (Stanford nuclear age series)
 Includes bibliographical references and index.
 ISBN 978-0-8047-8942-4 (cloth : alk. paper)—ISBN 978-0-8047-9275-2 (pbk. : alk. paper)
  1. African American political activists—History—20th century. 2. African Americans—Politics and government—20th century. 3. Antinuclear movement—United States—History—20th century.
4. Civil rights movements—United States—History—20th century. 5. Anti-imperialist movements—United States—History—20th century. 6. United States—Politics and government—1945-1989. I. Title.
II. Series: Stanford nuclear age series.
 E185.61.I64 2014
 323.1196'0730904—dc23
                                                                                            2014031670
 ISBN 978-0-8047-9348-3 (electronic)
 Designed by Bruce Lundquist
 Typeset by Classic Typography in 10.25/15 Brill

For Natalie

Contents

Acknowledgments

IN THE SUMMER OF 2005, I MADE MY FIRST TRIP TO HIROSHIMA as part of American University's Nuclear Studies Institute. Up to that point, my research had focused primarily on African American history. However, I was not prepared for the impact the atomic bomb survivors would have on my life. Hearing the testimony of Koko Kondo and witnessing firsthand what my country had done, I returned determined to continue studying the effects of nuclear weapons. Soon after, I met with Peter Kuznick, director of the Nuclear Studies Institute, and explained my desire to now focus on both African American history and the bomb. Peter asked one question: "What did African Americans think of Truman's decision?" It was finding the answer to that question which ultimately led to this book.

This entire journey began at SUNY Oswego, a small state school in upstate New York whose history department remains a hidden gem. Attending SUNY Oswego, I was fortunate to have the support and guidance of Gerry Forbes, Judith Wellman, and David Conrad. I am deeply thankful to David. Even as the years passed, while I was in Washington and he in Africa, David's words of encouragement always reached my inbox at the right moments. He was one of the first scholars to put me on this path, and I truly appreciate all he has done to make this possible.

American University's history department is what ultimately brought me to the nation's capital. Beyond that department, I would also like to acknowledge American University's College of Arts and Sciences for providing the fellowships and support that provided much-needed sustenance throughout this process. Eileen Findlay and Alan Kraut deserve special thanks for extending my thinking and for their expansive scholarship, generous natures, and insightful advice. They are not just brilliant scholars. They are great people.

Librarians and archivists at many institutions assisted my research efforts. Thank you to Wendy Chmielewski and the staff at the Swarthmore College Peace

Collection, and to Clement Ho at American University, for your constant assistance and expertise.

Many scholars and individuals have publicly supported my work and believed this book should be published. Tom Hayden, Daniel Ellsberg, Oliver Stone, Gerald Horne, and Derek Turner have all helped in their own way to get this book out, and I am truly thankful. Martin Sherwin and Carol Anderson are two scholars who also deserve special thanks and praise. Marty and Carol supported my work from the beginning, made it known, and were willing to fight to make this book a reality. Their scholarship helped make this book stronger. Their passion for my work helped get it published.

I would also like to thank Lisa Stokes, Danny Gilmartin, Marilyn Wells, and Bobby Bell at Seminole State College. Being able to walk down the hall every day, pop into Danny's office, and discuss my work, with John Coltrane playing in the background, meant more to me than he will ever know. In addition, I am thankful for my current home, Montgomery College. Teaching at a school where you cannot wait to arrive each morning, receive constant support from colleagues and staff, and have the opportunity to teach some of the most amazing students in the world made all the difference throughout this process.

Were it not for my close friends, who always knew when to make me laugh, when to offer words of encouragement, and who constantly reminded me to keep my eye on the prize, this book may not have been completed. A special thanks to Eric Singer, Paul Detor, Chris Ruding, Liam and Shannon Delaney, John and Laurie Chappell, Robert Williams, and Daniel Persons.

Fellow historian David Ekbladh deserves a special mention. Even with two little ones at home and with his own research work, no matter when the phone rang or e-mail arrived David never hesitated to offer guidance. His knowledge of the craft makes him a treasure, not only for Tufts but for the entire academy. He is a dear friend to whom I am deeply thankful.

Peter Kuznick was the foremost reason I chose to study at American University. Peter has taught me more about the profession and writing than any other individual. While I am enormously grateful for Peter's unwavering belief in me as a scholar and activist, it is his constant example of a professional, dedicated historian who fights for change that I most appreciate. His commitment to students, scholarship, and to ensuring the world is free of nuclear weapons is truly inspiring. I will never be able to thank Peter enough for his continued passion for my work—even when *The Untold History of the United States* avalanche hit.

It is unlikely that this book would have been published without my family. I am grateful for all the Skype sessions with my cousin John Pitonzo in Florence. John's expertise in Shakespeare undoubtedly made this book stronger as he edited my work. Special thanks to my sister, niece, brother-in-law, and grandparents who all reminded me throughout the years what is truly important and never doubted this day would arrive.

Most especially, I would like to thank my parents, the two most important people in my life. I cannot begin to describe their patience, compassion, love, and willingness to sacrifice so that I could complete this book. I am eternally grateful and proud to call them Mom and Dad.

Besides my parents, no single person deserves more credit for making this book happen than my wife, Natalie. I honestly cannot put into words my gratitude for her willingness, since we first met, to sacrifice as I wrote, edited, rewrote, and reedited. Her smile, laugh, strength, and courage are what got me to this point. Every day I am awed by her good nature, huge heart, and love for humanity. For me the sun rises and sets with her, which is why it is to her that this book is dedicated.

African Americans Against the Bomb

Introduction

IN AUGUST 1945, ONLY A FEW DAYS AFTER THE UNITED STATES dropped two atomic bombs destroying the Japanese cities of Hiroshima and Nagasaki, the Reverend J.E. Elliott, pastor of St. Luke Chapel, stepped up to the pulpit and began his Sunday sermon. The pastor condemned the use of atomic bombs in Japan and suggested that racism played a role in President Truman's decision. "I have seen the course of discrimination throughout the war and the fact that Japan is of a darker race is no excuse for resorting to such an atrocity," Elliott said.[1]

Twenty-three years later, on February 6, 1968, Dr. Martin Luther King, Jr., also stepped up to the pulpit to warn against the use of nuclear weapons. Addressing the second mobilization of the Clergy and Laymen Concerned About Vietnam, King urged an end to the war, and warned that if the United States used nuclear weapons in Vietnam the earth would be transformed into an inferno that "even the mind of Dante could not envision."[2] Then, as he had done so many times before, King made clear the connection between the black freedom struggle in America and the need for nuclear disarmament:

> These two issues are tied together in many, many ways. It is a wonderful thing to work to integrate lunch counters, public accommodations, and schools. But it would be rather absurd to work to get schools and lunch counters integrated and not be concerned with the survival of a world in which to integrate. And I am convinced that these two issues are tied inextricably together and I feel that the people who are working for civil rights tare working for peace; I feel that the people working for peace are working for civil rights and justice.[3]

Almost fifteen years later, on June 12, 1982, nearly one million activists and concerned citizens gathered in New York City for what became known as the largest antinuclear demonstration in the history of the United States.[4] A large contingent of minority groups organized under the Reverend Herbert Daughtry's

National Black United Front was among the thousands of protesters. Marching through Harlem, these activists, including prominent African Americans Harry Belafonte, Chaka Kahn, Toni Morrison, Ossie Davis, and Ruby Dee, demanded an end to the nuclear arms race and a shift from defense spending to helping the poor. When asked why they were marching, Dick Gregory responded, "to write the unwritten page of the Constitution, dealing with the right to live free from nuclear terror."[5]

From 1945 onward, many in the African American community actively supported nuclear disarmament, even when the cause was abandoned by other groups during the McCarthy era. This allowed the fight to abolish nuclear weapons to reemerge powerfully in the 1970s and beyond. Black leaders never gave up the nuclear issue or failed to see its importance; by doing so, they broadened the black freedom movement and helped define it in terms of global human rights.

African Americans Against the Bomb examines those black activists who fought for nuclear disarmament, often connecting the nuclear issue with the fight for racial equality and with liberation movements around the world. Beginning with the atomic bombings of Hiroshima and Nagasaki, this book explores the shifting response of black leaders and organizations, and of the broader African American public, to the evolving nuclear arms race and general nuclear threat throughout the postwar period. For too long scholars, viewing slavery, Jim Crow, and the Civil Rights Movement as national phenomena, have failed to appreciate the black freedom struggle's international dimensions. Because of the understandable focus on African Americans' unique oppression, historians have often entirely ignored African American responses when addressing other important issues, such as the nuclear threat. This omission comes despite the fact that African Americans, as part of the larger human community, have as great a stake as any other group of citizens. In fact, given the increasing urban concentration of African Americans, they face a greater risk when it comes to nuclear war and terrorism than do other groups.

The question of how African Americans have responded to nuclear issues is therefore of great historical consequence. Did African Americans respond differently to the atomic bombings of Hiroshima and Nagasaki compared to other Americans, and if so, to what extent was this related to the fact that the victims were nonwhite? Did African Americans' discrimination-induced estrangement from American life allow for a more critical attitude toward the Cold War, and U.S. nuclear policy in particular? Did the left-oriented social and political activism inspired by black Popular Front groups translate into a broader critique of U.S. militarism and foreign policy, both of which were undergirded by the American nuclear arsenal?

While African Americans immediately condemned the atomic bombings of Hiroshima and Nagasaki, not all of the activists protested for the same reason. For some, race was the issue. Many in the black community agreed with Langston Hughes's assertion that racism was at the heart of Truman's decision to use nuclear weapons in Japan. Why did the United States not drop atomic bombs on Italy or Germany, Hughes asked.[6] Black activists' fear that race played a role in the decision to use atomic bombs only increased when the United States threatened to use nuclear weapons in Korea in the 1950s and in Vietnam a decade later. For others, mostly black leftists ensconced in Popular Front groups, the nuclear issue was connected to colonialism. From the United States' obtaining uranium from the Belgian-controlled Congo to France's testing a nuclear weapon in the Sahara, activists saw a direct link between those who possessed nuclear weapons and those who colonized the nonwhite world. However, for many ordinary black citizens, fighting for nuclear disarmament simply translated into a more peaceful world. The bomb, then, became the link that connected all of these issues and brought together musicians, artists, peace activists, leftists, clergy, journalists, and ordinary citizens inside the black community.

Examining the role of black antinuclear activists is part of a larger narrative that challenges the idea that the black freedom struggle was an isolated movement in a narrowly defined set of years. The past two decades have seen a rise in new scholarship that challenges the accepted narrative of the black freedom movement. Historians have begun to rediscover the forgotten history of black Popular Front groups, Communist Party members and labor organizers, as well as anticolonial and peace activists. A number of these studies suggest that the black freedom movement's origins date back to the 1930s and 1940s, were much more global in scope, and were influenced by those who consistently combined their plight with those seeking peace and an end to colonialism.[7] From the Italo-Ethiopian War of 1935 to the Bandung Conference twenty years later, historians have convincingly shown that black activists consistently connected foreign affairs to their struggle for freedom, often demonstrating an anticolonial and Pan-African perspective. Scholars have reexamined the roots of black radicalism and by doing so have taken African Americans out of the neat categorical boxes in which they were trapped for so many years and have offered a history of the black freedom movement that is much more complex. As Jason Parker explains, scholarship on colonization and the black freedom struggle has "coalesced into a synthesis of international history," and it is important to examine these subjects through a lens of a "global race revolution."[8] How then does the inclusion of black antinuclear activism alter or reaffirm this emerging narrative?

While scholars have provided a valuable service by shedding light on these connections, many have failed to appreciate the role of nuclear weapons. From 1945, the bomb is what in many cases connected various groups and individuals inside the black community. Nuclear disarmament was a main part of the platform at the Bandung Conference in 1955. In the middle of the Civil Rights Movement, Bayard Rustin led a team in Ghana to stop the French from testing a nuclear weapon in the Sahara. Two years later, Kwame Nkrumah, joined by African American activists, held the "World Without the Bomb" conference. Dr. King began connecting the nuclear issue to black freedom as early as 1957. Therefore the role of the bomb is essential when examining the length and scope of the black freedom movement.

Throughout this new line of study scholars continue to disagree as to the length and influence of black radical activism. Historian Robbie Lieberman contends that Joseph McCarthy's anticommunist crusade dramatically stymied black leftists' progress and thus broke the chain connecting the black freedom movement to peace and colonialism, causing it to largely disappear. Clearly McCarthyism was a major factor in the decline of activists working within Popular Front or peace groups. The federal government targeted black leftists like W.E.B. Du Bois and Paul Robeson, and as anticommunism swept through the country many activists fell silent or disavowed their earlier actions. Indeed, Lieberman concludes that not until the late 1960s did activists once again connect the black freedom movement to peace.[9] Brenda Gayle Plummer disagrees, contending that "militant international racial discourse" continued even after the purges of the "conventional Left" in the 1950s. In examining black antinuclear activism, I am suggesting that while connections between the black freedom movement and peace were damaged, they were not completely severed. Rather, there was a consistent voice inside the black community making the case that freedom, peace, and colonialism were links in the same chain. At times the voice was faint, at other times quite loud, but it was always present.[10]

As Carol Anderson and Mary Dudziak have shown, this was in part due to the fact that liberals also continued to speak out against colonialism past the 1950s.

Parker agrees, arguing that the links survived the "anticommunist witch hunters" of the 1950s. This was largely because the nuclear issue resonated in both liberal and radical circles. Beyond the "usual suspects," artists, clergy, and ordinary citizens cared deeply about nuclear disarmament. Therefore, these connections do not disappear in the 1950s as some have suggested. Indeed, by focusing on the bomb, it is clear that they not only remained but in some ways strengthened throughout the 1980s and into the present day.[11]

While this is not the first book to address black activists' participation in the Peace Movement and foreign affairs, my intent is to focus on the role nuclear weapons played in linking these issues together. The black freedom struggle cannot be properly understood without exploring antinuclear campaigns. African Americans' views of nuclear weapons directly influenced their response to other international issues. Therefore, examining the African American response to the nuclear threat will not only add to the rich body of scholarship dedicated to African Americans and global affairs, but will alter the way we discuss these subjects.

African Americans Against the Bomb explains how the fight for freedom, coupled with the desire to avoid nuclear annihilation, blended together and united human beings. Connecting racial equality to nuclear disarmament and colonialism broadened the black freedom struggle, specifically the modern Civil Rights Movement. This book focuses on those activists who refused to stay quiet and continued to fight for freedom and nuclear disarmament when they had much to lose. It discusses those African Americans who joined with nonwhite peoples around the world in an effort to save humanity. From Du Bois to King, and Harold Washington to Barack Obama, this is a study of those in the black community who believed that equality, liberation, and a world free of nuclear weapons were, and would remain, links in the same chain.

African Americans' initial response to the atomic bombings of Hiroshima and Nagasaki was quite different from that of the general public. Chapter 1 traces the reactions of black activists, organizations, journalists, and others to the atomic bombings. Historians have compiled polls, surveys, and data to analyze Americans' reactions to the atomic bombings. Some data account for racial differences; however, no one has explored the response of the black church, press, entertainment industry, or ordinary black citizens. This chapter also begins to examine black leftists like Du Bois and Robeson who worked for nuclear disarmament through the new communist-led peace movement, analyzing how this affected the black freedom movement and the political landscape of the late 1940s.

Chapters 2 and 3 detail black antinuclear activism throughout the 1950s. With the early 1950s came the rise of McCarthyism. Antinuclear became synonymous with pro-communism. However, black leftists refused to remain silent on the nuclear issue and they were not alone. Throughout the black community, citizens were protesting the use of nuclear weapons. They were not motivated by a directive from Moscow but, with the start of the Korean War, by fear that nuclear weapons would again be used on a "darker nation." As the 1950s progressed, the connections between peace, colonialism, and freedom did not cease. Chapter 3 reviews black participation in new antinuclear groups like the Committee for Non-Violent Action (CNVA) and the Committee for a Sane Nuclear Policy (SANE), and details Bayard Rustin's leading a team, including Kwame Nkrumah and William Sutherland, in Africa to stop the French from testing a nuclear weapon. Perhaps no other event more clearly illustrates the connections between colonialism, civil rights, and nuclear weapons than the Sahara Project.

Dr. Martin Luther King, Jr., began connecting nuclear disarmament to black freedom in the late 1950s. Chapter 4 challenges those scholars who suggest that King did not combine peace and freedom until 1967 when he spoke out against the war in Vietnam. This chapter also focuses on those African American activists who again witnessed the United States wage war on a "darker nation," threaten to use nuclear weapons, and at the same time continue to deny African Americans equality at home. These activists included a number of black women who began to make their voices heard as members of the Women's International League for Peace and Freedom and of Women Strike for Peace. Throughout the 1950s and 1960s, Coretta Scott King, Lorraine Hansberry, Erna Harris, and others traveled around the world attending disarmament conferences, even confronting the Pope, to achieve nuclear disarmament. This chapter considers the impact of these women, along with Dr. King and others, who not only spoke out vociferously against the Vietnam War but also criticized U.S. foreign policy and the use of nuclear weapons.

Following the Vietnam War, many black activists saw a direct link between presidents Carter's and Reagan's increased spending for nuclear weapons and the elimination of funds for social programs that most benefited the poor. As antinuclear activism reached new heights in the 1980s, black participation was also at an all-time high. Black politicians, athletes, activists, entertainers, and clergy consistently made the case that Reagan's nuclear ambitions negatively affected their community. These men and women not only participated in antinuclear events but in some cases took the lead in the movement to ban the bomb. Again the black freedom movement was connected to issues of peace and colonialism. Again the bomb was the key link in that chain. The book concludes by analyzing whether President Obama's policies have strengthened or weakened the chances for global human rights and a world free of nuclear weapons.

Chapter 1

The Response to the Atomic Bombings of Hiroshima and Nagasaki

Are we to show our strength in guns and tanks—in atom bombs? Or, in food for the hungry, plows to till the field, and in bringing peace to men of good will?

—Mary McLeod Bethune, 1947

AS WORD SPREAD THAT PRESIDENT TRUMAN had instructed Emperor Hirohito to surrender, Chicago's South Side erupted in approval. "I'm the happiest woman in the world," exclaimed Mary Johnson, an African American South Sider. On August 18, 1945, the *Chicago Defender* declared, "America Hails End of War!" stating, "Everywhere Negro Americans welcomed the victory." The *New York Amsterdam News* reported, "Harlem exploded with uncurbed joy upon hearing of Japan's surrender." In Pittsburgh, Laura Dillard sat on her stoop watching the V-J Day parade pass by. She exulted, "The prayers of the righteous bear fruit." Described by the *Pittsburgh Courier* as representative of the "old South and new East," Dillard said, "Maybe I'm not so righteous, but I have prayed for peace ever since the war started. We have all prayed . . . and our prayers have at last been answered."[1] Throughout the country, it appeared that African Americans shared the same joyous response as most of the American public upon hearing the news that Japan had surrendered.

Much of the black community's enthusiastic support for the war, however, came from a hope that African Americans' loyalty, ability, and overall contribution to the war effort would be recognized and rewarded with progress toward gaining full equality. Many black soldiers shared these hopes. In March 1943, 42 percent of black soldiers thought they would be better off when they left the army. The same percentage foresaw better treatment for all African Americans after the war, with 43 percent anticipating "more rights and privileges." One soldier commented, "If we lose, the Negro's lot can't improve; but if we win there is a chance." Another declared, "By virtue of our valor, courage, and patriotism, things will be better for the Negro."[2]

African American journalists even highlighted black scientists' contribution to the atomic bomb to bolster the case for equality. On August 18, the *Courier*'s headline read, "Negro Scientists Played Important Role in Atomic Bomb

Development." The *Defender* also published a front-page article bearing the headline "Negro Scientists Help Produce 1st Atom Bomb." The *Washington Afro-American* announced that seven thousand black workers at Oak Ridge, Tennessee, had assisted in creating the atomic bomb; the article included photos of black men and women working in the plants.[3] In each story, though, the writers reserved praise for the workers, not the bomb. The *Courier* published biographies of black chemists who had contributed to the development of the bomb. Journalists stressed the scientists' education levels and ability to work side by side with white scientists. Writing for the *Atlanta Daily World*, the Reverend John C. Wright pointed out that black scientists who worked on the bomb were equal to whites in "scholastic backgrounds, research experience, and in the type of contribution they made to the project." These men had become "masters in the fields of mathematics, chemistry, and physics, and showed the true potential of a liberal education from Negro Colleges and Universities in the South." The *Norfolk Journal and Guide* described Dr. Ernest Wilkins, an African American chemist, as a "wizard of mathematics," who received his PhD at nineteen and was recruited by the government from Tuskegee to work full time on the atomic bomb.[4] Commenting on the level of black participation, Private First Class Jimmy Williams, in a letter to the editor, wrote: "We can truthfully say that the making of it [the atomic bomb] was in the hands of the Negro. In other things that we have accomplished why are we so still denied our advantages?"[5]

The black press also highlighted African Americans' role in protecting classified information about the atomic bomb. The *Courier* reported that twenty-three African Americans were working for the Atomic Energy Commission (AEC) and an additional "nine carefully selected Negroes" were in charge of guarding the building, safes, vaults, and confidential file cabinets of the AEC. The nine guards, veterans of both world wars, were described as "the sole custodians of the world's top secrets." Again, journalists reserved praise for the workers, not the bomb, calling them "the cream-of-the-crop personnel staff of Negro employees." The *Courier* made clear that African Americans worked with whites, sharing the same locker room, and the atmosphere was "completely free of segregation." The government's hiring of African Americans showed "color was not an important factor" in a job that required loyalty and trust, the *Courier* concluded.[6]

The Criticism Begins

Most Americans justified the atomic bombings, many seeing them as revenge for Pearl Harbor. While many white Americans differentiated between Nazis and

Germans, fascists and Italians, when it came to Japan, the entire country was responsible for Pearl Harbor. Historian John Dower explains that following the bombing of Pearl Harbor a majority of Americans developed a genocidal race hatred toward the Japanese. Ronald Takaki agrees, arguing that the anger over Pearl Harbor "aroused a national bloodthirstiness that seemed unquenchable until the enemy had been totally vanquished." In January 1945 *Newsweek* reported, "Never before has the nation fought a war in which our troops so hate the enemy and want to kill him." Indeed, a motto of the U.S. Marines stated, "Remember Pearl Harbor— keep'em dying." Admiral William Halsey, commander of the South Pacific Force, gave his men a direct and simple message: "Kill Japs, kill Japs, kill more Japs."[7]

The U.S. military, press, and public at large routinely described the Japanese as apes, gorillas, "yellow monkeys," demons, savages, subhumans, and beasts. General Joseph Stilwell wrote his wife, "When I think of how these bowlegged cockroaches have ruined our calm lives it makes me want to wrap Jap guts around every lamppost in Asia." *Time* magazine declared, "The ordinary unreasoning Jap is ignorant. Perhaps he is human. Nothing . . . indicates it."[8] These attitudes help explain why less than a week after the atomic bombings, a Gallup poll showed that 85 percent of respondents approved of Truman's decision to use the atomic bomb. Two months later, a Roper poll reported the following results when Americans were asked which of four statements best expressed their opinion about the dropping of atomic bombs on Japan.

1. We should not have used any atomic bomb at all: 4.5%
2. We should have dropped one first on some unpopulated region, to show the Japanese its power, and dropped the second one on a city only if they hadn't surrendered after the first one: 13.8%
3. We should have used the two bombs on cities, just as we did: 53.5%
4. We should have quickly used many more of the bombs before Japan had a chance to surrender: 22.7%
5. Don't know: 5.5%

Historian Lawrence Wittner notes that no poll in late 1945 ever revealed more than 4.5 percent of respondents being opposed to the use of atomic bombs under any circumstances, concluding that after four years of war one out of four Americans' primary concern was not to secure surrender, but to kill as many Japanese as possible.[9]

While much of the general public celebrated Truman's decision, a smaller number immediately condemned the use of atomic bombs in Hiroshima and

Nagasaki. Some were members of traditional peace groups, such as the Women's International League for Peace and Freedom (WILPF). Others came from the religious community, like the Catholic Church and the Fellowship of Reconciliation (FOR). However, atomic scientists were among the earliest and most vociferous critics of the bomb.[10]

In November 1945, atomic scientists formed the Federation of Atomic Scientists (FAS). A month later, the FAS reorganized itself into the Federation of American Scientists and created the National Committee on Atomic Information (NCAI), an umbrella group that brought together labor, religious, educational, and professional organizations. The FAS distributed educational information to libraries, scientific organizations, and the media, including the *Bulletin of Atomic Scientists*, which became the definitive source for antinuclear information.[11] Like many atomic scientists, Jasper Jeffries, an African American physicist and member of the Atomic Scientists of Chicago, believed that a world government through the United Nations was necessary to deal with the challenges of the nuclear age. He envisioned international control as the only safeguard against atomic energy coming under the control of national militaries. Without control, he warned, there would ultimately be a "mad race to arm with atomic weapons." However, Jeffries concluded the best way to ensure peaceful uses of atomic energy was to "banish war entirely."[12]

Jeffries was not alone. Inside black communities, pastors, poets, intellectuals, artists, and musicians condemned the atomic bombings and immediately criticized Truman's decision to use nuclear weapons. Many of these men and women were not lifelong peace activists, and for the first time they began to view colonialism, racism, and the bomb as links in the same chain.

African Americans were among the first to envision what historian Peter Kuznick refers to as the "apocalyptic narrative."[13] In late August, Gordon Hancock, a columnist for the *Atlanta Daily World*, warned readers that with the development of the atomic bomb, life on earth will "eventually be totally destroyed . . . Mankind will be the loser in the great game of human destructiveness." He argued that unless mankind had a moral awakening, "we are all doomed." Atomic weapons had made the world a "slaughter pen," as children would be "snatched from their mothers' knees to face a horrible destruction." Hancock predicted that "wicked men" and the "science of human destruction" would end the world in the "twinkle of an eye."[14] William Fowlkes, managing editor and columnist for the *World*, described the atomic bomb as "a ghastly war weapon." He told his readers that the atomic bombings left him with "a new horror of the future of mankind and respect for the Biblical Revelations of the destruction of earth's creatures and their creations by man himself."[15] A few days after the atomic bombings, the *Defender* warned, "When the frightful horror and devastation of the new atomic bomb was unleashed on Japan, that shock was not only felt in Hiroshima but in every city and hamlet throughout the world. A tremor of foreboding fear must have shaken the spirits of men everywhere—an awesome dread lest this most formidable weapon of destruction turn out to be a Frankenstein to be turned against its democratic creators at some future date."[16] An editorial in the *Washington Afro-American* explained, "Each time a new weapon of offense is developed it becomes necessary to develop a new instrument of defense. All efforts are then bent toward the development of an even more lethal offensive weapon and so the vicious circle is perpetuated."[17]

A little over a week after the atomic bombings, the *Baltimore Afro-American* polled African Americans in Newark, New Jersey, on the atomic bomb and its effect upon the future of the world. Of the statements the *Afro-American* printed, most expressed concern over the use of the atomic bomb. Muriel Blackburn, a student, said, "It is rather terrifying that it [the atomic bomb] should come out as a war weapon and not as an instrument to benefit mankind." Beauty shop owner Mary Hall warned that the atomic bomb "will cause the other powers to create or release something even more stupendous. I do not think it will cause wars to cease but rather to be more destructive." Edward Lewis, a truck driver, worried that the atomic bomb would "force civilization to thrive below the earth." Even those who showed minor support for the bomb stressed the importance of controlling and monitoring its use. Martin Erwin Jr., a wholesale house manager, hoped that "men who will be in control of that bomb have the interest of humanity in their hearts."[18]

Respondents to a similar question posed by the *Norfolk Journal and Guide* reacted more favorably to the use of the bomb. The paper asked five women, "What do you think of the atomic bomb?" All of the women praised the role of the bomb in bringing the war to an end. Selena Harris called the atomic bomb "the greatest destructive force of scientific discovery," but also explained that when atomic energy was "directed into proper channels" the entire civilized world "would benefit greatly." When Constance Quiero first heard of the bomb, she thought that "no nation could withstand the devastating effects of such a weapon" and thus the war would quickly end. Janette Spencer showed the most enthusiasm: "This deadly weapon of war can easily be termed the greatest discovery of the century . . . and if diverted to the good of mankind it will change completely the pattern of civilization. I think it has undreamed of possibilities."[19]

Criticism of the bomb, however, could be found on both sides of the political aisle. Conservative journalist George Schuyler wrote a scathing critique of U.S. foreign policy, connecting the atomic bombings to race and colonialism:

> The atom bomb puts the Anglo-Saxons definitely on top where they will remain for decades . . . This means that the Anglo-Saxons, led by the U.S.A., will have their way in the world until other people discover and perfect a weapon more devastating than the uranium bomb. That way, it must be admitted, is the way of white imperialism which firearms enabled them to establish two centuries ago. Controlling this tremendous power for evil are second-rate and small-minded men filled with racial arrogance such as Truman, Tom Connally, Jimmy Byrnes, Stimson, Bilbo and our military naval officer clique, who believe in racial segregation and color discrimination with religious fanaticism and have not the slightest intention of lowering the color barriers their forefathers established.[20]

Schuyler referred to the bombings as the "murder of men wholesale" and "the supreme atrocity of all time." He made sure to mention that those killed were civilians—mothers, fathers, and children. Killing people by the thousand no longer satisfied the United States, Schuyler argued. "Now the country achieved the supreme triumph of being able to slaughter whole cities at a time."[21]

As these sentiments emerged in the black consciousness, members of the clergy began to speak to their parishioners about the atomic bomb. Concerned about the role race played in Truman's decision, the Reverend J. E. Elliott, pastor of St. Luke Chapel, argued, "I have seen the course of discrimination throughout the war and the fact that Japan is of a darker race is no excuse for resorting to such an atrocity." The Reverend Louis F. Lomax of Taber Presbyterian Church referred to the bomb as a "diabolical weapon" and claimed that "man has more scientific knowledge than religion to control it." Expressing a similar perspective, the Reverend A. Joseph Edward, pastor of Zion Baptist Church, stated, "We were taught to hate this enemy, and our hatred has made us barbarous and inhumane as our enemy."[22] The Reverend Samuel Gandy, chaplain of Virginia State College, warned that racial domination could lead to nuclear war and destroy the world. The atomic bomb made racial equality and brotherhood "social mandates." For the future of mankind, "no longer could one racial group dominate," Gandy maintained.[23]

Poet Langston Hughes also joined the initial chorus of protest against the bomb. Hughes questioned the justification for using the atomic bomb through his fictional character Jesse B. Semple, known also as "Simple," who appeared regularly in his column in the *Defender*. Drawing on conversations in bars, Hughes used Simple as a wise fool of Harlem to comment on a variety of topics that affected the black community. To address the issue of the atomic bomb, Hughes recalled a conversation between himself and Simple. The story begins with Simple and Hughes trying to change the topic of discussion from race relations to human relations. However, as Simple points out, "The only trouble with that is that we will not have no human relations left when we get through dropping that new atomical bomb on each other. The way it kills people for miles around, all my relations and—me too—is liable to be wiped out in no time." Simple then asks, "How come we did not try them [atomic bombs] on Germany?" "Perhaps they were not perfected before V-E Day," Hughes responds. "You know better than that. They just did not want to use them on white folks. Germans is white. So they wait until the war is over in Europe to try them out on colored folks. Japs is colored," explains Simple.[24]

Hughes's onetime colleague, Zora Neale Hurston, who many describe as apolitical, did not remain silent on the issue of the atomic bomb. Writing to Claude Barnett, Hurston expressed her outrage at Truman and at African Americans' complacency: "Thruman [*sic*] is a monster. I can think of him as nothing else but the BUTCHER OF ASIA. Of his grin of triumph on giving the order to drop the Atom bombs on Japan. Of his maintaining troops in China who are shooting the starving Chinese for stealing a handful of food . . . Is it that we are so devoted to a 'good Massa' that we feel that we ought not to even protest such crimes?"[25]

In 1946, the National Association for the Advancement of Colored People (NAACP) called for nuclear disarmament at its annual conference. The group also adopted a resolution supporting "civilian control of atomic energy" and "the rapid development of the United Nations into a world government."[26] Archibald Carey Jr., a minister from Woodlawn A.M.E. church in Chicago, was the conference's keynote speaker. Describing atomic bombs as "devastating," Carey warned that the next war, with the use of nuclear weapons, would destroy "two-thirds of all the people of the world." "They will not be bruised, injured, or maimed for life, but verily dissolved," he predicted. Carey told the audience that those who believed atomic bombs made the country safe were "fools" since "everyone would die" in the next war. The minister stated that this "new violence" meant "we must live in a new world which transcends color, class, and creed," and he pleaded for peace and unity.[27]

NAACP leader Walter White had been an early critic of the atomic bombings. In September 1945, White described the atomic bomb as "the most terrible weapon of them all." He criticized the Western world for "letting a genie out of the bottle" and warned, "The atomic bomb in the future would be responsible, on the nationalist, economic, and racial stage, for much more damage than it did in Japan."[28] In March 1946, the National Committee on Atomic Information invited White to a meeting of antinuclear organizations, where Leo Szilard, Albert Einstein, and Robert Oppenheimer weret among the featured speakers. The National Committee for Civil Control of Atomic Energy also recruited White to work on nuclear issues. White enthusiastically supported these groups, joined their committees, and participated in fund-raising efforts.[29] Thus, the NAACP initially protested the atomic bombings before the antinuclear movement had gained wide support. However, while many rank-and-file members of the organization remained staunchly anticolonial and antinuclear, White's criticism of the bomb would later decrease considerably when he, along with other moderate black leaders, pivoted to the right, condemned communism, and openly supported President Truman's bid for reelection in 1948.

In January 1946, the Truman administration announced that in July the United States would conduct an atomic bomb test on Bikini Atoll, located in the Marshall Islands. The announcement came just after the president appointed a blue-ribbon panel chaired by David Lilienthal and Dean Acheson to draft a comprehensive proposal for international control of all uses of atomic energy.[30] Clearly wanting to make the test a major event, the Joint Chiefs of Staff planned to have ninety-seven ships and 20,000 men participate. By the time of the test, the numbers had risen to two hundred ships, 42,000 men, 150 planes, and 4,400 test animals. Officially named Operation Crossroads, the test had the goal of examining the blast effects on naval vessels, although army weapons and equipment were not excluded. To add to the drama, the Joint Task Force included a host of famous battleships and carriers that had been used in one or both world wars.[31]

While the government planned its show, the *New Yorker* published John Hersey's *Hiroshima*, and for the first time many people learned about the horrors of the atomic bomb on a human level and began to shift their opinions. Born in

China, Hersey graduated from Yale and wrote for Time-Life publications during World War II. His essay *Hiroshima*, which originally appeared in the August 31, 1946, edition of the *New Yorker*, focused on six citizens living in Hiroshima before, while, and after the atomic bomb fell. Hersey described in detail the effects of radiation exposure and the psychological impact on those who survived the horrific conditions that followed the bombings. The book version became a best seller, was read in four half-hour segments over the ABC radio network, and won the Peabody Award for the outstanding educational broadcast of 1946. Examining Americans' reactions to the atomic bombings, Paul Boyer contended that in reading *Hiroshima*, most Americans for the first time transformed "subhuman Japs back into Japanese human beings."[32]

In response to the governments' plans, the Federation of American Scientists issued a statement flatly denying that there was any need for the Bikini tests. "Nothing of scientific value and little of technical value" would be gained from such explosions, it argued. In May, Albert Einstein expressed his concern. As chairman of the Emergency Committee of Atomic Scientists, he wrote: "Our world faces a crisis as yet unperceived by those possessing power to make great decisions for good or evil. The unleashed power of the atom has changed everything [except] our mode of thinking and thus we drift toward unparalleled catastrophe."[33]

The nuclear test also elicited a response from the black community, due in large part to Plummer Bernard Young Jr., editor of the *Norfolk Journal and Guide*. The Joint Task Force had selected Young to attend the nuclear test as a representative of the Negro Newspaper Publishers Association. Following the test, Young wrote in great detail about his experiences, never hiding his concern for the future:

> I have seen at first hand the results of atomic bombing and what it can do to huge warships is a terrible thing to behold. Do not be misled by off the cuff first reports. That was the unanimous feeling of eleven of us correspondents who were first to be permitted aboard the cruelly battered, twisted, burned hulk that once was the proud *USS Pensacola* . . . and the bomb did not hit the *Pensacola* as would the ordinary bomb. It obviously exploded obliquely against the starboard side and some considerable distance to the rear. The detonation might have been a mile or more away and, of course, was above the cruiser. I am convinced that an atomic bomb actually striking any warship would simply vaporize it into nothingness. Seeing the Bikini targets impels a solemn prayer that the American people—in fact any people—will never be subjected to another war in which it would be used. For there is no defense against this weapon except peace.[34]

Bayard Rustin and the Bomb

While African Americans began to protest the use of nuclear weapons, combining peace and freedom was certainly not a new concept. Black leftists had, since the 1930s, connected racial equality in America to liberation movements around the world. In addition, Bayard Rustin, Bill Sutherland, and other black activists had been active for years in the American Peace Movement. These men and women fought on multiple fronts and paved the way for the antinuclear activism that was now appearing throughout the black community.

In 1943, Bill Sutherland initiated a conscientious objector (C.O.) strike against segregation at Lewisburg Penitentiary in Pennsylvania. Sutherland, who was serving time for violating the Selective Training and Service Act, refused to sit at the cafeteria table designated for African Americans. In support of Sutherland, other C.O.'s, including peace activist David Dellinger, willingly took their trays into the cafeteria but refused to eat. After a few days, weakened from not eating, they also refused to work. At that point, Sutherland recalls, "we were put in the 'hole,' so to speak. I think there were about nineteen of us, altogether, who were put in the hole. Then after we made this protest, we filled up all the holes for the recalcitrants, . . . so we did get integrated in the sense that they put us all—I think there may have been over time two or three of us who were African American— but they put us all into a dormitory."[35]

By August 1943, three months after the strike began, the C.O.'s broadened their demands to include an end to censorship at the prison. James Tracy explains that combining various demands was typical, since many C.O.'s felt that racial injustice was only one aspect of the broader struggle for freedom. While the strike continued, pacifist groups such as the Fellowship of Reconciliation (FOR) and the War Resisters League (WRL) began to publicize the force-feeding of the prisoners. Caving from the pressure, Bureau of Prisons director James Bennett urged Lewisburg's warden to ease censorship regulations. Although this was far short of the strikers' demands (the prison remained segregated), the exhausted prisoners declared a victory and the strike ended.[36] More importantly, out of these strikes a new and influential organization was about to emerge—the Congress of Racial Equality (CORE).

Released from prison in 1941, peace activist George Houser moved to Chicago to complete his seminary training at the University of Chicago. Due in part to his experience in the prison strikes against segregation, Houser became interested in exploring direct action tactics as the basis for a movement for racial equality. Houser began to meet with a small group of graduate and undergraduate students at the University of Chicago who shared these same concerns. Most of them were white middle-class members of the FOR. The group met every Saturday to study readings on Mohandas Gandhi and discuss how nonviolence could defeat racism in the United States.[37]

In March 1942, the group organized a preliminary committee that attempted to desegregate the White City Roller Rink in Chicago using direct action techniques and a team of twenty-four interracial activists. While the group failed to integrate the rink, it generated excitement and publicity among activist circles. Thus, a month later, fifty people met to form a permanent organization committed to the use of nonviolent direct action in combating racial discrimination, and CORE was formed. At CORE's first national conference, a year after its inception, the group reported that it had organized actions against segregation in seven cities across the country.[38]

Bayard Rustin was one of CORE's first field organizers. Rustin began his journey into activism in the 1930s as a member of the Young Communist League (YCL). However, when Hitler invaded the Soviet Union in June 1941, the Communist Party decided to cease fighting for racial equality to focus more on "national unity against fascism." This was a defining moment for Rustin, as he decided to leave the YCL rather than give up the fight against racism.[39] By late June, Rustin embraced pacifism through Norman Whitney, his mentor from Syracuse, New York, and came to the attention of FOR executive secretary A. J. Muste. Muste knew virtually every radical and liberal leader in the country on a first-name basis, having personally spanned the activist spectrum of the left over the previous three decades.[40] He aggressively recruited the young activist to the staff, and Rustin soon began working for the FOR. As a youth secretary, Rustin taught the principles of pacifism and nonviolence to the younger activists. Rustin biographer John D'Emilio writes that Rustin spent much of his time on the road, "rallying the spirits of local FOR groups, lecturing on college campuses and at high schools, running workshops at conferences of church-affiliated youth organizations, or speaking at the Sunday school of churches whose ministers were FOR members." When the United States formally entered the war, he also began to visit C.O.'s in the Civilian Public Service camps and Japanese Americans in the internment camps.[41]

Following the nuclear test in 1946, Rustin started speaking out against the bomb. Rustin took umbrage with the Emergency Committee of American Scientists, who set out to raise $200,000 for a Campaign of Education on the Atomic

Bomb. The committee stated that the time had come to "let people know that a new type of thinking is essential in this atomic age" if mankind is to survive. The next day, the Federation of American Scientists said, "Scientists seek by education to teach men that they must abandon atomic weapons to preserve civilization." Pointing out what he viewed as blatant hypocrisy, Rustin questioned the validity of scientists who were building "stockpiles of atom bombs" and contending they could also "teach men that they must abandon atomic weapons to preserve civilization." "How can scientists expect the man on the street to follow their leadership?" Rustin asked. He explained that although the Federation of American Scientists sought to educate the public on the bomb, it stated, "in these matters we must submit to the guidance and orders of the military." Rustin argued that although scientists warn that the atom bomb could destroy civilization and appeal for funds to avoid nuclear war, they ultimately ignore their conscience and "submit to the orders of the military." Thus, "men who cry out that atomic weapons will destroy civilization, continue to make them because national allegiances demand it. They announce that they work with 'heavy hearts and without enthusiasm' but they do not answer the heart."[42]

Over the next two years, Rustin's commitment to the nuclear issue continued to grow. Delivering the William Penn lecture at the Arch Street Meeting House in Philadelphia, Rustin maintained that the atomic bomb showed once again that "violent force" had become the "greatest problem of our time." He questioned why the American press so quickly criticized Mussolini for using flamethrowers on Ethiopians yet remained silent when it came to dropping the atomic bombs. Rustin blamed not only "those responsible for deciding to use the bomb," but also those who continued to "depend on violence."[43]

In April 1948, Rustin, Muste, Houser, Dellinger, and fellow peace activist Dwight McDonald joined two hundred men and women in Chicago for a "Conference on More Disciplined and Revolutionary Pacifism." Out of this meeting came Peacemakers, an ad hoc group that urged young men to refuse to register for the draft, championed tax refusal, and campaigned against building nuclear weapons.[44] However, a debate within Peacemakers ensued over how to best achieve its goals.

Dellinger advocated a simple, nonconsumerist lifestyle that focused on the personal and spiritual side of pacifism. Rustin had hoped that Peacemakers would become an organization with the discipline of the Communist Party. D'Emilio explains that Rustin "saw extremism as a prelude to engagement" and

was drawn to it, as were other members of Peacemakers. He wanted a radicalism that provoked action and was a particularly zealous advocate of unilateral
disarmament.[45]

Antinuclear versus Anticommunist

The most far-reaching criticism of the atomic bombings came from black leftists. Since the 1930s black Popular Front groups had sought to connect the black
freedom movement in America to peace, labor, anticolonial, and antifascist
movements around the world. For many of them, the Italo-Ethiopian War was
a critical moment. Historian Penny Von Eschen argues that black leftists viewed
the Italian invasion as "a piece of an overall race war of European (and Japanese)
colonial expansion, in which Ethiopia was the last holdout of real independence
in Africa." Indeed, Paul Robeson maintained that since the Italian invasion, "the
parallel between his [African Americans'] own interests and those of oppressed
peoples abroad had been impressed upon him daily."[46]

In the 1930s, Robeson traveled to London, the Soviet Union, and Spain. It was
on this trip that the singer claimed he discovered Africa. At the University of London, Robeson studied African linguistics, customs, and music. He met with various African leaders and befriended Jawaharlal Nehru. These experiences helped
convince Robeson to embrace the left and raise the anticolonialist banner.[47]

In 1937, Robeson along with YMCA field secretary Max Yergan formed the International Committee on African Affairs (ICAA). The ICAA, renamed the CAA
five years later, was primarily an educational organization. Comprising twelve
activists, seven black and five white, the group lobbied for colonial reform, circulated petitions, distributed educational information, and organized programs in
support of various African independence movements. It also coordinated state-
side scholarship opportunities for Africans and provided links to anticolonial
networks and African liberation groups around the world. [48]

Mark Solomon suggests that the CAA combined the cause of anticolonialism with a pro-Soviet outlook. Solomon asserts that by constitutionally banning
racism, the Soviet Union convinced activists like Robeson that it had become
the leader in the fight against colonialism. Indeed, according to Robeson, the
Soviet Union was the "real friend" of the African people. "Africa remembers that
it was [Maxim] Litvinov who stood alone beside Haile Selassie in Geneva, when
Mussolini's sons flew with the blessings of the Pope to drop bombs on Ethiopian
women and children," Robeson said.[49]

Communist involvement in anticolonial organizations like the CAA, however, often caused rifts among members, hindering various groups' overall effectiveness. Black labor leader A. Philip Randolph resigned from the National Negro Congress (NNC), an umbrella group founded in 1935, because of the organization's communist involvement. Yergan took over leadership duties of the NNC, but his ties to the Communist Party coupled with the CAA's lack of direction, caused Ralph Bunche to resign from the organization along with a group of Howard University professors who also sought to distance themselves from Yergan and the Communist Party.[50]

Nevertheless, black leftists held firm in their belief that the atomic bombings of Hiroshima and Nagasaki were inextricably linked to colonialism and racial equality. Jacqueline Castledine maintains that for many black leftists, "Jim Crow, European colonization, institutional racism, and international imperialism each grew from the same seed and represented a form of violence."[51] The bomb encompassed all of these and represented the most deadly form of violence. Calling the bomb a "measureless act of aggression," W.E.B. Du Bois explained, "We have seen through this war, to our amazement and distress, a marriage between science and destruction; a marriage such as we had never dreamed of before. We have always thought of science as the emancipator. We see it now as the enslaver of mankind." Du Bois warned that Western nations would use atomic energy to maintain power, setting back progress for "the majority of the people of the world." "If power can be held through atomic bombs," Du Bois wrote, "colonial peoples may never be free." He welcomed the use of atomic energy for electricity, heat, light, and power, as long as first and foremost it was universally outlawed for making bombs.[52]

For Du Bois, the fact that the victims of the atomic bombings were nonwhite only further validated the idea that race, peace, and colonization were connected and the black freedom struggle was indeed global. In June 1946, Du Bois took part in a massive "Big Three Unity Rally" organized by the Council on African Affairs (CAA) at Madison Square Garden. Between 15,000 and 19,000 heard Du Bois, Robeson, Yergan, Mary McLeod Bethune, William Hayes (president of the New England Baptist Convention), Michael Quill (head of the Transport Workers Union), and others condemn the exploitation of Africa by colonial powers, especially the United States through its importation of uranium to make atomic bombs. Organizers called for "anti-imperialist and democratic forces" to influence American foreign policy. Yergan urged Americans to unite in the demand that "colonialism—that bankrupt, plundering and wasteful system of the past—be done away with," and replaced by a "new relation, amongst the peoples of the earth, characterized by dignity" and working for the welfare of all people.[53]

The most stinging condemnation came from Robeson. At the time, Robeson was coming off a successful run of *Othello* and was described as America's "number one Negro" in several publications. Thus, Robeson spoke out when he had much to lose.[54] "In Africa, in the West Indies, and in Asia, the colonial peoples wage a desperate struggle for recognition simply as human beings—as human beings to whom human rights are due," he said.[55] Addressing the racism aimed at Japanese Americans, Robeson noted that "it is all part of one problem, this matter of discrimination and it may be the foremost question facing us today in the atomic age."[56] Robeson embraced the notion that nuclear weapons, colonialism, and the black freedom struggle were connected, emphatically stating:

> Our government is getting uranium from the Belgian Congo for atomic bombs. American companies are prospecting for oil in Ethiopia and for minerals in Liberia . . . these manifestations of a new and heightened interest in Africa on the part of American Big Business represent a challenge to the rest of us . . . We on the anti-imperialist side are handicapped by lack of money, lack of powerful organization, lack of influence in state and international affairs. But, although the enemy has all the advantage and has a head start in the race, it is yet possible for us to catch up and win. It is possible to win if the majority of the American people can be brought to see and understand in the fullest sense the fact that the struggle in which we are engaged is not a matter of mere humanitarian sentiment, but of life and death. The only alternative to world freedom is world annihilation.[57]

Since 1945, many in the black community had expressed outrage over the use of atomic bombs. However, their commitment to the nuclear issue would soon be tested with the rise of a communist-led peace offensive and the emergence of the Truman Doctrine.

On March 12, 1947, President Truman announced to a joint session of Congress that the world had changed and there was a need to combat a growing Soviet menace. The president asked Americans to choose between nations with "free institutions, representative government, free elections, guarantees of individual liberty, freedom of speech and religion, and freedom from political oppression" and those governments that rely on "terror and oppression, a controlled press and radio, fixed elections, and the suppression of personal freedoms." The choice was too often not a free one, Truman declared. A cornerstone of U.S. policy was now to support "free peoples" from "aggression," and Americans had to accept the "great responsibilities" that came with fighting communism.[58]

The Truman Doctrine was intended, according to Senator Arthur Vandenberg, to "scare hell" out of the American people. Nine days later, the president went a step further by establishing a program that required federal employees to ensure their "complete and unswerving loyalty" to the country. These policies had devastating effects. Lines became blurred. Words such as "enemy," "communist sympathizer," or "subversive" now applied to those who expressed an opinion different from that of the federal government. Civil liberties were often trampled on. Men and women could now face imprisonment for their beliefs as much as for crimes they had committed.[59]

Less than a year later, the international communist movement launched a "peace offensive" aimed at building a worldwide movement to prevent war between the United States and the Soviet Union and eliminating nuclear weapons. The communist-led peace campaign consisted largely of a series of congresses and an international petition campaign to "ban the bomb."[60] The first major conference took place in Wroclaw, Poland, in August 1948. The Polish-led World Congress of Intellectuals for Peace brought together communists and prominent noncommunists, including former U.S. assistant attorney general O. John Rogge, French priest Abbé Jean Boulier, and Julian Huxley, the director general of the United Nations Educational, Scientific, and Cultural Organization (UNESCO). Robbie Lieberman explains that the communists tried to combine their hard line on the issues with a broad-based approach to organizing, hoping that intellectuals might lead popular resistance to Western government measures, such as the rearmament of Germany and the formation of the Atlantic Alliance, which threatened Soviet security. The Wroclaw Congress elected an international committee to continue the work of attracting intellectuals to the communist approach to peace. In the United States such work meant mobilizing scientists who objected to nuclear war, writers and artists concerned about the anticommunist climate, and religious leaders who opposed the Cold War on moral grounds.[61]

While the communist-led peace movement gained momentum, a number of its events, including the Cultural and Scientific Conference for World Peace in March 1949, only solidified the notion that anything related to peace or nuclear disarmament was "Red." A month later, nearly two thousand people, representing over fifty nations, gathered in Paris and Prague to launch a "peace offensive" against the threat of nuclear war. Renowned French physicist Frédéric Joliot-Curie, who helped organize the gatherings, stated, "We are not here to ask for peace, but to impose it." He then declared, "One of the most spectacular misappropriations of science is the atomic bomb, produced . . . as a weapon of mass destruction."[62] The meetings resulted in the formation of the World Peace Congress, which became the World Congress of the Partisans of Peace. Du Bois and Robeson attended the Paris meeting with Du Bois as head of the American delegation and Robeson a featured speaker.[63]

With the emergence of the Cold War and the new "peace offensive," black activists were now forced to make some important decisions. As antinuclear was rapidly becoming synonymous with anti-American, African Americans had to consider the repercussions of continuing to speak out against the bomb. For many black moderates, the decision was clear: embracing Truman and anticommunism meant a greater possibility of gaining civil rights. For others, the decision was not that simple.

The 1948 presidential election counterposed President Truman, and the belief that containing communism was necessary for America's security, to Henry Wallace, and the belief that peace between America and the Soviet Union was both possible and necessary. Wallace supporters tended toward left-leaning, international-minded activism and looked to Wallace and the Progressive Party as viable alternatives to the Truman administration. From the outset, Wallace supported nuclear disarmament and favored full voting rights for African Americans and an end to segregation—embracing a civil rights platform much stronger than Truman's.[64]

Wallace garnered significant support from the black community. Indeed, ten thousand people, the majority of whom were African American, packed the Golden Gate Ballroom in Harlem to hear Wallace kick off his presidential campaign.[65] Seventy percent of the NAACP's national office staff "favored Wallace."[66] Former United Negro Improvement Association (UNIA) activist Charlotta Bass, then publisher of the *California Eagle*, mobilized African Americans in Los Angeles for Wallace. Heavyweight boxing champion Joe Louis gave money to Wallace's campaign.[67] Paul Robeson, Lena Horne, and newspaper publisher George Murphy also worked for the Wallace campaign. Robeson told supporters that he first began to connect issues of peace and freedom when he joined the Wallace campaign in 1948. Wallace, Robeson explained, had made a tremendous contribution time and again to the cause of peace, freedom, and black equality. "Peace," Robeson concluded, "was and is the issue."[68]

African American support also came from within the Progressive Party's counterpart, the American Labor Party (ALP). Originally founded in New York to help ensure President Roosevelt's 1936 reelection, ALP members and Wallace supporters Eslanda Goode Robeson, Shirley Graham, Ada B. Jackson, and Thelma Dale consistently made the case that peace, freedom, and racial equality were inextricably linked. Graham, a respected author and future wife of Du Bois, warned that children could live in peace only in a world "without battleships, atom bombs and lynch ropes."[69]

A peace activist, journalist, and the wife of Paul Robeson, Eslanda Goode Robeson worked with the Council on African Affairs (CAA), traveled numerous times to Africa, and supported Henry Wallace and the Progressive Party. Robeson was a vocal and active member of the party's platform committee and helped draft the 1948 platform, which reflected many of her political values. Speaking around the country on Wallace's behalf, Robeson constantly made clear that "there are no points which do not refer back to peace." Both "Essie" and her husband were among the earliest proponents of the view that the struggle for civil rights at home, independence movements in Africa, and the efforts of working-class people worldwide were inextricably linked. Describing Robeson as a "vociferous defender of the right of colonized people to self-rule, an unwavering critic of U.S. racism, and a strong advocate of disarmament," biographer Barbara Ransby explains that Robeson was "an important advocate for internationalizing the Black freedom struggle in the U.S. and for drawing parallels with socialist, communist, and anti-colonial movements abroad."[70] Describing Robeson as only "one of several influential black leftist women who in the postwar years shaped the discourse of decolonization by linking it to the issue of world peace," Jacqueline Castledine asserts that these women were instrumental in placing efforts to end Jim Crow in the American South within a larger anticolonial liberation movement for peace and freedom.[71]

Ada Jackson was perhaps the most critical of Truman. The Georgia native and NAACP member had a rich history of activism working as a community organizer for much of her life. After earning her degree from Langston University, Jackson was president of the Brooklyn Interracial Assembly and chair of the Brooklyn YWCA's Negro Communities Committee. Throughout the 1940s she ran for public office in New York and then focused largely on the American Labor

Party and the Wallace campaign. She was the vice chair of the New York State Wallace for President Committee. In 1948, Jackson spoke at the "Yankee Doodle Rally" at Yankee Stadium. Organized by the ALP, Progressive Party, and a number of black activists, the rally addressed the issues of peace and racial inequality. Calling the president a "paper progressive," Jackson unloaded on Truman, daring him to emulate Wallace, who refused to speak to segregated audiences.[72]

Black moderates, however, rejected Wallace and publicly endorsed the president. Walter White and John H. Sengstacke, editor and publisher of the *Defender*, both became staunch supporters of Truman's foreign policy. Penny Von Eschen explains that White knew that under the Truman administration, criticizing the president was becoming unacceptable and at the same time new opportunities were emerging to make progress on domestic civil rights. In short, White's support of Truman's foreign policy was at least in part strategic.[73]

The election also reignited the lingering tensions between the NAACP and Du Bois. White had made his dislike for Wallace quite clear. The NAACP leader described Wallace as devious, unelectable, and a communist dupe. Following White's lead, the NAACP broke its own rules of nonpartisanship and openly supported Truman, even though many of its members favored Wallace. Determined to stifle support for Wallace, White demanded Du Bois's silence. Du Bois questioned how the NAACP could want to stop a private citizen from supporting and voting for whomever he or she wanted. This was the beginning of the end of Du Bois's involvement with the organization he had helped build. From fights over desk space and salary to Africa, colonialism, and human rights, Du Bois and White's relationship deteriorated until it was beyond repair.[74]

At the same time, Truman was well aware that he needed black support to defeat Republican Thomas Dewey. Thus, on February 2, 1948, in front of a Southern-dominated Congress, the president announced plans for a civil rights package that included anti-lynching and anti–poll tax measures, and the creation of a Fair Employment Practices Commission. Truman also made public his decision to soon end segregation in the armed forces and discrimination in the federal government, all the while hiding his own deep-seated racism and bigotry.[75]

It worked. The black press and prominent black leaders praised Truman. Channing Tobias hailed Truman's recommendations as a "bold" and "courageous" decision. Walter White congratulated Truman for his "courage." The *Norfolk Journal and Guide* declared, "No president, not even the great Franklin D. Roosevelt, ever called upon the nation, through its elected lawmakers, to enact so sweeping and vital a corrective program." The *Guide* described Truman as "Lincolnesque" and concluded that he had done a "great and selfless thing" and it was up to all citizens to help carry out Truman's wishes.[76]

Truman's image as a president dedicated to civil rights resonated in the black community. In many areas, including Harlem, where Truman addressed a crowd of 65,000 three days before the election, the president received a greater portion of the black vote than Roosevelt had in 1944. Truman received 108,643 votes to Wallace's 28,903 in the Harlem districts. In four black wards of St. Louis, only 4,151 African Americans cast ballots for Wallace, while Truman received almost 30,000 votes. In Pittsburgh, only 2,000 African Americans voted for Wallace. In California, Ohio, and Illinois, black voters provided the decisive electoral edge for Truman over Dewey. Overall, Truman carried about two-thirds of the black vote and, with that margin, won reelection.[77]

In the end, Truman's promises of black equality, which would go largely unfulfilled, gave him the presidency. As Manning Marable made clear, Truman himself was virtually silent from 1946 to 1953 as white racist vigilante groups proliferated. In addition, by refusing to work with leftists, groups like the NAACP lost some of their most principled organizers and activists.[78] Rather than challenging Truman on civil rights and his use of the bomb, leaders chose to support an administration that tolerated racial injustice and the threat of nuclear annihilation.

By the late 1940s, faced with the risk of being labeled "Black and Red," many traditional activists shifted their focus solely to the domestic front while distancing themselves from the international stage in hopes of receiving civil rights legislation. However, for Du Bois, Robeson, and other black activists, peace and freedom were not bargaining chips. Rather than shy away from the nuclear issue, they embraced it. Some scholars have concluded that the rise of anticommunism in the United States broke the chain that connected peace, freedom, and colonialism.[79] But they underestimate the power of the bomb. For it was the bomb that motivated many in the black community to continue to fight for peace and equality as part of a global struggle for human rights, even as McCarthyism and the Korean War loomed on the horizon.

Chapter 2

"We Will Not Go Quietly into the Night"

Fighting for Peace and Freedom During the McCarthy Era

I've got a child, and I don't want that child to die. I would like to take the plans of the H and
A bombs and make sure they were destroyed. The power to decide whether humanity is
destroyed or lives lies in the hands of the people—all of the people—not the political few.
—Charlie Parker, 1950

BY THE EARLY 1950S, THE STRAIN ON U.S.–SOVIET RELATIONS had grown considerably. In a climate shaped by the Korean War and Joseph McCarthy's anticommunist crusade, black activists faced an atmosphere in which antinuclear activism was depicted as procommunism. Individuals who voiced opposition to the bomb suddenly went mute, and organizations that had brought the nuclear issue to the forefront fell into disarray. As Mary Helen Washington explains, African Americans, simply "by virtue of their blackness," were now deemed subversive. However, as some activists retreated, others refused to conform, alarmed over the rising threat of nuclear war and fearing another Hiroshima in Korea.[1]

Concern over the United States exploding a nuclear weapon in Korea was not unfounded. The secretary of the navy and the commandant of the Air War College were among the first to publicly favor the use of nuclear weapons in Korea. U.S. chief of operations, General Bolte, proposed using between ten and twenty nuclear weapons in Korea. In July, General Douglas MacArthur, at a meeting in Tokyo with the U.S. Army and Air Force chiefs of staff, suggested using atomic bombs to destroy supply routes into Korea from China and the Soviet Union. He then proceeded to ask for authorization to use nuclear weapons at his discretion, and noted in his journal that it would take between thirty and fifty atomic bombs to end the war.[2]

Truman acknowledged the possibility four months later. During a press conference, the president stated, "The forces of the United Nations have no intention of abandoning their mission in Korea." Then, in response to a question, Truman announced that the United States would "take whatever steps are necessary to meet the military situation, just as we always have." A reporter asked, did that "include the atomic bomb?" It included "every weapon that we have," Truman replied. Had there been "active consideration of its use?" the reporter queried. "There has always been active consideration of its use," Truman assured him.

Upon hearing Truman's statements, French prime minister Rene Pleven and foreign minister Robert Schuman, along with Dutch officials, shared their concerns with British prime minister Clement Attlee and foreign secretary Ernest Bevin. They agreed that Western Europe must urge the United States to show restraint and decided to send Attlee to Washington to relay the message.[3]

Leaders around the world expressed similar sentiments. Sir Girja Bajpai, secretary general of the Ministry of External Affairs in India, told U.S. ambassador Loy Henderson that the critical immediate objective in Korea was to avoid the spread of hostilities. Jawaharlal Nehru sent a message to Sir Benegal Rau at the United Nations calling for a meeting of representatives of the great powers, the linkage of a settlement in Korea to one on Taiwan, and the "absolute necessity" of avoiding use of the atomic bomb. The pro-U.S. foreign minister in Australia, Sir Percy Spender, issued a statement in support of the United States, but made clear that the atomic bomb should be used "only after the fullest consultation." Although U.N. delegates from Greece, Turkey, Iran, Afghanistan, Saudi Arabia, and Liberia, as well as from Latin American countries, approved Truman's nuclear threats, those from the "Arab-Asian group" expressed concern both that the bomb might be used once more against Asian peoples and that it would precipitate a third world war.[4]

A year later, the press reported that "high-level" discussions were taking place throughout the government to decide if the United States should use atomic bombs in Korea. Moreover, senators on both sides of the aisle publicly advocated using nuclear weapons on the Koreans and Russians. Senator Henry Cabot Lodge Jr. (R-MA) called for an "atomic artillery barrage" against the Koreans. There could be no "moral disapproval of using atomic weapons in Korea. As a matter of fact, a strong argument could actually be made for using the atomic bomb strategically so as to permit a defensive line of craters to be made at some point across the Korean peninsula," Lodge said. Senator Lyndon Johnson (D-TX) suggested that the United States unleash a "full-scale atomic attack" on Russia if it perpetuated "one more act of aggression." As late as 1953, Defense officials conceded that the Eisenhower administration was considering using nuclear weapons in Korea.[5]

The Korean War added a sense of urgency, especially for African Americans. After World War II, war-weary Americans, black and white, recoiled at the thought of another conflict. While the threat of being labeled "Red" kept the traditional black press and moderate organizations away from protesting the Korean War, some in the black community became vocal in their opposition.

They resented being told to fight for the freedom of others abroad while being denied basic civil rights at home. Others objected to African Americans again fighting against people of color. Du Bois argued that while France was using the "black Senegalese to conquer Vietnam," and Britain had used troops of "every race and hue to hold the remains of her empire," perhaps worst of all was the use of "American Negro troops in Korea." Lastly, there were those who viewed U.S. involvement in Korea through the lens of colonialism. Robeson warned, "If we don't stop our armed adventure in Korea today—tomorrow it will be Africa."[6]

Langston Hughes combined all of these sentiments in the *Defender*. Convinced these actions would only speed up the end of the world, Hughes wrote that dropping another atomic bomb in Asia would be a "very great mistake for the white world." In any event, using nuclear weapons may be inevitable, Hughes contended, since "stupid men in the capitols of the Western World" still do not understand colonialism. "Almost anybody would know by now that colored peoples do not like to be ruled by outside forces, Jim Crowed, segregated, or told what to do by aliens, and in general kicked around," Hughes warned. He asked how Americans could view Asians as human beings when "there are still a great many Americans who cannot see their way clear to granting human dignity to the millions of Negro citizens in the United States?" "The Negro problem is one thing that makes it so hard for them to look clearly at Asia, because their racial specs are still very cloudy at home." Hughes concluded that until African Americans were viewed as human beings, "it is going to be very hard for some Americans not to think that the easiest way to settle the problems of Asia is by simply dropping an atom bomb on colored heads there. I wish, for all our sakes, they could realize that things are not that simple."[7]

Like Hughes, many African Americans deplored the possibility that nuclear weapons would again be used on a "darker nation." "The American people are deeply concerned that Dixiecrat Congressman (Lucius Mendel) Rivers of South Carolina and many others have urged President Truman to drop the atomic bomb on the Koreans in the attempt to spread World War III," Du Bois said.[8] Over one hundred black leaders issued a "protest and a plea," condemning the war and the use of atomic weapons:

> Peace in Korea, in Malaya, in Indo-China, and in other parts of Asia, Africa, and America does not mean that powerful nations can force their policies and demands upon weaker people . . . The United States has no right to force on Koreans a government or way of life, which Koreans do not want. The awful thing, which we are facing

today is the attempt of the United States to replace Europe in the enslavement of Asia and Africa. This American policy the colored people of the world resent and oppose, and this is the real cause of upheaval in Korea. We maintain that it is not treason for us to protest against using Negro soldiers to reduce free people to slavery. It is not yet treason to work for Peace. The jails of the United States today are filled with Negroes whose chief crime is being black, and hundreds of Negro boys and girls are daily sentenced to crime and disgrace because they are the grandchildren of slaves. Problems like these are not answered by the charge of "communism," nor is this nation justified in leading the world to war in order to make men accept our economic system, which millions of Americans know is itself in desperate need of betterment and reform.[9]

These activists were not alone. Indeed, millions of concerned citizens, including many in the black community, refused to accept the possibility of nuclear annihilation. They fought back by signing a pledge to "Ban the Bomb."

The Stockholm Peace Appeal

On March 15, 1950, alarmed by President Truman's decision to proceed with the development of a hydrogen bomb, the Permanent Committee of the Partisans of Peace, an extension of the World Peace Congress, gathered in Stockholm, Sweden. Under the leadership of Joliot-Curie, the meeting adopted a resolution aimed at banning nuclear weapons, which became the Stockholm Peace Appeal.[10] The "Ban the Bomb" pledge, as the appeal was also known, contained simple but strong language, which demanded a ban on all nuclear weapons and holding those who refused to comply accountable:

> We demand the outlawing of atomic weapons as instruments of intimidation and mass murder of peoples.
>
> We demand strict international control to enforce this measure.
>
> We believe that any other government, which first uses atomic weapons against any other country whatsoever will be committing a crime against humanity and should be dealt with as a war criminal.
>
> We call on all men and women of good will throughout the world to sign the appeal.[11]

Following the meeting, the Partisans of Peace embarked on a mission to obtain as many signatures as possible in hopes of "Banning the Bomb."

A few weeks later, Du Bois and thirty-six other activists gathered for the Provisional Committee of Americans for World Peace, an outgrowth of the Paris conference. Du Bois chaired the meeting. One of the participants, Elizabeth Moos, suggested establishing the Peace Information Center (PIC) to supply information on peace actions to the press and other activist groups, as well to send American delegations to peace conferences around the world. The group accepted the proposal. It chose Du Bois as the chairman of the Advisory Council and Moos as the executive director. Headquartered in New York City, the Peace Information Center circulated news about peace actions and provided organizations with speakers, posters, supplies, and petitions. However, the PIC's most notable campaign involved promoting the Stockholm Peace Appeal.[12]

The appeal gained wide support inside the United States, especially in the black community. Duke Ellington declared, "It is quite unimaginable that people should think of using the A-Bomb."[13] Dancer and anthropologist Pearl Primus, E. Franklin Frazier, chair of the Department of Sociology at Howard University, Mary Church Terrell of the National Association of Colored Women, and Armand V. Boutte Sr., president of the Negro Business League of New Orleans, all backed the appeal. Boutte commented, "Under no circumstances should the atomic bomb be thought of as a weapon of warfare. It is a weapon of madness." Clarie Collins Harvey, Charlie Parker, and Marian Anderson also endorsed the petition. Parker said, "I've got a child, and I don't want that child to die. I would like to take the plans of the H and A bombs and make sure they were destroyed. The power to decide whether humanity is destroyed or lives lies in the hands of the people—all of the people—not the political few." Anderson expressed similar sentiments, adding, "I have the honor of knowing Einstein and the pleasure of meeting him often. He is never tired of saying that the use of the atom bomb in another war could mean the annihilation of all life on earth. This terrible threat must be avoided by outlawing the atom bomb."[14]

As a member of the Peace Information Center, Paul Robeson focused on gaining the support of the labor movement. In June 1950, Robeson addressed a meeting of the National Labor Conference for Negro Rights:

> Shall we have atom bombs and hydrogen bombs and rocketships and bacteriological war, or shall we have peace in the world; the hellish destruction of the men, women and children, of whole civilian populations, or the peaceful construction of the good life everywhere?
>
> I have just this past week returned from London where the Executive Committee of the World Partisans for Peace met to further their crusade against atomic destruction. And there, spokesmen of millions of men and women from all parts of the

globe—Europe, Asia, Africa, North and South America, Australia—pledged themselves anew that the Truman plan for the world shall not prevail—that peace shall
conquer war—that men shall live as brothers, not as beasts.

These men and women of peace speak not merely for themselves, but for the
nameless millions whose pictures do not adorn the newspapers, who hold no press
conference, who are the mass of working humanity in every land. Did I say nameless? Not any more! For one hundred million have already signed their names in all
lands to a simple and powerful pledge, drawn up in Stockholm. The Soviet Union and
China are signing this pledge. People in all nations of the world are signing it. Will you
take this pledge now? Your meeting tonight as men and women of American labor
is in good time because it places you in this great stream of peace-loving humanity,
determined to win a world of real brotherhood. It will enable you, I hope, to place
the Negro trade unionists in the front ranks of a crusade to secure at least a million
signatures of Negro Americans to this Stockholm appeal for peace.[15]

Organized labor responded favorably. In New York, the National Labor Conference for Peace enthusiastically supported efforts to ban the bomb. The Brooklyn Peace Committee obtained 25,000 signatures in shops and on docks. The total
number of Brooklyn signers reached 145,000. Rallies were held in the garment
district while fur workers gathered 75,000 signatures. Local unions throughout
New York City organized peace committees to drum up support. The United
Electrical Workers, Baker and Confectionary Workers, Local 13 of the American Federation of Labor, International Longshore and Warehousemen's Union,
Woodworkers Union, Ship Scalers and Dry Dock Workers, International Association of Machinists, Marine Cooks and Stewards Union, and the United Office and
Professional Workers Union of America (UOPWA) all backed the appeal.[16]

Robeson's activism, however, stretched beyond the Stockholm Peace Appeal.
Throughout the 1950s Robeson consistently emphasized that African Americans
would only gain their freedom through fighting for peace—a peace that would
include a chance for their "colonial brothers" to "build and grow."[17] Robeson explained, "In fighting for the full civil rights and equality of my folk, I entered the
struggle for peace." "Peace meant some opportunity to wage major battles around
freedom for my people here in the United States and for an end to colonialism in
Africa and elsewhere," he said.[18]

Robeson spoke at yearly May Day parades in New York City. While the parades' main focus was organized labor, they often combined workers' rights with

the need for racial equality and banning nuclear weapons. In 1951, Robeson told the crowd, "There can be no more important day in our lives, for we march for world peace, friendship and cooperation with the peoples of the world." He asked the demonstrators to remember "colonial peoples throughout the world" while they marched for a "peace we must and shall win." Turning his attention to the black community, Robeson declared, "If fifteen million Negroes spoke out for peace, there will be peace. If fifteen million Negroes speak out against anti-Semitism, there will be no anti-Semitism. If fifteen million people speak out against persecution of the Mexican people, that persecution will end."[19]

By the start of the summer, support for the Stockholm Peace Appeal had spread far and wide. Over 1.5 million Americans had signed the petition, including Nobel Prize Laureate Thomas Mann, assorted religious leaders, and members of the NAACP. The Peace Information Center organized activities in Philadelphia, Boston, and Denver. In Detroit, a giant "peace bomb" loaded with petitions calling for Truman to outlaw the atomic bomb was set up in front of City Hall. Three thousand signatures were collected in four days. The PIC declared that the call for an end to atomic weapons had "Swelled to a Mighty Chorus!" Indeed, there were 10 million signatories in France, 60 million in China, and 115 million in the Soviet Union. Among Brazil's 3.75 million signers were 2,000 illiterate peasants who signed by making thumb prints with the juice of crushed poppy leaves. Two hundred fifty million signed worldwide. [20]

The religious community lent its support. The 131st Annual Conference of the Methodist Church and the 162nd General Assembly of the Presbyterian Church both called for an end to nuclear weapons. French Protestant pastors, cardinals, and bishops, Italian bishops, and the Polish Roman Catholic Episcopate also endorsed the appeal. Support, both financial and political, also came from Jewish communities in Israel and the United States.[21]

While many inside the religious community reacted favorably to the petition, others, including various leaders of the Protestant and Catholic faiths, publicly denounced the appeal. Moreover, ten Jewish organizations, including the American Jewish Congress, American Jewish Committee, Association of Jewish Chaplains in the Armed Forces, Jewish War Veterans, and the National Council of Jewish Women, rejected the petition. The Commission of the Churches on International Affairs, in a statement to 350 religious leaders in seventy countries, warned against supporting the Peace Appeal. The letter emphasized that in speaking out on the atomic crisis, the churches "should guard against the possibility that their utterances may be used for propagandist purposes quite different from those, which they intend."[22]

Some atomic scientists found the appeal's connection to communism sufficient grounds for opposition. Eugene Rabinowitch criticized the appeal and Joliot-Curie in the *Bulletin of Atomic Scientists*. Niels Bohr argued that he could not join any appeal that did not include "the clearly expressed demand of access to information about conditions in all countries and of fully free exchange of ideas within every country and across the boundaries." In September 1950, delegates of the American and British Federation of Atomic Scientists concluded that the appeal was "a very effective piece of propaganda," which provided "no help" on the issue of how to control nuclear weapons.[23]

The executive council of the American Federation of Labor called it "spurious" and a "rank fraud." The War Resisters League, which already repudiated the communist-led peace offensive, condemned the petition, saying, "The CP [Communist Party] use of the term 'peace' is not peace at all."[24] The Austrian government warned against "peace-mongering." The International Socialist conference in Copenhagen, a meeting of Europe's socialist parties, adopted a resolution repudiating the appeal and described the whole "Moscow-led peace campaign" as a "camouflage for a totalitarian policy of militarism and domination." Communist involvement also convinced some signers to withdraw earlier endorsements.[25]

Representative Peter Rodino Jr. (D-NJ) called on the clergy of all faiths to make God-fearing Americans aware of "the insidious danger of atheistic communism as exemplified by the so-called Stockholm peace petition." Rodino described it as "a war petition calculated to give Soviet Russia time to stockpile atomic weapons while we are lulled into a false sense of security." Rodino then requested that the State and Justice Departments provide churches and schools lists of communist-front organizations. Representatives Bernard Kearney (R-NY) and Harold Velde (R-IL) vehemently denounced the petition as treasonous. Kearney maintained that the goal of the Stockholm Appeal was "to confuse and divide the American people and paralyze their resistance to Communist aggression."[26]

Some in the black community also voiced opposition. Conservative writer George Schuyler called the Peace Appeal a "Moscow hustle" and remained convinced the Soviets were using the petition to divide Americans. He accused Du Bois of moving in a "totalitarian direction" and becoming a puppet of the Soviet Union.[27] A. Philip Randolph's Brotherhood of Sleeping Car Porters deemed the petition "a colossal hoax and fraud," but also pointed out that the petition showed that people all over the world were "hungry for peace."[28]

Secretary of State Dean Acheson vigorously went after Du Bois. Acheson declared that communists could care less about peace or disarmament, opportunistically exploiting those issues to spread their ideology. The secretary of state reiterated that the United States would not refrain from using atomic weapons simply because activists like Du Bois would consider it a criminal act.[29]

Du Bois responded to all the charges, particularly those by Acheson. He suggested that the secretary of state's remarks might be interpreted "as foreshadowing American use of the atom bomb in Korea." He challenged Acheson to "let the world know that in the future the Government of the United States will never be the first to use the atom bomb, whether in Korea or in any other part of the earth."[30] Du Bois asked, "Must any proposals for averting atomic catastrophe be sanctified by Soviet opposition? Have we come to the tragic pass where, by declaration of our own Secretary of State, there is no possibility of mediating our differences with the Soviet Union? If we worked together with the Soviet Union against the menace of Hitler, can we not work with it again at a time when only faith can save us from utter atomic disaster?"[31] Du Bois later insisted that the people who signed the appeal were moved "not by the thought of defending the Soviet Union so much as by the desire to prevent modern culture from relapsing into primitive barbarism."[32]

Soliciting signatures proved to be a risky business. Police harassed, beat, and jailed petitioners. In New York, police officers arrested four individuals for disorderly conduct when they refused to stop circulating the petition and move from the street corner. In Los Angeles, twelve construction workers threatened four activists who were collecting signatures. Security guards working at the site stepped in to prevent a physical altercation. One of the guards, a retired Los Angeles policeman, said he feared that the petition circulators would be injured if he did not intervene. A twenty-four-year-old man was arrested for circulating the appeal in Columbus, Ohio, and in Durham, North Carolina, a judge ordered the police to arrest anyone gathering signatures. When the New York Labor Conference organized a demonstration in Union Square Park attended by over ten thousand people, New York police responded forcefully. Mounted officers charged protesters on the sidewalk and badly beat those who refused to move. Fourteen demonstrators were arrested and countless others injured.[33]

When it was reported that four thousand American seamen signed the petition, a number of them were removed from ships and from the Merchant Marine for being "bad security risks." Three workers were forced to quit under pressure from fellow union members at a Milwaukee factory. One man who returned to work suffered a broken back when he was literally thrown out in the street by four coworkers. The Reverend Robert M. Muir, interim rector of two Protestant Episcopal churches in Quincy, Massachusetts, was dismissed for supporting the petition.[34]

By October 1950, the Peace Information Center had folded due to financial difficulties and government pressures. Four months later, the Justice Department, in a clear attempt to halt the circulation of the Stockholm Peace petition, indicted Du Bois and four of his associates—Elizabeth Moos, Kyrle Elkin, Abbot Simon, and Sylvia Soloff—for failure to register as foreign agents. If convicted, each faced up to five years in prison and a ten thousand dollar fine.[35] Outraged over the charge, Du Bois emphatically stated, "We were an entirely American organization whose sole objective was to secure peace and prevent a third World War. We felt then, and feel now, that our activities for peace, and in particular to outlaw atomic warfare, could not conceivably fall within the purview of such a statute." Du Bois made clear that in this atmosphere, citizens must support the Korean War, be ready to fight wars anywhere or anytime, and believe in the use of nuclear weapons, or risk imprisonment.[36]

African Americans initially responded tepidly to the Du Bois arrest. However, as the black press began to focus on Du Bois's case, many in the black community enthusiastically defended their leader. In his 1952 book *In Battle for Peace*, Du Bois discussed the level of support he received:

> The response of Negroes in general was at first slow and not united, but it gradually gained momentum. At first, many Negroes were puzzled. They did not understand the indictment and assumed that I had let myself be drawn into some treasonable acts or movements in retaliation for continued discrimination in this land, which I had long fought. They understood this and forgave it, but thought my action ill-advised. Support came in tied directly to Pan-Africanism and anticolonialist activists, specifically George Padmore and South Africa, West Africa, Nigeria, World Federation of Scientific Workers, French West Indies, British Guiana, British West Indies, China, Southeast Asia Committee, Indonesian students, Vietnamese students.[37]

Throughout the black press, columnists and readers voiced their concern over Du Bois's arrest and trial. The case showed "what alarming and absurd lengths hysteria-ridden Department of Justice officials will go," the *Afro-American* argued. Du Bois said no more about the government "than abolitionists said during slavery," and "it is a shameful period in American history when the government feels it necessary to imprison a patriotic and loyal citizen like Du Bois simply because he speaks out for world peace," the *Afro-American* concluded.[38] *Courier* columnist P. L. Prattis suggested that if the government treated African Americans equally, it would not have to fear the influence of communism on the black community.[39] Prattis's column triggered a strong response. Readers expressed disgust over the lack of African American support for Du Bois and appreciation for Prattis's "courage to speak out" in such "dangerous times."[40]

When a banquet was held in New York to celebrate Du Bois's birthday and protest the indictment, Langston Hughes bravely sent a telegram: "YOUR BOOK DARKWATER GREATLY INFLUENCED MY YOUTH. I GREW UP ON YOUR EDITORIALS. AS EDITOR OF THE CRISIS YOU PUBLISHED MY FIRST POEM. IN GRATITUDE ON YOUR EIGHTY THIRD BIRTHDAY I SALUTE YOU AS ONE OF AMERICAS GREAT MEN AND THE DEAN OF NEGRO WRITERS AND SCHOLARS."[41]

While the NAACP's rank-and-file members voted overwhelmingly to support Du Bois, the leadership did not. Roy Wilkins was already in the process of "cleaning out" the organization of suspected communists. Walter White did not want the NAACP anywhere near the communist-led peace campaign.[42] He labeled the peace offensive "communist-inspired propaganda" and tried to tie Russian money to the Peace Information Center. Regardless of White's accusations, there was no money trail, no interlocking secretariat, and no formal links between the PIC and the Soviet Union.[43]

Du Bois and the Peace Information Center were acquitted of all charges. Citing the lack of evidence offered by the prosecution, Judge Matthew McGuire, who presided over the case, said that he did not want the jury to "speculate on a speculation." Many viewed the decision as a win not only for Du Bois but also for those fighting for peace and equality. The *National Guardian* declared, "For the first time since Harry S. Truman set off the greatest witch-hunt of modern times with his loyalty purge in March 1947, the government last week took a stunning defeat." The *New York Daily Compass* termed the acquittal "[the] biggest victory for peace and civil liberties to be seen around these United States in many months."[44]

Lawrence Wittner, who has written extensively on the global antinuclear movement, downplays the effectiveness of the Stockholm Peace Appeal. He argues that the petition ignored the complex problems involved in banning the bomb.[45] Wittner questions organizers' claims regarding the number of signers of the deliberately inoffensive petition, most of whom, in any case, came from communist bloc nations. He concludes that little good came from the communist-led peace campaign and it "produced limited results in the three major NATO powers."[46]

Given the political climate of the early 1950s, it is striking that many Americans were willing to sign a petition that demanded an end to nuclear weapons. Robbie Lieberman shows that while the appeal originated with the communist-led peace campaign, it took on a life of its own in that those people who agreed with its sentiments rarely questioned its origins and signed it out of a genuine desire for peace. Indeed, some people even wrote their own version of the petition and circulated it.[47] A Protestant Episcopal bishop in Oregon stated:

> If I signed a thing sponsored by a subversive group that is too bad. But I would rather find myself shoulder to shoulder with a group working for peace than in a camp of warmongers who think we can settle the present world difficulties only by bloodshed ... Americans seem to be dominated by a group of militarists whose only aim is to bring us into war ... I deplore the present tendency to call everyone a Communist who is making a plea for peace.[48]

A member of the First Methodist Church in Everett, Washington, made clear that he would do it again. "I have heard that the World Peace Appeal is supposed to be Communist-inspired, but I'm not convinced of that. Even if it is, I would sign it anyway, because I am so desperately anxious to find peace that I'm for finding it through any channel," he said.[49] Even the House Un-American Activities Committee (HUAC) conceded that most of the signers were loyal Americans expressing a desire for peace.[50] By focusing solely on the appeal's origin, historians fail to discuss the courage it took to protest nuclear weapons and the Korean War during the McCarthy era. Many Americans (black and white) who had previously expressed little concern over the atomic bomb began to examine the nuclear issue and added their names. The millions of signatories represented the collective outrage of Americans who denounced the atomic bomb as a weapon of mass murder. With McCarthyism in full swing and the modern Civil Rights Movement approaching, it remains quite remarkable that the "Ban the Bomb" pledge in America was led by Du Bois, enthusiastically supported by African Americans, and signed by millions.

Beyond Stockholm

Du Bois continued to connect the black freedom movement with nuclear disarmament as a candidate for the U.S. Senate. Following the 1948 presidential election, unlike many supporters, Du Bois stayed loyal to the Progressive Party. As he indicated to Henry Wallace and told readers of the *Chicago Globe*, Du Bois saw the Progressive Party as a latter-day Liberty Party, just as he saw communists as heirs to the abolitionists. Thus, Du Bois ran for the New York Senate seat on the American Labor Party ticket, the Progressive Party's local counterpart.[51]

Du Bois made clear from the beginning that he was going to campaign around peace and racial equality. In September 1950, at a press conference at Harlem's Hotel Theresa, Du Bois announced, "Big business wants war to keep your mind off social reform; it would rather spend your taxes for atom bombs than for schools because in this way it makes more money; it would rather have your sons dying in Korea than studying in America and asking awkward questions. The system, which it advocates depends on war and more war."[52] He praised former president Franklin Roosevelt while calling for the admission of the People's Republic of China to the United Nations Security Council, decolonization in Asia, Africa, and Puerto Rico, and the banning of atomic weapons.[53]

While Du Bois campaigned tirelessly, he was no match for his opponent, Senator Herbert Lehman (D-NY). Du Bois had a budget of $35,000, compared to the $600,000 spent by Republicans and $500,000 by the Democrats. Lehman received a bevy of endorsements from prominent African Americans, including civil rights, political, and labor leaders, as well as local clergy members. The Reverend Moran Weston praised Lehman's favorable position on the Fair Employment Practices Commission. A. Philip Randolph's Brotherhood of Sleeping Car Porters staunchly supported Lehman. Mary McLeod Bethune served as a member of the executive committee of the Lehman reelection campaign. Channing Tobias noted that Lehman appointed the first State Committee Against Discrimination. Walter White was more cautious. While he deemed Lehman's civil rights record "exceptional," he referred back to the NAACP's rule of nonpartisanship and refused to endorse him. However, Lehman's well-publicized telegram to President Truman calling for an "executive order barring discrimination in defense industries" and his ability to flood radio stations geared toward black listeners all but guaranteed his reelection. In that tense political climate, many African Americans were convinced, as Gerald Horne writes, "to swing behind the incumbent."[54]

Although Lehman won reelection, Du Bois had garnered considerable support. Out of five million votes cast, he received roughly 37,094 in the Bronx, 52,453 in Brooklyn, 18,480 in Queens, 1,637 in Staten Island, 55,935 in Manhattan, and 29,000 Upstate. In Harlem, he received approximately 12.6 percent of the total vote cast. Following his unsuccessful bid, Du Bois and his new wife, Shirley Graham, continued for years to travel and speak out in favor of peace and freedom.[55]

In that same year, Bayard Rustin became extremely frustrated with what he saw as peace activists' complacency toward the hydrogen bomb. Writing to A. J. Muste, Rustin suggested that Peacemakers take drastic action to call attention to the development of the new thermonuclear "super-bomb." Rustin was especially troubled by the muted response of religious and labor groups. In his view, they were "little prepared to question the H-bomb." The refusal of these groups to sponsor meetings on "The Quaker Plan for Peace with the Soviet Union" outraged Rustin. "Labor leaders are afraid. They admit it is bad but give in," he wrote. Rustin wanted to increase the size and scope of their actions: "We must find some way to let people know that *now* we are prepared to go to jail or even to give up all—to get shot down if necessary—but to cry out." He suggested traveling to Los Alamos to "obstruct the coming in of materials" or renouncing citizenship to raise awareness about the H-bomb. Rustin believed such dramatic actions would show people "the price we are willing to pay."[56]

Rustin received a less-than-enthusiastic response from his pacifist friends. Al Hassler contended that Rustin's idea would do little to awaken the conscience of the American people and mentioned that he was neither impressed nor moved by Rustin's suggestions. While he could not offer a viable alternative, Hassler warned that lying down in front of the gates at Los Alamos would only earn them the label of "crackpot" or "communist sympathizer." George Houser and Roy Kepler were also unsure of how to proceed. While neither flatly rejected Rustin's proposals, they warned about acting hastily and about the repercussions of such tactics. "I do not agree with putting my body at a Los Alamos gate or giving up national citizenship, or chaining myself in the U.N., or smuggling my way into Russia . . . I haven't rejected these ideas yet, but I haven't accepted them," Kepler said. He concluded that their actions must not simply resist the production of hydrogen bombs, but "must show that there is an alternative to hydrogen bombs." Connie Muste was the most receptive. While she questioned some of the direct action techniques, she supported the idea of renouncing citizenship and thought it could become an international movement with real impact.[57] For the most part, however, Rustin faced a group of predominantly white, middle-class pacifists, who balked at adopting a more radical approach. This difference in strategy between black and white activists would play out many times over the years.

Rustin, though, continued to work on nuclear issues, and in the spring he, along with Sutherland, Dellinger, Muste, Francis Hall, and Winifred Rawlins, formed the Working Committee for the "Fast for Peace." The activists, forty-four in total, planned on fasting for eight days in Washington, D.C., to protest the use of nuclear weapons. Focusing the action around Holy Week, the committee asked how people could consider themselves Christian while preparing to use hydrogen bombs? "If we conquer the world with hydrogen bombs, we shall lose our souls," it argued. The committee made clear that individuals, and indeed the nation, had to choose between "carrying the Cross or the H-bomb."[58]

The "Fast for Peace" grew much larger than any of the organizers expected. Parallel actions began popping up throughout the United States and the world. Dozens of individuals notified the committee of their plans to fast. A six-year-old boy offered to give up two meals a day "so as to ask people not to drop bombs on other people besides it would be better to share." An eighty-year-old woman from Westchester, Pennsylvania, wrote to organizers that although she was not in good health, she would still fast on Good Friday and Saturday. Sixty-four activists in Fukuoka, Japan, notified the committee of their intent to join the fast, as well as groups in Puerto Rico, Hawaii, and England.[59] On Good Friday, Rustin and others held a six-hour silent vigil on the steps of the Pentagon and outside Secretary of Defense Louis Johnson's office. In addition, the committee sent telegrams and letters to President Truman, Sumner Pike (chair of the Atomic Energy Commission), and Alexander Panyushkin (Soviet ambassador to the United States), among others, pleading for nuclear disarmament.[60]

Rustin also headed up Caravans for Peace. Organized by the college section of the Fellowship of Reconciliation (FOR), the project consisted of caravans of eight to ten young people and adult leaders who lived and trained together in local communities where they worked with local activists and organizations. According to the fellowship, the project sought to "stimulate discussion, arouse people to act, urge action for disarmament, and promote peace." Rustin was convinced that Caravans for Peace was an important project at a time when "nuclear weapons threatened mankind with extinction and the arms race was becoming ever more dangerous."[61]

Caravans for Peace organizers planned a series of events to commemorate the fifth anniversary of the Hiroshima bombing. Participants held an all-night vigil on August 5, which included readings from *A-Bomb Fell on America* and other works, leading up to 8:00 the next morning. The vigil ended at the exact time the bomb fell, while FOR executive secretary Francis Hall read a prayer and an account of the experiences of atomic bomb survivor the Reverend Kiyoshi Tanimoto, pastor of the former Central Methodist Church in Hiroshima. The group also presented choral readings and included a message of peace to six hundred high school girls in Hiroshima signed by sixty persons at the vigil. The message read: "We add our voices and prayers to yours in the plea for peace. We ask President Truman and Premier Stalin to outlaw atomic and bacterial weapons; to enter into a pact for complete disarmament and to use the savings in constructive work for the well being of all people."[62]

After 1951, African Americans' efforts to stop the bomb greatly declined. Caravans for Peace lacked the necessary organization and funds to produce any significant results. [63] The intimidation, repression, and fear that accompanied McCarthyism caused a dramatic downturn in peace activity. However, as the decade wore on, activists from Martin Luther King, Jr., to Lorraine Hansberry argued that these issues were inextricably linked. These men and women remained committed to the notion that the fight for racial equality, the abolition of nuclear weapons, and anticolonialism were part of the same struggle. They would be proven right when the French government decided to test a nuclear weapon in Africa.

Chapter 3

"Links in the Same Chain"

Civil Rights, Anticolonialism, and the Bomb in Africa

There must be unilateral [disarmament] action by a single nation, come what may. There must be no strings attached. We must be prepared to absorb the danger.

—Bayard Rustin, 1958

EARLY IN THE MORNING ON MARCH 1, 1954, the Atomic Energy Commission detonated a hydrogen bomb, code-named "Bravo," on the northwestern corner of Bikini Atoll in the Marshall Islands. A flash of blinding light illuminated the area as a fireball of intense heat shot skyward at a rate of 300 miles an hour. Within minutes, an enormous cloud filled with radioactive debris rose up more than twenty miles, generating winds hundreds of miles per hour. The gusts blasted the surrounding islands and stripped the branches and coconuts from trees. The explosion sent sand, coral, plant, and other sea life from Bikini's reef and the surrounding lagoon high into the air. A little over an hour after the explosion, twenty-three fishermen aboard the Japanese fishing vessel *Daigo Fukuryu Maru* (Lucky Dragon No. 5) watched in awe as radioactive dust began to fall on them. The men aboard the ship were oblivious to the fact that the ash was fallout from a hydrogen bomb test. Shortly after, the men's skin began to itch, while they vomited from the fallout. One man, Aikichi Kuboyama, died six months later. Three to four hours after the blast, the same ashy dust began to rain down onto the sixty-four people on Rongelap Atoll (located about 125 miles east of Bikini) and also onto the eighteen people residing on Ailinginae Atoll. The thermonuclear weapon test was a thousand times more powerful than the atomic bombs that were dropped on Hiroshima and Nagasaki and far exceeded the commission's expectations.[1]

Two months after the hydrogen bomb test, Supreme Court Justice Earl Warren wrote for a unanimous court that "the doctrine of 'separate but equal' has no place" in the nation's public schools. All over the world, people celebrated the *Brown v. Board of Education* decision as a victory in African Americans' fight for equality. However, for Warren the *Brown* decision was about more than civil rights. The chief justice firmly believed that the judiciary had a role to play in the Cold War. Viewing the Cold War as a battle of ideas, Warren told the judges of the

Fourth Circuit Court of Appeals in June 1954 that the world needed "a sense of justice instead of a sense of might." He asserted that the American conception of justice "separates us from many other political systems of the world." If the judiciary would uphold the ideals of American justice, "you and I can make our contributions to justice at home and peace in the world." Later that year, in a speech at the American Bar Association, Warren further explained his position:

> Our American system, like all others, is on trial both at home and abroad. The way it works; the manner in which it solves the problems of our day; the extent to which we maintain the spirit of our Constitution with its Bill of Rights, will in the long run do more to make it both secure and the object of adulation than the number of hydrogen bombs we stockpile.[2]

A peaceful world, he argued, "will be accomplished through ideas rather than armaments; through a sense of justice and mutual friendships rather than with guns and bombs and guided missiles."[3]

A few months after the *Brown* decision, in December 1954, five newly independent Asian countries (Burma, Ceylon, India, Indonesia, Pakistan) announced plans for an unprecedented conference of African, Asian, and Middle Eastern states. On April 19, 1955, twenty-nine nations of Asia and Africa gathered in Bandung, Indonesia, and declared that "freedom and peace are interdependent." The Asian-African Conference, or the Bandung Conference as the gathering became known, highlighted the need to eliminate European colonialism, white supremacy, and nuclear weapons.[4] Delegates at the Bandung Conference declared that nuclear weapons threatened the human race and that disarmament was imperative to save mankind from "wholesale destruction." Nuclear disarmament was "an absolute necessity for the preservation of peace" and it was their "duty" to bring it about. Delegates requested the United Nations and all concerned countries to prohibit the production, testing, and use of nuclear weapons as well as establish international control to ensure this outcome.[5]

The significance of the first Asian-African meeting was not lost on African Americans. Richard Wright and Adam Clayton Powell attended the Bandung Conference. The NAACP sent a message of support, and members of the American Labor Party offered "warm greetings" to the delegates.[6] Paul Robeson, who had been denied a passport to travel, sent the following message:

> Discussion and mutual respect are the first ingredients for the development of peace among nations. If other nations of the world follow the example set by the Asian-

African nations, there can be developed an alternative to the policy of force and an end to the threat of H-Bomb war. The people of Asia and Africa have a direct interest in such a development since it is a well-known fact that atomic weapons have been used only against the peoples of Asia. There is at present a threat to use them once more against an Asian people. I fully endorse the objectives of the Conference to prevent any such catastrophe, which would inevitably bring about suffering and annihilation to all the peoples of the world. Throughout the world all decent people must applaud the aims of the Conference to make the maximum contribution of the Asian and African countries to the cause of world peace.[7]

The *Afro-American* reported that there was a real possibility the conference could be the birthplace of a workable and honorable plan for world peace: "Amid all the rattling of nuclear weapons, if it [the Bandung Conference] does no more than hold out a slim hope for this greatest of all human desires, all mankind could rejoice and call it blessed."[8]

Since 1945, black activists had made the case that nuclear weapons, colonialism, and the black freedom struggle were connected. Ten years later, it never seemed clearer. From 1954 to 1955, African Americans witnessed a rise in nuclear weapons tests, the emergence of a new civil rights movement, and the first conference of nonwhite nations, which focused on colonialism, racism, and the bomb. However, the rabid anticommunism that had swept through the United States in the early 1950s destroyed most black leftist organizations (Council on African Affairs, American Labor Party, National Negro Labor Council, Civil Rights Congress) that were at the forefront of connecting the bomb to colonialism and racial equality.[9] As a result, many activists turned their attention solely to civil rights.

Alarmed over this development, writer Eugene Gordon began to criticize the black community's complacency in the battle to stop nuclear war. He pleaded with African Americans to take an interest in nuclear testing, warning, "The calcium properties of strontium 90 tend to introduce it into the body's bone structure—be it a black or a white or a yellow or a brown body—and certain quantities produce bone cancer and leukemia." He asked:

Why aren't U.S. Negro newspapers as quick to report on and to stir up excitement around the worldwide anxiety over the fallout of ashes of death as these papers are—and should always be—to report and editorialize on lynchings and denials of civil rights? Don't our editors and publishers wants us to know that a generation of Negro children with bone cancer and blood diseases would be less able to continue our fight for human rights? Or less able to enjoy those rights when won? Shouldn't we therefore pay some attention to less tangible but more sinister evils than those we meet daily face to face?

Something is going on which you and I had better look into when the U.S., having scared up enough votes in the United Nations to defeat resolutions demanding suspension of nuclear test explosions in the far Pacific, [*sic*] the daily commercial press crows as if we had won a great moral victory.[10]

As antinuclear activism declined, the number of nuclear weapons tests increased. Indeed, by the end of 1958, the American, Soviet, and British governments had exploded an estimated 307 nuclear weapons, the vast majority of them in the atmosphere. This news, coupled with the early success of the Civil Rights Movement, inspired citizens across the country to once again rise up against the bomb. Inside the black community, activists were ready to heed Gordon's call. However, instead of working in Popular Front groups, they found a new home inside the Peace Movement.[11]

On April 22, 1957, War Resisters League (WRL) member Lawrence Scott organized a meeting with Bayard Rustin, A. J. Muste, Norman Thomas, and others, in Philadelphia, to launch a campaign against nuclear weapons testing. The group talked about a "Proposed Committee to Stop H-bomb Tests" and decided that the committee would include both pacifists and nonpacifists. A subsequent meeting held a month later in Washington, D.C., solidified the group's desire for a new antinuclear campaign. As the pacifists were planning to protest upcoming Nevada nuclear tests, the Southern Christian Leadership Conference held a "Pilgrimage of Prayer," which brought 25,000 people to the Lincoln Memorial to urge equal rights for African Americans. For the pacifists, the fact that these two events occurred simultaneously was no coincidence and only further proved that the issues were connected.[12]

Two organizations formed as a result of the meetings, both dedicated to halting nuclear testing and ultimately abolishing nuclear weapons. The first group, the Committee for a Sane Nuclear Policy (SANE), appealed to the more moderate middle-class base of supporters and focused on publicizing the dangers of nuclear weapons while calling for nuclear disarmament. The other group, Non-Violent Action Against Nuclear Weapons (NVAANW), later called the Committee for Non-Violent Action (CNVA), comprised those activists who wanted to focus on more radical, direct action forms of protest.[13]

Rustin played a pivotal role in the renewed Peace Movement. As a prominent member of the CNVA, he was active in most discussions involving tactics, strategies, and objectives. Rustin's commitment to nonviolence during World War II earned him much respect, and his opinion carried weight with religious groups as well as the left. But most of all, D'Emilio writes, the longtime activist effectively transmitted the experience of the black freedom struggle to peace activists.[14]

The Committee for Non-Violent Action

In June 1957, Rustin traveled to Britain for the War Resisters International triennial gathering, which brought together pacifists from twenty-one nations. Rustin discussed the success of the Montgomery Bus Boycott and urged delegates to turn their focus on banning H-bomb tests. He returned to the United States just as CNVA members were completing their first major protest on the nuclear testing issue.[15]

In August, the Atomic Energy Commission decided to conduct a nuclear weapons test in Nevada. To commemorate Hiroshima Day, thirty pacifists held a twenty-four-hour "Prayer and Conscience Vigil" two hundred yards from the entrance of the test site. Eleven activists intentionally entered the military territory, Camp Mercury, and were arrested. While the group did not stop the test, it found success in that the events were covered by the mainstream press and attracted international attention. Indeed, the Third World Conference Against the A and H Bombs and for Disarmament, which was held in Tokyo at the same time, adopted a resolution in support of those who were arrested.[16]

Motivated by the energy and publicity of the Nevada protest, CNVA activists decided to sail into the South Pacific, where the Eisenhower administration planned another round of nuclear tests, and travel to Moscow to make clear that they were also holding the Soviet Union accountable for its nuclear activities. Rustin worked tirelessly on publicizing and coordinating the events and was one of the delegates who traveled to Moscow.[17]

On February 10, 1958, the *Golden Rule*, a thirty-foot ketch with a crew of four captained by Albert Bigelow, set sail from California to protest American nuclear weapons tests scheduled off Eniwetok Island. Bigelow, a World War II veteran, had been deeply affected by the atomic bombings of Hiroshima and Nagasaki. He participated in the Nevada protest and hosted two of the "Hiroshima maidens" when they arrived in the United States. Explaining his reasons for skippering the *Golden Rule*, Bigelow wrote, "I am going because it's time to do *something* about peace, not just *talk* about peace. I am going because I know *all* nuclear explosions are monstrous, evil, unworthy of human beings. I am going because it is cowardly and degrading for me to stand by any longer, to consent, and thus to collaborate in atrocities. I am going because I have to—if I am to call myself a human being."[18]

While the *Golden Rule* voyage became a major antinuclear event and received significant publicity, the activists never halted the tests. Following multiple mishaps, Bigelow and the crew made it to Honolulu by mid-April. Ignoring a federal injunction, they set sail for the Eniwetok testing area on May 1 but were greeted by the Coast Guard, who ordered the crew to stop and towed the *Golden Rule* back to Honolulu. After a week in jail, each crew member received a sixty-day suspended sentence. Crew members made another attempt in June, but again they were halted, arrested, and tried. This time they served thirty days in Honolulu City Jail.[19]

As the crew awaited trial, protests spread around the country and another ketch, the *Phoenix of Hiroshima*, arrived in Honolulu. Earle Reynolds—an anthropologist who had spent three years in Japan studying the effects of radiation—along with his wife, Barbara, their two teenage children, and a Japanese sailor were on board. The Reynolds crew continued the protest of the *Golden Rule*; on July 2, they entered the test area, notifying the authorities. Earle Reynolds was arrested and sentenced to six months in jail.[20]

As the *Golden Rule* sailed to Honolulu, Rustin was on his way to Moscow. Traveling through Europe, Rustin took part in a historic Easter weekend march from London to Aldermaston, the location of a nuclear weapons facility. As thousands gathered in Trafalgar Square, Rustin took his place at the microphone and told the activists:

> There must be unilateral [disarmament] action by a single nation, come what may. There must be no strings attached. We must be prepared to absorb the danger. We must use our bodies in direct action, non-cooperation, whatever is required to bring our government to its senses. In the United States, the black people of Montgomery said, "We will not cooperate with discrimination." And the action of those people achieved tremendous results. They are now riding the buses with dignity, because they were prepared to make a sacrifice of walking for their rights.[21]

Antinuclear activist Michael Randle recalled, "Bayard Rustin delivered what many regarded as the most powerful speech of that Good Friday afternoon, linking the struggle against weapons of mass destruction with the struggle of blacks for their basic rights in America."[22]

Witnessing thousands of protesters march in the rain for nuclear disarmament made an especially big impression on Rustin. Indeed, Lawrence Wittner contends that Rustin's motivation to propose and organize the 1963 March on Washington came from this demonstration.[23] Rustin's trip also proved to be a forerunner of another significant event: the Sahara Project.

The Sahara Project

In the summer of 1959, France announced plans to test a nuclear weapon in the Sahara. Frightened and angered, many Africans saw the French test as another form of European colonialism. Those who lived in Ghana feared that nuclear fallout would devastate their cocoa industry, a vital source of national revenue. The independent states of Africa asked France to cancel the test plans and the United Nations passed a resolution urging France to abandon the test. France ignored the pleas and argued that unless other nuclear powers gave up their weapons, it had to proceed.[24]

Upon learning of France's plans, British Direct Action Committee members April Carter and Michael Randle proposed sending an international protest team to the test site to raise awareness, ignite antinuclear activism throughout Africa, and halt the bomb tests. The two activists made clear that the Sahara Project would employ direct action in protesting against both nuclear weapons and colonialism. More than merely undertaking a symbolic act, the activists were to "place their lives in the way of the nuclear instrument that may ultimately wipe out thousands of lives."[25]

In some ways the Sahara Project did not seem realistic. Even reaching the test site in Algeria would pose a serious challenge. If they started from Morocco, they risked the chance of being caught or shot by French paratroopers. If they came through French West Africa, starting at Nigeria or Ghana, the trip was three times as long as through Morocco and meant the protesters would have to journey days through the Sahara. While Carter received initial support from the African community, French and American pacifists balked at the idea. CNVA leader George Willoughby described the project as "in the dream stage." Al Hassler at the Fellowship of Reconciliation agreed, arguing that the project was "completely unrealistic and fanciful" and activists should not "waste any time" debating it.[26]

Carter and Randle did however receive backing from the Reverend Michael Scott, a well-respected British antiapartheid activist, and from Bill Sutherland, who was working as an assistant to the finance minister in Ghana. The two also managed to garner support from the War Resisters League and CNVA, as well as from Rustin and Muste. Rustin, who was intrigued by the idea of linking the campaign to abolish nuclear weapons and the African struggle for independence, became an important member of the protest team. Lobbying for Rustin to join the team, Sutherland explained that Rustin had more direct action experience than the British activists and that having an African American who was active in the Civil Rights Movement participate in the project would bring much needed credibility among Africans. As a result, Rustin headed to Britain and then Africa to organize the protest.[27]

The fact that France chose Africa to test its first nuclear weapon played an especially significant role. Ghana had become independent in 1957 and under the leadership of Kwame Nkrumah remained committed to fighting colonialist rule. Nkrumah had avoided taking sides in the Cold War and stood for nonalignment along the lines enunciated at the Bandung Conference. In addition, Ghana's campaign for independence had been based on Nkrumah's strategy of nonviolent "positive action." Since Ghana's leaders and the protest team both favored disarmament and nonviolence, Carter explains, "Neither had to compromise their principles despite the need to adjust to the political circumstances inside Ghana, and the attitudes of the Government."[28]

In 1958, Ghana hosted the Conference of Independent African States. It resolved that "nuclear testing should be suspended and means taken to reduce the arms race. It called for African representation in international arms control agencies."[29] The next year, Ghana established the Ghanaian Campaign for Nuclear Disarmament (CND). Ghana CND included representatives of the main organizations in the country and was an unofficial government body. In late August, Ghana CND decided to support the Sahara Project; as a result, Sutherland's role in the project increased. He became the bridge between Africa, Britain, and America. "It was so exciting because we felt that this joining up of the European antinuclear forces, the African liberation forces, and U.S. civil rights movements could help each group feed and reinforce the other. Then to be sponsored by a majority political party in government clearly marked a unique moment in progressive history," Sutherland recalled.[30]

Rustin Heads to Africa

Rustin departed for London in October. Less than a week after he left, he sent the CNVA a report expressing his frustration with the lack of organization and funds for the project. He estimated that the necessary costs would be double what the British Direct Action Committee had budgeted and was concerned that the Ghanaian government "did not understand the full implications of the project." African leaders were unaware of planned civil disobedience and not clear on the protest team's position on nuclear weapons. The Committee of African Organizations stopped working with the London committee, and African participation was clearly in jeopardy. Rustin was also vexed about Canon Collins's attempts to stymie the project. Collins, a moderate activist in Britain's Campaign for Nuclear Disarmament (CND), had urged African leaders to disassociate themselves from the project, calling Rustin and others "irresponsible" and "crackpot."[31]

Rustin worked tirelessly to gain African support. Upon arriving in Accra on October 20, he received the full backing of the Ghanaian government and interest from Nigeria, Guinea, Nyasaland, Basutoland, and Cameroon. Rustin spoke to thousands at various assemblies, including the All African Trade Union Congress. The congress had passed a resolution in favor of the project and invited Randle and Rustin to address delegates at its meeting in November. Moroccan officials offered financial support and suggested the protest set off from their territory, 300 miles from the test site and 1,200 miles closer than Ghana.[32]

Rustin knew, however, that once he began to accept funding and support from other countries he had to question their motives. Rustin did not want the colonialism issue to overshadow nuclear weapons, which was the protest group's first priority. He feared that Morocco would use the project as an opportunity to highlight France's colonial rule. While Rustin and others were staunchly anticolonial, they maintained that the purpose was for universal nuclear disarmament and to protest colonialism in a general sense, not to focus solely on France.[33]

Rustin received a less-than-enthusiastic response at home. He became distressed upon finding out that A. Philip Randolph did not support the project. Randolph's response seemed odd considering that in October he had expressed support for Kenyan labor leader and politician Tom Mboya, telling him, "Negro citizens of America are keenly interested" in aiding African students because "of our African roots."[34] Randolph, however, had avoided internationalizing the black freedom struggle since the 1940s. He resigned from the National Negro Congress when Max Yergan became president and refused to support the Stockholm Peace Appeal. Randolph wanted Rustin to return to the United States to focus solely on civil rights and help organize protests for the 1960 presidential conventions. Protest organizers, though, made clear they were "united in the conviction that work for PEACE and CIVIL RIGHTS must go on year round." Voting was not enough, they argued, and activists "must be serious about ending the threat of nuclear war" and "racial discrimination." The activists called on the United States to adopt a foreign policy aimed at disarmament and global human rights. Randolph, however, failed to make the obvious connections between Rustin's actions in Africa and the protests in the United States.[35]

In an attempt to remedy the situation, Rustin wrote to Muste, Willoughby, and Stanley Levison. Rustin felt he was "making a real contribution to the Sahara Project" and it was "one of the most potentially important projects that the pacifist movement has been associated with." Rustin knew, though, that Randolph mistrusted many pacifists. To keep the peace, Rustin suggested that all those involved, especially "others in the Negro community," get together and decide the best course of action. "This is sound, not only for me, but for the pacifist organizations and the role that we can play in the Civil Rights Movement," he wrote. Rustin was "deeply, very deeply concerned" that he not be placed in a position where he "could be accused of irresponsibility or shirking in duty in the Civil Rights struggle," fearing that "any such interference will play directly into the hands of those who basically disagree with our non-violent and mass approach to the civil rights struggle and the solution thereof."[36]

By the end of November, Rustin received news that several pacifists and civil rights leaders had met in Randolph's office to discuss the situation, but could not come to a consensus. One of the attendees, Jim Peck, told Rustin that he "emphasized that the Sahara Project goes far beyond the scope of a peace project: It is a demonstration of brotherhood because of the interracial makeup of the team and it is a demonstration against colonialism, whose ugly manifestation of recent times is the explosion of this bomb." He added, "The main theme music throughout the meeting was your [Rustin's] indispensability for ALL non-violent action projects." However, Peck also thought it was a "sad situation" and did not "speak well for Randolph, King or the Civil Rights Movement" that they relied so much on Rustin. In short, the group remained deadlocked: Randolph wanted Rustin to return, while others thought he should stay.[37]

Rustin concluded from subsequent memos that the decision was ultimately his to make. While he was crucial to the potential success of the project, Rustin decided to return to the United States and urged Muste to oversee the Sahara protest. Muste obliged and on November 23 left for Ghana, freeing Rustin to leave.[38]

Once Muste arrived, he better appreciated Rustin's importance to the project. "Bayard is magnificent," Muste wrote to Willoughby. "Don't see how project could possibly have got off the ground without him." Rustin had raised more than $25,000 and the publicity in Africa exceeded anything pacifists had achieved in the United States. "An immense propaganda job for the idea of nonviolence has been done among the masses," Muste observed. Rustin had also succeeded in giving the project as much of an African focus as a pacifist one, and he was now too invested to leave without participating in the actual event. Rustin continued to work with the Sahara Project, but left Africa after the first stage of the protest.[39]

The Protest

On December 5, the night before the team began its journey, Michael Scott told Radio Ghana listeners that the desert "was being prepared as a base for nuclear war in North Africa and the Middle East." Their journey, he said, would be "a holy war, a non-violent war, against the inhumanity of nuclear war."[40] Thus, on Sunday morning, December 6, the Sahara protest team set off to stop the French from exploding a nuclear weapon on African soil. Rising before dawn, the group headed to a farewell rally at Accra Arena. Traveling with two Land Rovers, a truck carrying supplies, and an extra jeep, the team was greeted by waving Ghanaians along the roadside. A thousand spectators filled the arena for the send-off. Among the speakers, the finance minister, K. A. Gbedemah, forcefully spoke out in favor of the protest: "It seems nowadays that when Frenchmen assume high government office, they become mad. This is the only word one can apply to much of French policy today and especially to its fatuous effort to become a nuclear power." The French had no right to interfere on African soil while "an international team [was] traveling to the Sahara on a mission for all mankind." As the team drove through the city, hundreds lined the streets waving and shouting, "Sahara!" and "Freedom!"[41]

After a seven-hour drive, the group arrived in Kumasi to enthusiastic supporters and another massive demonstration. For the next three days, the group traveled hundreds of miles from Accra to Navrango and Bawku, approaching the Upper Volta border where French jurisdiction began.[42] On December 9, participants finally set off for the border and crossed into French Upper Volta. At Bittou, sixteen miles beyond the border, three French officials detained team members and attempted to collect their passports. While the French officers wanted to avoid a confrontation, they would not let the protesters through, and the team refused to leave. As the officers deliberated about their next move, large numbers of Africans eagerly watched the development. One of them said, about the test, "If it's harmless, why not hold it in the country outside Paris, so all the French people can see the wonder?" "This confirmed the impression, that whether they say so openly or not, Africans are afraid of and against the Sahara tests," Muste concluded. On Thursday, tensions finally built up between the French officers and protesters. A hundred police, armed with revolvers, rifles, and machine guns, surrounded the team and sealed off the area so that Africans could not get within fifty yards of the group, thus ensuring that support would be limited.[43]

The Sahara Project gained the attention of the African, British, and U.S. media and inspired solidarity demonstrations in Europe, Africa, and the United States. The War Resisters League urged France not to violate the moratorium on nuclear tests and not to join the "nuclear club." Such action, the league warned, would cripple disarmament efforts by encouraging other nations to develop atomic arsenals. In New York City, the group led a protest from the United Nations to the French mission, while others demonstrated at the French embassies in London and Lagos.[44]

The project continued into January with multiple efforts to penetrate the French territory, each resulting again in apprehension and removal from the area. While team members explored alternative routes, they never reached the test site; in early 1960, France exploded several nuclear bombs in Africa. Protests erupted throughout the African continent. Most North and West African states issued statements denouncing the test and its effects. Egypt's president, Gamal Abdel Nassar, and the Arab League Council immediately condemned the action. The Moroccan Cabinet met to discuss measures against France, while the Istiqlal Party called for breaking off diplomatic relations. Ghana froze the assets of French firms. African states that were part of the French community, however, refrained from overt protest, and Ivory Coast and Chad went so far as to congratulate France on the test.[45]

Even though the team failed to stop the French tests, one could conclude that the Sahara Project was a success. After the initial round of tests, the Algerian war intensified and antinuclear sentiment spread. Eventually, the French decided to abandon nuclear testing in Africa. There can be no doubt, Richard Taylor explains, that because of Nkrumah's support the protests against the French tests and, to a lesser extent, the team's direct action tactics gained large-scale public support in Ghana. Bill Sutherland maintained that the Sahara Project was a victory since the French eventually halted nuclear testing in Africa. Rustin concluded that the Sahara protest was "the most significant non-violent project" in which he had participated.[46]

After the French tests, Nkrumah focused his energy on organizing a special All-African Conference to coordinate action against further nuclear tests and to develop ongoing forms of peace activism in Africa. Michael Scott proposed the idea to Nkrumah, and the Ghanaian government took the initiative in planning the Conference on Positive Action for Peace and Security in Africa, in Accra in April 1960. The meeting brought together overseas peace groups with representatives of African governments, liberation movements, and union federations and drew prominent pacifists from around the world.[47]

While the conference was originally planned as a response to the French tests, events that occurred throughout Africa in 1960 forced organizers to add to the agenda. On March 21, South African police fired on a group of unarmed, nonviolent demonstrators who were protesting the government's increasingly harsh and racist policies. In what became known as the Sharpeville Massacre, officers killed sixty-three demonstrators and wounded over 180. Combining this with the increasingly violent struggle for independence in Algeria, the conference addressed much more than was previously planned. However, amid concerns by some government officials who had supported the conference in its original format, Nkrumah declared that the threat of nuclear weapons was of the utmost importance. The African leader reassured delegates in his opening address that they had come to Accra "first to discuss and plan future action to prevent further use of African soil as a testing ground for nuclear weapons." Moreover, Nkrumah explained, the conference would focus on ways to prevent further bloodshed in South Africa and Algeria.[48]

Ralph Abernathy, Dr. King's top aide in the Southern Christian Leadership Conference, joined with advocates of armed struggle like Frantz Fanon to unanimously applaud the Sahara team, urge further protests against nuclear testing, and support the establishment of training centers in nonviolent resistance. At the gathering's outset, the Sahara protest team presented a manifesto to the delegates, calling not only for an end to nuclear testing and arms, but for a thousand volunteers for a renewed protest movement: "By joining with Africans from other parts of our Continent in positive non-violent action against nuclear imperialism they can make a decisive contribution to the liberation of all Africa." According to Bill Sutherland, the conference represented "the height of influence of the world pacifist movement on the African liberation struggle."[49]

In June 1962, with financial assistance from Nkrumah's government, a week-long assembly on disarmament convened in Accra. "The World Without the Bomb" conference included 130 participants from nonaligned countries and formed the Accra Assembly. Speaking on the conference's opening day, W.E.B. Du Bois stated:

> If we can conceive of a world without atomic bombs, then we can conceive of a real world peace. The only hope of mankind today is Peace, and the development, which Peace permits. Atomic powers and war make Peace impossible. We strive therefore for a world without bombs, for world peace; for a world where men thinking and acting for the social good of all will be able to achieve this aim which war makes impossible. Africa, which is just at the point of recovering its past greatness after centuries of domination and oppression, faces the danger of having its bright future blotted out before it can even attempt to realize it. It seems curious that some of the great modern discoveries, and inventions, instead of being used to help mankind, are used for its destruction or certainly to threaten its destruction. I beg you, therefore, let us all strive for a world without atomic bombs—which means a world of Peace.[50]

Christine Johnson, director of Muhammad University of Islam in Chicago and president of the African American Heritage Association, attended the gathering. "The purpose of the conference was to call the attention of the world and particularly the U.S.A. and Russia to the fact that we want peace in our time; that the bomb must be banned and nuclear power used for peaceful purposes," she said. In the months following the meeting, the Accra Assembly protested further French nuclear tests, sponsored a "Peace Week" in Ghana, and sent delegates to represent Africa at various international disarmament meetings.[51] Julian Mayfield, former member of the Harlem-based Committee for the Negro in the Arts, edited *The World Without the Bomb*, a collection of papers from the gathering. A black-nationalist and an important writer in the Black Power Movement, Mayfield had moved to Ghana to work with Nkrumah. Speaking at Howard University years later, Mayfield called out black moderates like Randolph, who he said embraced anticommunism while ignoring colonialism and nuclear weapons. "The older leaders had long discouraged our taking an interest in controversial foreign policy matters, or even traveling to socialist countries on the disapproval list of the State Department. But we went to those forbidden countries anyway," he said.[52]

African leaders remained focused on the bomb throughout the 1960s. Two years after the French test, Haile Selassie and Kwame Nkrumah openly objected to the Soviet Union's plan to test a nuclear weapon. In a message sent to Soviet ambassador A. V. Budakhov, Selassie stated, "We have learned with dismay of the Soviet Union's stated intention to explode a 50-megaton bomb on October 31. We must express to your excellency our deep concern with the potential consequences for those who find themselves in its path." Nkrumah also expressed "deep concern" over the plans and asked Nikita Khrushchev to reconsider.[53] Dr. Nnamdi Azikiwe, governor general of Nigeria, urged President Kennedy to redouble U.S. efforts to prevent nuclear war, explaining, "It is the fervent hope of the people of Nigeria that you will use your country's stupendous strength and wealth to prevent the onset of nuclear annihilation."[54]

Committee for a Sane Nuclear Policy

By 1960, activists had sailed into nuclear weapons testing zones, blocked entrances to missile bases, and traveled to Africa to stop the bomb. Building on this new momentum, activists took to the streets and antinuclear demonstrations began cropping up in major cities around the country. In May, three thousand Americans demonstrated in San Francisco's Union Square for an end to the arms race. The same month, two thousand people in New York City resisted the yearly nuclear bomb drill, including five hundred in City Hall Park who refused to take shelter.[55] SANE organized many of these actions.

Throughout the late 1950s and into the 1960s, SANE provided a much needed organizational focus for the Peace Movement. It consistently placed advertisements in various publications, urging a ban on nuclear testing.[56] On November 15, 1957, a full-page advertisement in the *New York Times* was headlined, "We Are Facing a Danger Unlike Any Danger That Has Ever Existed." Suggesting that Americans become the leaders in world peace, SANE demanded that all nations suspend nuclear tests immediately, because no nation had the right to "contaminate the air that belongs to all peoples, devitalize the land, or tamper with the genetic integrity of man himself." While stopping nuclear bomb testing would not solve all the problems, SANE argued that it would "eliminate immediately at least one real and specific danger." The "challenge of the age," SANE contended, was not to acquire new and more powerful weapons but "to develop the concept of a higher loyalty—loyalty by man to the human community." Martin Luther King, Jr., and Dorothy Height, president of the National Council of Negro Women, were among the many notable signers.[57]

When world leaders met in Geneva to discuss nuclear disarmament, SANE gathered thousands of signatures urging a test ban and delivered them to the delegates. SANE also published a full-page advertisement, "To the Men at Geneva," in the *New York Times* on October 31, 1958, the day the one-year halt in U.S. nuclear testing went into effect and the nuclear powers commenced their meeting. The ad addressed the dangers of nuclear fallout as well as the problem of nuclear proliferation and was signed by nineteen world leaders, including Albert Schweitzer, Bertrand Russell, Eleanor Roosevelt, and King.[58]

SANE sponsored and organized many antinuclear demonstrations, including a massive rally at New York City's Madison Square Garden. The group planned the event to coincide with summit talks between President Eisenhower and Premier Khrushchev in hopes of influencing the leaders to "end nuclear testing, fully disarm, and work towards a genuine peace." Over 17,000 joined Norman Cousins, Eleanor Roosevelt, former Republican presidential nominee Alfred M. Landon, Norman Thomas, and Walter Reuther of the United Auto Workers in demanding an end to nuclear testing. In what can be considered a reversal of his earlier positions, A. Philip Randolph also took part in the demonstration. Singer and actor Harry Belafonte headlined the entertainment, along with Elaine May, Tom Posten, and Orson Bean. Senators Hubert Humphrey (D-MN), Jacob Javits (R-NY), and Adlai Stevenson sent messages of support. Stevenson expressed his regret for not attending, but stated his "emphatic belief that a world under law entails essentially an end to the settlement of disputes by violence and this in the context of 1960 means first of all a dedicated search for disarmament." Following the rally, five thousand protesters marched through Times Square to the United Nations for a midnight prayer, led by Reuther, Thomas, and Belafonte. They demanded that Eisenhower and Khrushchev not abandon the path to peace, and protesters held signs reading "Ban the Bomb" and "Don't Start Testing" and circulated anti-testing petitions.[59]

In September 1959, SANE started "Hollywood for SANE," targeting those celebrities who supported nuclear disarmament. Nat King Cole, Sammy Davis Jr., Sidney Poitier, and Belafonte were just some of the prominent African American members. In June 1960, Hollywood for SANE presented "An Evening with Belafonte." Held at the Shrine Auditorium, the event sold out two weeks in advance and was attended by 6,500 persons. The singer was on stage by himself for more than two hours, raised more than $52,000, and drew one of the largest audiences in the history of the Shrine Auditorium. It was Belafonte's only appearance on the West Coast for the year.[60]

Later that month, Belafonte, Steve Allen, and Robert Ryan asked for a nuclear test ban before a Democratic national platform committee that was seeking "grass roots" opinions on major issues. Allen told the panel: "A recent Gallup poll . . . indicated that 77 percent of the American people are in favor of banning further nuclear tests, as compared to earlier surveys, which showed that the great majority had consistently opposed the halting of H-bomb tests. We feel this clearly indicates a growing public awareness of the dangers of both nuclear bomb testing and war itself." He argued that the question of radiation danger was a medical and moral issue rather than a political one. Belafonte drew heavy applause from the more than one hundred persons present when he asked the committee to adopt a resolution that brought the matter "to the people" and "let them have their say," since it was "the people's fate at stake." "I think it is well and good," he added, "for people in high places to make plans for protection, but it is another thing to make plans and not inform the mass of the people of what is going on."[61]

By 1960, longtime activists like Bayard Rustin, as well as Hollywood celebrities, civil rights leaders, and ordinary citizens, had consistently made the case that the black freedom movement was part of the larger fight for global human rights. However, with the start of the Vietnam War and emerging Civil Rights Movement, the question again became, How would activists keep this chain together? Two people led the way. Both had the last name of King.

Chapter 4

"Desegregation Not Disintegration"

The Black Freedom Movement, Vietnam, and Nuclear Weapons

What will be the ultimate value of having established social justice in a context where all people, Negro and White, are merely free to face destruction by strontium 90 or atomic war?
—Dr. Martin Luther King, Jr., 1959

ON APRIL 1, 1961, THE PROMINENT BLACK WRITER JAMES BALDWIN addressed a large group of peace activists at Judiciary Square in Washington, D.C. Baldwin, who had recently become a member of the advisory group of SANE, was one of the headlining speakers for the rally, which focused on "Security Through World Disarmament." When asked why he chose to speak at such an event, Baldwin responded: "What am I doing here? Only those who would fail to see the relationship between the fight for civil rights and the struggle for world peace would be surprised to see me. Both fights are the same. It is just as difficult for the white American to think of peace as it is of no color . . . Confrontation of both dilemmas demands inner courage." Baldwin considered both problems in the same breath because "racial hatred and the atom bomb both threaten the destruction of man as created free by God."[1] The rally was part of a larger antinuclear campaign organized by Witness for Peace, which began with Easter weekend.

Baldwin's comments were strikingly similar to those of Dr. Martin Luther King, Jr., just four years earlier. Many scholars who have examined King's later years argue that in the mid-1960s King began to shift his focus from civil rights to issues relating to peace and economic justice.[2] However, King began protesting the use of nuclear weapons a decade *before* 1967 and made the case much earlier than has previously been written, that civil rights was inextricably linked to peace.

When asked in December 1957 about the use of nuclear weapons, King replied:

> I definitely feel that the development and use of nuclear weapons should be banned. It cannot be disputed that a full-scale nuclear war would be utterly catastrophic. Hundreds and millions of people would be killed outright by the blast and heat, and by the ionizing radiation produced at the instant of the explosion . . . Even countries

not directly hit by bombs would suffer through global fall-outs. All of this leads me to say that the principal objective of all nations must be the total abolition of war. War must be finally eliminated or the whole of mankind will be plunged into the abyss of annihilation.[3]

A year later, King was asked again about nuclear weapons. Echoing his earlier sentiments, King stated, "I definitely feel that there should be a cessation of nuclear tests. It cannot be disputed that full scale nuclear war would be utterly catastrophic . . . The principal objective of all nations must be the total abolition of war, and a definite move toward disarmament."[4]

King remained committed to the antinuclear cause throughout the Civil Rights Movement. In 1959, five months after being stabbed in Harlem, King addressed the War Resisters League's thirty-sixth annual dinner, where he praised its work and linked the domestic struggle for racial justice with the campaign for global disarmament: "Not only in the South, but throughout the nation and the world, we live in an age of conflicts, an age of biological weapons, chemical warfare, atomic fallout and nuclear bombs . . . Every man, woman, and child lives, not knowing if they shall see tomorrow's sunrise." He asked, "What will be the ultimate value of having established social justice in a context where all people, Negro and White, are merely free to face destruction by strontium 90 or atomic war?"[5] A month later, King visited India to study nonviolence as a guest of Prime Minister Jawaharlal Nehru. Giving his farewell statement for All India Radio, he declared:

> The peace-loving peoples of the world have not yet succeeded in persuading my own country, America, and Soviet Russia to eliminate fear and disarm themselves . . . It may be that just as India had to take the lead and show the world that national independence could be achieved nonviolently, so India may have to take the lead and call for universal disarmament. And if no other nation will join her immediately, India may declare itself for disarmament unilaterally.[6]

Later that year, King ended up publicly defending his position on nuclear weapons to Robert F. Williams. Williams, an ex-marine and black radical, had become the NAACP branch leader in North Carolina. After a series of confrontations with white racists, Williams declared African Americans had no choice but to "meet violence with violence," and organized an armed self-defense group in Monroe. The NAACP's national office suspended Williams soon after. Williams appealed his case to delegates attending the group's national convention in July. Roy Wilkins persuaded delegates to uphold Williams's suspension, and King, who was scheduled to speak at the convention, focused his talk on the importance of remaining nonviolent.[7]

King felt compelled three months later to respond when Williams wrote in *Liberation* that nonviolence was an unrealistic strategy for African Americans. While he praised King as "a great and successful leader," Williams insisted that nonviolence was "made to order" for the Montgomery Bus Boycott. Conceding some ground to Williams, King admitted that even Gandhi had not condemned the principle of self-defense, even involving weapons and bloodshed. Indeed, Gandhi sanctioned armed self-defense for those "unable to master pure non-violence." However, King was convinced that armed self-defense would "mislead Negroes into the belief that this is the only path and place them as a minority in a position where they confront a far larger adversary than it is possible to defeat in the form of combat." King especially took umbrage with Williams's assertion that he did not speak out nearly enough against nuclear war. Williams argued that those like King who preached nonviolence were weak when it came to protesting "the warmongering of the atom-crazed politicians in Washington." For Williams, black-nationalism was synonymous with antiwar. King fired back saying, "I have unequivocally declared my hatred for this most colossal of all evils and I have condemned any organizer of war; regardless of rank or nationality. I have signed numerous statements with other Americans condemning nuclear testing and have authorized publication of my name in advertisements appearing in the largest circulation newspapers in the country, without concern that it was then 'unpopular' to so speak out."[8]

Whether addressing church parishioners or college students, King often demanded an end to the nuclear arms race.[9] In "Pilgrimage to Nonviolence," King explained that "the church cannot remain silent while mankind faces the threat of being plunged into the abyss of nuclear annihilation. If the church is true to its mission it must call for an end to the arms race."[10] Speaking at Spelman College, King pleaded that together they must work to end the arms race and bring about universal disarmament. He called it "a matter of survival": "Talk about love and nonviolence may have been merely a pious injunction a few years ago; today it is an absolute necessity for the survival of our civilization."[11] For these supporters, King's strong antinuclear views added credence to the notion that peace and freedom were connected.

Although Hollywood for SANE brought some well-known individuals into the fold, it was King's enthusiastic and committed support that largely helped SANE and the Peace Movement affect groups of people they may have otherwise never reached. King routinely worked with SANE and lent his name to many of its public ads and campaigns. He consistently preached a message of peace through disarmament and applied his philosophy of nonviolence to the threat of nuclear annihilation. In 1962, King argued that world peace would become secure, "not because of a balance of terror" but because people will have realized that "non-violence in the nuclear age was life's last chance."[12] A year later, in *A Strength to Love*, King stressed the dangers of nuclear weapons. "Man now has atomic and nuclear weapons that could within seconds completely destroy the major cities of the world. Yet the arms race continues and nuclear tests still explode in the atmosphere, with the grim prospect that the very air we breathe will be poisoned by radioactive fallout."[13] Discussing the possibility of nuclear annihilation, he stated:

> When confronted by midnight in the social order we have in the past turned to science for help. And little wonder! On so many occasions science has saved us. When we were in the midnight of physical limitation and material inconvenience science lifted us to the bright morning of physical and material comfort. When we were in the midnight of crippling ignorance and superstition, science brought us to the daybreak of the free and open mind. When we were in the midnight of dread plagues and diseases, science, through surgery, sanitation, and the wonder drugs, ushered in the bright day of physical health, thereby prolonging our lives and making for greater security, and physical well-being. How naturally we turn to science in a day when the problems of the world are so ghastly and ominous.
>
> But alas! Science cannot now rescue us, for even the scientist is lost in the terrible midnight of our age. Indeed, science gave us the very instruments that threaten to bring universal suicide. So modern man faces a dreary and frightening midnight in the social order.[14]

Shifting to the "culture of fear" in America, King maintained that nuclear weapons and fear of "death and racial annihilation" had risen to "morbid proportions." "The terrifying spectacle of nuclear warfare put Hamlet's words, 'To be or not to be,' on millions of trembling lips," King warned. "Witness our frenzied efforts to construct fallout shelters. As though even these offer sanctuary from an H-Bomb attack! Witness the agonizing desperation of our petitions that our government increase the nuclear stockpile. But our fanatical quest to maintain 'a balance of terror' only increases our fear and leaves nations on tiptoes lest some diplomatic *faux pas* ignite a frightful holocaust."[15] Fear, King predicted, would be the ultimate cause of nuclear war. "Our deteriorating international situation is shot through with the lethal darts of fear. Russia fears America, and America fears Russia. Like-wise China and India, and the Israelis and the Arabs. These fears include another nation's aggression, scientific and technological su-premacy, and economic power, and our own loss of status and power." In true Gandhian fashion, King concluded that only when countries work out their dif-ferences with love and peace would mankind be safe.[16]

King also used the Cuban missile crisis in October 1962 as an opportunity to connect nuclear disarmament to racial and economic justice. Since annihilation had been avoided, he argued, now was the time "to concretely seek common agreement on nuclear testing and disarmament." King maintained that since tensions had eased, this was the federal government's chance to turn its atten-tion and funds to education, a Medicare program for seniors, and civil rights. "If our nation is to survive abroad, she must first survive at home," he warned. King suggested the government take some of the "billions of dollars spent on nuclear devices" to increase teachers' salaries and build much needed schools. "Let us not misuse the success of the Cuban missile crisis, but instead strengthen the country by granting African Americans the right to vote, eliminate the poll-tax, and end the system of segregation in 1963."[17]

Receiving the Nobel Peace Prize in 1964, King explained that the "spiritual and moral lag" in modern man was due to three problems: racial injustice, pov-erty, and war. King warned that in the nuclear age man must eliminate racism or risk human annihilation. "Equality with whites will hardly solve the problems of either whites or Negroes if it means equality in a society under the spell of terror and a world doomed to extinction," he said. Nation-states were responsible for war and nuclear weapons which "threaten the survival of mankind," and both are "genocidal and suicidal in character." He concluded by pleading for a "peace race" rather than an arms race.[18]

Although the press often focused on outspoken male leaders, King's wife, Coretta, along with a number of female activists, followed in the footsteps of Shirley Graham, Marian Anderson, and others to fight for both peace and equal-ity. Prominent among them was Lorraine Hansberry, best known for writing *A Raisin in the Sun*, who linked freedom to anticolonialism and nuclear disarma-ment throughout her life. Indeed, Mary Helen Washington describes Hansberry as "militantly left-wing, antiracist, anticolonialist, and a social feminist." Steven Carter contends that Hansberry's passion for world peace began in her youth, when she was alarmed and outraged by world war and the atomic bombings of Hiroshima and Nagasaki. Her disdain for nuclear weapons only increased as she grew older. She vehemently opposed using atomic bombs in Korea and Vietnam. When Hansberry reviewed the Japanese film *Hiroshima*, she wrote, "Coming out of the movie house into the American streets one repeats it with the feeling: No more Hiroshimas—anywhere, ever." When asked about the type of future she envisioned, Hansberry answered, a world of peace. "Nobody fights. We get rid of all the little bombs—and the big bombs."[19]

Before she died, Hansberry worked on two plays, one antinuclear, the other anticolonial. In 1961, Hansberry began writing *What Use Are Flowers?* The play centers on a survivor of nuclear war who decides to teach the remaining children how to live in a new world—with love rather than hate, and peace instead of war. It was Hansberry's last plea to never again use atomic bombs. The second play, *Les Blancs*, focused on colonialism in Africa and challenged the notion that liberation could be achieved solely by nonviolence. The main character, Tshembe Matoseh, on returning to Africa for his father's funeral, is forced to choose between taking up arms to free his homeland from white colonialists and remaining nonviolent. Through the characters, Hansberry examines liberation struggles from all sides and, while not advocating violence, effectively demonstrates the danger in remaining complacent and passive.[20]

Many female activists were members of groups like Women's International League for Peace and Freedom (WILPF) and Women Strike for Peace (WSP). Established in 1915, WILPF focused mainly on disarmament, social and economic justice, and an end to all war.[21] The organization began with five African American members and by 1975 had about twelve times that many. Examining WILPF's black members, Joyce Blackwell maintains that African American women played a far more significant role in the Peace Movement than has been previously acknowledged and, despite their small numbers, exercised a considerable amount of influence.[22]

Following World War II, a new group of black women joined WILPF, including Sadie Sawyer Hughley, Coretta Scott King, Enola Maxwell, Erna Prather Harris, Fannie Lou Hamer, Angela Davis, Shirley Chisholm, Bessie McLaurin, Eartha Kitt, Inez Jackson, and Virginia Collins. Like earlier black members, these women argued that peace and freedom could not be achieved solely through ending war.

Fighting racial injustice remained a core element of their agenda. However, unlike their foremothers who focused largely on racial self-help, these activists attacked racism throughout American society, including in the Peace Movement. They took it upon themselves to challenge WILPF as a predominantly white, middle-class organization to ensure that members made good on their promise to eradicate racial injustice. While some white members wanted to confront racism, a larger majority felt that the organization should stay focused on peace and disarmament. As a result, racial discrimination persisted within the organization, causing some black women to leave the Peace Movement altogether and focus solely on civil rights. Others remained in WILPF and tried to change the culture from within.[23]

After 1945, WILPF dedicated a significant amount of time to nuclear disarmament.[24] Erna Harris, a member of the organization, actively worked on nuclear issues, often arguing that there was no such thing as a "peace-atom."[25] Raised in segregated Kingfisher, Oklahoma, Harris watched her father routinely stand up to the local Ku Klux Klan. A product of segregated schools, Harris attended the integrated Wichita State University, where she became one of the first black women to graduate with a degree in journalism in 1936. Breaking down racial barriers, Harris worked for various newspapers and in the 1940s regularly wrote editorials criticizing Japanese internment.[26]

In April 1964, Harris made headlines for her participation in the Soviet-American Women's Conference in Moscow. Twelve women from the U.S. section of WILPF joined twelve women from the Soviet Union to participate in the conference, the second of its kind.[27] Whereas the first conference had been held immediately following the Soviet resumption of nuclear tests in 1961, the second conference took place in a more favorable atmosphere created by the Partial Test Ban Treaty, the establishment of direct communication between Washington and Moscow, and the agreement not to put space vehicles carrying nuclear weapons into outer space. Therefore, the Moscow conference dealt with relaxing international tensions, the role of the United Nations, and universal disarmament. On returning to the United States, Harris traveled the country speaking about foreign affairs, often commenting that with all of the issues on the table, "nuclear disarmament was one of the most important."[28]

On November 1, 1961, Women Strike for Peace (WSP) took the Peace Movement by surprise when it began to organize women's antinuclear protests throughout the country with thousands in attendance. As female activists witnessed the

Soviet Union's decision to continue nuclear weapons testing, they made a conscious choice to focus on nuclear disarmament. Across the country, thousands of women picketed public facilities, issued antinuclear press releases, and implored public officials to "End the Arms Race—Not the Human Race."[29]

As in WILPF, black members of Women Strike for Peace faced internal racism and struggled to find their voice. For them, civil rights and nuclear disarmament were inextricably linked. Some white members disagreed. These differences surfaced on the first day of WSP's national conference. At the opening session, four Detroit women, representing a committee to "ban the bomb and end segregation," were refused admittance. This ran counter to the idea that all women who identified with the WSP movement were welcome, which was what the group had previously stated. It turned out that black women from Detroit were in conflict with the group that considered itself Detroit WSP. The African American women had insisted on carrying placards to WSP actions bearing the slogan "Desegregation Not Distintegration." The white women in Detroit, not in favor of combining the issues, banned the desegregation placards and excluded the black women from their delegation. However, Amy Swerdlow explains that the group's commitment to inclusion and repudiation of racism created sympathy and support for the black Detroiters, and they were seated immediately. Barbara Bick, an important member of WSP in Washington, D.C., and editor of *MEMO*, recalled several years later, "Everyone felt deeply about civil rights but, I think, most women there also felt deeply that WSP should be a peace-issue movement only." The black women, on the other hand, made it clear that for them the issues were linked and that any movement that refused to take a stand against segregation would lose African American support.[30]

In an effort to remedy the situation, WSP leaders reached out to one of their most well-known members, Coretta Scott King. King began her activism as a student at Antioch College. She played a crucial role in influencing her husband's views on war and nuclear weapons. Michael Eric Dyson contends that Coretta King was an earlier and more devoted pacifist than her husband. Her "principled pacifism," Dyson writes, nurtured her husband's beliefs and provided a source of "moral inspiration" as Dr. King ventured further into the Peace Movement his wife had independently supported for years. Throughout the 1950s and 1960s, Coretta King worked with WILPF, SANE, and WSP.[31]

In 1962, King traveled as a delegate for WSP to Geneva for the Conference of the Seventeen-Nation Committee on Disarmament. The gathering was part of a worldwide effort for a nuclear test ban treaty between the United States and the Soviet Union. On her return, she spoke to an audience of women at AME Church in Chicago. "It is of vital importance that we solve world tensions and bring about understanding between nations," she said. "If we fail in this, then the world is lost, and our efforts in race relations will have been in vain. We are on the brink of destroying ourselves through nuclear warfare, even though science has made one neighborhood of the whole world." For these reasons, King told the women, she felt compelled to attend the Geneva conference.[32] According to the *Detroit Free Press*, King indicated that the Civil Rights Movement should play a more active role in the Peace Movement. The "Peace Warrior," as the *Press* described her, explained that "the Civil Rights Movement and the Peace Movement work together because peace and civil rights are part of the same problem."[33]

Writing to King, WSP leaders made clear that "as women dedicated to bringing about a world where every child may live and grow in dignity, we identify ourselves with the heroic effort of Negro citizens to achieve this goal. As a movement working for an atmosphere of peaceful cooperation among nations, we support the movement for peaceful integration in our nation. Our goals are inseparable, the movement for civil rights is part of the movement for a world of peace, freedom, and justice to which we have dedicated ourselves."[34] Local groups were instructed to use this letter in place of a policy statement on civil rights, especially in communication with civil rights groups. However, there remained those who believed the two issues should remain separate. As WSP founder Dagmar Wilson explained, "The Civil Rights Movement has a tremendous emotional appeal—as it naturally would do to the kind of women who are motivated by a sense of indignation at the disregard for human rights which the arms race represents. It has been very tempting at times to drop everything and work for civil rights, except for the fact that we all realize that civil rights without nuclear disarmament won't do any of us any good. We realize that the two movements are different aspects of the same problem and that eventually the two will meet and merge."[35]

Clarie Collins Harvey joined Coretta King in Geneva as a member of Women Strike for Peace. A native of Jackson, Mississippi, Harvey held degrees from Spelman, Columbia, and New York University. Following college and her father's death, Harvey took over management duties for Collins Funeral Homes and Collins Insurance Company. In 1961, she and two others founded Womenpower Unlimited (WU), an interracial organization that worked on civil rights and peace issues. Harvey was a member of the Mississippi Advisory Committee to the United States Commission on Civil Rights and a life member of the NAACP and Urban League. Following her trip to Geneva in 1962, Harvey represented Women Strike for Peace at the "World Without the Bomb" meeting in Africa. A year later, Harvey traveled with a group of sixty women from eighteen nations to the Vatican to confront the Pope on nuclear issues.[36]

Many of these actions, including the Geneva gathering, were aimed at a nuclear weapons test ban, a goal of President Kennedy's since he took office. However, Kennedy had not met activists' expectations in his first two years, largely continuing the foreign policies of his predecessors. This all changed in 1963, when, as Peter Kuznick explains, Kennedy underwent a "stunning reversal, repudiating the reckless cold war militarism that defined his early presidency." Kennedy publicly displayed his "reversal" in June when he delivered American University's commencement address. Speaking to the young graduates, Kennedy declared his commitment to fighting for a peaceful world, free of nuclear weapons.[37] The president could not do it alone, however.

Throughout the summer, activists urged the president to respond decisively. A month before Kennedy's speech, two thousand women descended on the Capitol in Washington, D.C., demanding a nuclear test ban. The activists marched through the halls of Congress meeting with various members. Coretta King wired her approval of the demonstration, which she could not attend, assuring that she fully supported their actions and a nuclear test ban. "Peace among nations and peace in Birmingham, Alabama, cannot be separated," she stated.[38]

Her husband agreed. Dr. King explained that the SCLC and the Nuclear Test Ban advocates' objectives were indeed the same. "In supporting the philosophy of nonviolence, we feel that this is a philosophy which is remarkable [sic] similar to those persons who so strongly advocate a Test Ban Treaty," he wrote. King made clear that the SCLC would not "accept the premise that our engagement in a struggle for racial justice in America removes us from the arena of concern over the Test Ban Treaty."[39]

Their work paid off when the U.S. Senate approved the Nuclear Test Ban Treaty in September by a vote of 80 to 19, fourteen more than the required two-thirds needed to pass. Kennedy advisor Ted Sorenson noted that no other single accomplishment in the White House gave the president greater satisfaction.[40] He could not have done it without the work of these activists.

The victory of the Nuclear Test Ban Treaty was short-lived. By 1964, peace activists began to shift their attention to the Vietnam War while many in the black community remained focused on passing civil rights legislation. Specifically regarding the nuclear issue, Paul Boyer argued that opposition to the Vietnam War had an urgency that could not be denied. The bomb was a potential menace; Vietnam was an actuality. Therefore, Boyer wrote, "the nuclear issue was not simply set aside, but forcibly pushed to the background."[41] However, one could argue that the Vietnam War actually brought these issues together. Racism and colonialism were certainly present in Vietnam. And as in Korea, there were valid reasons to fear that the United States would again use nuclear weapons on a "darker nation." In 1967, facing the potential loss of six thousand marines at Khe Sanh, the Pentagon prepared plans and leaked warnings that if necessary nuclear weapons would be used to break the siege at Khe Sanh fortress. In addition, President Nixon and national security advisor Henry Kissinger repeatedly threatened and prepared to end the Vietnam War with nuclear weapons.[42]

Throughout the 1960s, every August, activists linked the conflict in Vietnam to nuclear disarmament by commemorating the atomic bombings of Hiroshima and Nagasaki. In 1964, one thousand demonstrators gathered in New York City, carrying signs that read, "No More Hiroshimas" and "End the War in Vietnam." Bayard Rustin and Miyoko Matsurbara, a *hibakusha* (atomic bomb survivor), were among those who spoke at the rally. Rustin compared the situation in Vietnam to the police brutality African Americans faced in Harlem. "People will no longer tolerate being without dignity and being poor," he said.[43]

From the start of the demonstrations, black and white activists appeared united in ending the war in Vietnam. In April 1965, Students for a Democratic Society (SDS) organized one of the first major anti–Vietnam War demonstrations in Washington, D.C. The protest brought together about 25,000 people from across the country, including a large contingent of African Americans. The Student Nonviolent Coordinating Committee's (SNCC) executive committee unanimously decided to support the march. SNCC chairman John Lewis argued that the United States should withdraw from Vietnam. SNCC leader Bob Moses, a featured speaker at the rally, compared killing in Vietnam to that in Mississippi. Congress of Racial Equality (CORE) leader James Farmer backed the demonstration and stated on CBS's *Face the Nation* that "persons who participate in the Civil Rights Movement have not only a right, but a duty to be interested in all activities of our government—domestic policies outside of the civil rights area and foreign policy." A group of black high school students from Mississippi, who had worked in the South during Freedom Summer, also participated in the protest. Otis Brown, a sixteen-year-old student leader from Indianola, explained that they had come to Washington "because we have to look beyond just Negro freedom. We don't want to grow up 'free' at home in a country which supports this kind of war abroad."[44]

Some began to assert that a new alliance had formed. One reporter stated, "The most important new liaison was that between the young, vibrant freedom workers of the South and the peace oriented students of the North." An SDS leader explained that the "breadth and urgency of the march could never have been achieved without the life instilled in the student movement by the Southern civil rights struggle."[45]

Two months later, SANE organized an "Emergency Rally on Vietnam" at Madison Square Garden. Since its inception, many SANE members had embraced the idea that combining civil rights with peace and nuclear issues was of mutual benefit. SANE leader and longtime pacifist Sanford Gottlieb asserted that since SANE and CORE members were both "humanitarians," they should work together. He urged SANE and other organizations to participate in activities sponsored by CORE, the NAACP, and the SCLC, in hopes that these groups would form a solid bond that would benefit all people.[46] In June, SANE issued a formal statement regarding the Civil Rights Movement and Peace Movement. It declared "the struggle for freedom—whether among Negroes in Mississippi, artists in Moscow, or villagers in Angola—inseparable from the effort to attain a world without war." Both hatred and H-bombs, the group argued, "can destroy humanity." SANE leaders highlighted the relationship between military spending and cutbacks in social programs for the poor:

> In the movement to achieve their immediate goals, Negroes will be handicapped by a shortage which affects all Americans; a civilian economy which is too small to satisfy the present needs of all the citizens of the United States. There are already too few schools, homes, jobs, and health and recreational facilities for the present population, with Negroes bearing the brunt of the deprivation. This undersized economic pie aggravates the plight of Negroes and complicates their struggle. When the economic pie becomes larger, Negroes will have a better opportunity to attain their rightful share.
>
> At a moment when the present armed forces of the United States have enough destructive power to wipe out all major Soviet cities many times over, further investment in the military sector can be reduced. A large part of the resources thus saved can and should be diverted to the strengthening of the civilian economy, a step, which would both meet pressing domestic needs and enhance the national security.

A cut in arms spending and a shift of resources to the civilian economy is one common interest currently shared in the Peace Movement and the most underprivileged groups in American society. While SANE must give highest priority to building public and political support for world disarmament, it cannot ignore opportunities to work cooperatively on shorter-range goals, which are consistent with its principles. The National Board and staff will therefore begin consultations with civil rights leaders, such as SANE Sponsors, Martin Luther King, Jr., James Farmer, and James Baldwin to explore the relationship of arms reduction, economic growth, and peace with freedom.[47]

SANE's Vietnam demonstration garnered significant black support. SNCC and the Northeastern Regional Office of CORE gave their endorsement. Ossie Davis served as cochair of the rally, and Coretta Scott King and Bayard Rustin were featured speakers. Rustin ignited the crowd of 18,000 declaring, "We must stop meeting indoors and go into the streets." After the rally three thousand protesters marched with King, Benjamin Spock, Norman Thomas, and Senator Wayne Morse (D-OR) through the theater district, Times Square, and across town to the United Nations Plaza.[48]

A year later, on the twenty-first anniversary of the Hiroshima bombing, activists again took to the streets to protest nuclear weapons and the war in Vietnam. Thousands of demonstrators participated in rallies across the nation. The black community in Roxbury took part in the Boston demonstration, while contingents of CORE and SNCC members chanted "Black Power" and carried signs reading "No Fighting for the Racist USA" and "Our Fight Is Here Not There" as they marched through New York City. Lincoln Lynch, associate national director of CORE addressed the crowd and described the United States as "a nation of cynical hypocrites, a place where we preach peace yet wage war in all its starkest horrors." However, not all civil rights leaders endorsed these actions. A silent vigil was planned outside the church where President Lyndon Johnson's daughter was to be married. Dr. King, Roy Wilkins, Whitney Young, and A. Philip Randolph asked organizers not to follow through on the vigil. SNCC leaders rejected their plea, accused Johnson of deliberately setting his daughter's wedding date on the anniversary of the Hiroshima bombing, and continued as planned.[49]

Black moderates' negative response to the vigil was not uncommon. Wilkins, Randolph, and Young strongly disagreed with the antiwar movement. They maintained that the antiwar movement was communist inspired and urged African Americans to refrain from supporting the National Liberation Front. Thus, civil rights groups became divided as to whether they should formally support the antiwar movement. While members of the NAACP individually protested U.S. actions in Vietnam, the group's leadership refused to publicly speak out against the war effort. CORE was also split on the issue. James Farmer argued that while civil rights was an autonomous movement, it was proper for civil rights people "as concerned citizens" to be interested in such issues as peace. He had participated in antiwar activities dating back to the 1940s; now he joined Ossie Davis, Ruby Dee, and Rustin in organizing a mass protest in Washington, D.C., in November. Farmer also worked with John Hersey, playwright Arthur Miller, Benjamin Spock (SANE), and Carl Oglesby (president of SDS) in calling for a negotiated settlement in Vietnam and in organizing a successful demonstration. However, Farmer was reluctant to have CORE adopt a formal antiwar position, fearing it would lose support in the black community and damage any efforts on the civil rights front.[50]

One could argue that Dr. King's April 4, 1967, speech was his "Vietnam moment." However, King began speaking publicly about Vietnam in the spring of 1965. Addressing an audience at Howard University, King predicted that Vietnam would "accomplish nothing." Following his speech, King told reporters, "War had always been a negative concept, but nuclear weapons made it totally unacceptable." In August, without prior approval of his board or its members, King gave a speech at the SCLC's annual convention and called for direct negotiations between Washington and Vietnam and the halting of U.S. bombings.[51] In February 1967, a month before his "Beyond Vietnam" address, King devoted an entire speech to the Vietnam War.[52] Speaking in Los Angeles, King discussed the mounting casualties in Vietnam. "I tremble for our world," he said. "I do so not only from dire recall of the nightmares wreaked in the wars of yesterday, but also from dreadful realization of today's possible nuclear destructiveness, and tomorrow's even more damnable prospects." King continued:

> There may have been a time when war served as a negative good by preventing the spread and growth of an evil force, but the destructive power of modern weapons eliminates even the possibility that war may serve as a negative good. If we assume that life is worth living and that man has a right to survive, then we must find an alternative to war. In a day when vehicles hurtle through outer space and guided ballistic missiles carve highways of death through the stratosphere, no nation can claim victory in war ... So if modern man continues to flirt unhesitatingly with war, he will transform his earthly habitat into an inferno such as even the mind of Dante could not imagine.[53]

A month later, speaking from New York City's Riverside Church, King delivered his most famous comments on the Vietnam War. Unleashing a scathing critique of U.S. military actions in Vietnam, King referred to the government as the "greatest purveyor of violence in the world today." He argued that African Americans were disproportionately dying in Vietnam, and still treated unequally at home. King urged the United States to stop the bombing and end the war, while stressing the dangers of using nuclear weapons. He concluded that citizens had a choice: nonviolent coexistence or violent co-annihilation.[54]

King's antiwar statements were met with harsh reactions from the liberal establishment, the mainstream press, and even from some elements within the black community. Presidential advisor John Roche told Lyndon Johnson that King had "thrown in with the commies," while Johnson referred to King as that "goddamned nigger preacher." Hubert Humphrey told University of Georgia students that King had "acted in error." "I think it will hurt the Civil Rights Movement. I don't think it will promote peace in Vietnam," he said. The *New York Times* charged King with damaging both the civil rights and antiwar movements. *Life* magazine described his speech as "a demagogic slander that sounded like a script for Radio Hanoi."[55]

Black moderates pounced on King's statements with a vituperation that was sadly reminiscent of the assault on Paul Robeson in 1949. Wilkins bitterly attacked King, charging him with "downgrading the Negro cause" by linking peace and civil rights issues. "I don't believe Dr. King . . . as leader in the Civil Rights Movement has the right to mix up the civil rights fight with the Vietnam fight," Wilkins argued. He made clear that the Viet Cong were "no brothers" of the "American Negro soldier" and King's charge that the United States was using African Americans as mercenaries was "hogwash."[56] Five days after his speech, the NAACP adopted a resolution, clearly aimed at King, which stated that "any attempt to merge the Civil Rights Movement with the Peace Movement . . . is, in our judgment, a serious tactical mistake, that would serve the cause neither of civil rights nor peace," and pledged to "stick to the job for which it was organized."[57]

Rustin also expressed concerns over King's comments. Discussing the speech in the *Amsterdam News*, Rustin at first argued that as a Nobel Peace Prize Laureate, King had a moral obligation to work for peace and speak out against the war. However, in a striking departure from his deeply held views of just a few years before, Rustin questioned whether African Americans should join peace organizations and spend time working on issues other than civil rights. "I must say that I would consider the involvement of the civil rights organizations as such in peace activities distinctly unprofitable and perhaps even suicidal," Rustin wrote.[58] Dyson accurately points out that "King and Rustin's trajectories of antiwar criticism were now inverted: As Rustin assumed leadership of the A. Philip Randolph Institute, his priorities accordingly shifted to racial and economic concerns. As King became immersed in the fight to end economic inequality and racial oppression, he embraced the Peace Movement as a logical and moral extension of his expanding social concerns."[59]

Feeling the pressure, King responded to his critics stating that he "held no such view" that the Civil Rights Movement and Peace Movement should formally merge. However, he also made clear that the overarching issue remained universal human rights:

> We [SCLC] do not believe in any merger or fusion of movements, but we equally believe that no one can pretend that the existence of the war is not profoundly affecting the destiny of civil rights progress. We believe that despite the war our efforts can produce results and our strength is fully committed to that end. But it would be misleading and shallow to suggest that the role of the war is not hampering it substantially and can be ignored as a factor.
>
> Loud and raucous voices have already been raised in Congress and elsewhere suggesting that the nation cannot afford to finance a war against poverty and inequality on an expanding scale and a shooting war at the same time. It is perfectly clear the nation has the resources to do both, but those who oppose civil rights and favor a war policy have seized the opportunity to pose a false issue to the public. This should not be ignored by civil rights organizations. The basic elements in common between the Peace Movement and Civil Rights Movement are human elements.[60]

When the *New York Times* condemned King, readers flooded the newspaper with letters defending the civil rights leader. William Hixon Jr., an instructor at Michigan State University, wrote: "The implication made by many of his critics that, as a civil-rights leader, Dr. King departs radically from precedent in speaking out against American foreign policy, cannot bear historical examination." Citing Oswald Garrison Villard (first treasurer of the NAACP) and James Weldon Johnson (former executive secretary of the NAACP), Hixon argued that the NAACP had a history of attacking U.S. foreign policy. "While serving as [NAACP] president between 1910 and 1929, [Moorfield] Storey continued his anti-imperialism, publicly condemning American interventions in the Dominican Republic, in

Haiti, and in Nicaragua," Hixon wrote.[61] John Matthews of Princeton, New Jersey, labeled the *New York Times'* criticisms "an unfortunate disservice to a great American and a great Christian." "The two issues are fused in Dr. King because he is a man of peace," Matthews wrote.[62] Benjamin Spock also disagreed with the *Times* assessment. A member of SANE and outspoken critic of the Vietnam War, Spock argued: "Our mistreatment of Negroes and our lawlessness in Vietnam are both manifestations of the same self-deceptive kinds of thinking. And they require similar solutions . . . I believe that the civil rights and Peace Movements should cooperate closely in their educational and organization work. Their common aim is to save the world literally by fostering the brotherhood of man. In the long run their greatest gains will come, I think, from patient political organization beginning at the grass roots, within or outside the existing parties."[63]

In the face of all the criticism, King refused to back down and he continued to protest the war. Moreover, King publicly spoke about the very issue that caused much of the controversy. At a rally in the Chicago Coliseum, King called for combining the "fervor of the Civil Rights Movement with the Peace Movement." "It isn't enough to be concerned about integration, but about the survival of a world in which to have integration," King said. At the same event, Spock stated that "one of the great needs" was an "alliance of civil rights groups" that would form what could be referred to as a "Brotherhood of Man" group, and "Dr. King should be its leader."[64] On April 15, King joined Spock, James Bevel, Harry Belafonte, and between 400,000 and 500,000 others in New York City for one of the largest peace demonstrations in U.S. history. The demonstrators marched from Central Park to the United Nations, where King, Stokely Carmichael, and Floyd McKissick addressed the crowd. At the same time, Coretta Scott King joined Julian Bond and about 75,000 others in San Francisco to protest the war. One journalist noted that the Civil Rights Movement was "represented more conspicuously than before." King told the crowd that "freedom and justice in America" were "bound together with freedom and justice in Vietnam," while Bond attacked the "growing cancer" of American militarism. He urged that the "screams of the children in Harlem and Haiphong" be replaced with "cheerful, loving laughter."[65]

The Spring Mobilization Committee organized the demonstrations in New York and San Francisco. An antiwar coalition founded in November 1966, Mobe (National Mobilization Committee), as it became known, attempted to gather antiwar, peace, and civil rights groups under one umbrella to protest the war. SNCC, SCLC, and CORE all supported Mobe. Cleveland Robinson, president of the Negro American Labor Council, and SCLC vice president Ralph Abernathy became vice-chairs of the organization, while Julian Bond, Stokely Carmichael (SNCC), Ivanhoe Donaldson (SNCC), James Farmer, Floyd McKissick (CORE), Ruth Turner (CORE), Fred Shuttlesworth (SCLC), Wyatt T. Walker (SCLC), Harry Belafonte, and John Lewis individually offered their endorsement and support.[66]

A month before he died, King addressed the second mobilization of Clergy and Laymen Concerned About Vietnam. Urging an end to the war, King explained that the United States' involvement in Vietnam demonstrated the "spiritual lag of Americans":

> It does not help America nor its so-called image to be the most powerful and the richest nation in the world at war with one of the smallest and poorest nations in the world, which happens to be a colored nation. And this is something that must be said over and over again, for a predominately white nation to be at war with one of the poorest and smallest nations that happens to be a colored nation. This only leads a nation, leads America to a point of losing its own soul if something is not done.[67]

Then King made clear that the black freedom movement and nuclear disarmament were indeed part of the same fight:

> We have played havoc with the destiny of the world and we have brought the whole world closer to nuclear confrontation . . . It is no longer a choice between violence and non-violence. It is either non-violence or non-existence, and the alternative to disarmament, the alternative to a great suspension of nuclear tests, the alternative to strengthening the United Nations and thereby disarming the whole world will be a civilization plunged into the abyss of annihilation, and our earthly habitat will be transformed into an inferno that even the mind of Dante could not envision. We have to see that and work diligently and passionately for peace.
>
> I am still convinced that the struggle for peace and the struggle for civil rights as we call it in America happen to be tied together. These two issues are tied together in many, many ways. It is a wonderful thing to work to integrate lunch counters, public accommodations, and schools. But it would be rather absurd to work to get schools and lunch counters integrated and not be concerned with the survival of a world in which to integrate. And I am convinced that these two issues are tied inextricably together and I feel that the people who are working for civil rights are working for peace; I feel that the people working for peace are working for civil rights and justice.[68]

Examining the relationship between the Civil Rights Movement and the anti–Vietnam War movement, some scholars suggest the rise of the Black Power Movement in the mid-1960s was a major factor in the low number of African American participants in the antiwar movement. David Colburn and George Pozzetta maintain that as black activists began to focus on social and economic justice, white activists expressed resentment. "Rather than working together," Charles DeBenedetti argues, "the Black Power and anti-Vietnam war movements ran parallel to one another." Simon Hall contends that the Black Power Movement acted as "a double-edged sword. While black radicals shared both the New Left's critique of liberalism, and its analysis of the war in Vietnam, black-nationalism made the task of constructing an interracial antiwar movement more difficult and provided white activists with a convenient excuse to focus solely on the war."[69] Therefore, the Black Power Movement, at least in part, contributed to a split between those fighting for peace and those fighting for freedom. However, many historians have reexamined the roots of the Black Power Movement, dating it back to the early twentieth century. In so doing, these scholars have demonstrated that the Black Power Movement has historically linked domestic and international issues as part of the same fight for universal human rights. The Black Power Movement's history of internationalism is evident in some of its most prominent leaders' antinuclear efforts. For many, the Black Power Movement did not contribute to a split in movements, but rather continued to combine the black freedom struggle with peace and nuclear abolition.[70]

On June 6, 1964, three Japanese writers and a group of *hibakusha* arrived in Harlem as part of the Hiroshima/Nagasaki World Peace Study Mission. Speaking out against nuclear proliferation, the group had traveled to at least five other countries before reaching the United States. However, traveling to Harlem was the high point for the *hibakusha*, who were thrilled at the prospect of meeting Malcolm X.[71]

Yuri Kochiyama, a Japanese American activist, organized a reception for the *hibakusha* at her home in the Harlem Manhattanville Housing Projects. In an effort to make the *hibakushas'* wish come true, Kochiyama contacted Malcolm's office months before their arrival, but she received no response and remained doubtful that Malcolm would attend the reception. Throughout the day, the *hibakusha* walked around Harlem, visiting a black school and church, eating lunch at a restaurant Malcolm X frequently visited, passing by the "World's

Worst Fair," and finally making their way to Kochiyama's apartment. Little did they know whom they were about to meet.[72]

Shortly after the reception began, there was a knock at the door. Kochiyama opened it, and there stood Malcolm X. On entering the house, Malcolm first apologized to Kochiyama for not responding, explaining he did not have her address. He further remarked that if he traveled again, he would remember to write. (He did, and wrote to Kochiyama eleven times from nine different countries.) Malcolm thanked the *hibakusha* for taking the time to go the "World's Worst Fair." He said, "You have been scarred by the atom bomb. You just saw that we have also been scarred. The bomb that hit us was racism." He went on to discuss his years in prison, his education, and Asian history. Turning to Vietnam, Malcolm said, "If America sends troops to Vietnam, you progressives should protest. America is already sending American advisors." He argued that "the struggle of Vietnam is the struggle of the whole Third World: the struggle against colonialism, neo-colonialism, and imperialism."[73] The group then met with comedian and activist Dick Gregory and made such an impact that he joined them on their tour to Berlin and Russia.[74]

Three months before meeting the *hibakusha*, Malcolm X formally broke with the Nation of Islam and soon after created a new organization, Muslim Mosque, Inc. (MMI). The organization's first goal, he stated, was to submit "the case of the American Negro before the United Nations." In April, Malcolm addressed an MMI gathering and again insisted that the black freedom movement had to refocus from a quest for "civil rights" to a demand for "human rights."[75]

After leaving the Nation of Islam, Malcolm traveled, as he had previously done, to Africa and the Middle East. Influenced by Nkrumah and other African leaders, Malcolm adopted a Pan-Africanist, anticolonialist philosophy. Writing to MMI supporters in 1964, Malcolm explained that the highest priority was now building "unity between the Africans of the West and the Africans of the fatherland [which] will change the course of history."[76] Addressing over five hundred supporters in December, he said, "We're living in a revolutionary world and in a revolutionary age." We must realize "the direct connection between the struggle of the Afro-American in this country and the struggle of our people all over the world." He warned, "You'll never get Mississippi straightened out. Not until you start realizing your connection with the Congo."[77] He maintained that the Congo's misery was a result of the attempts of "imperialist nations" to acquire and control its "immense wealth." Malcolm's arguments were not only Pan-Africanist in nature but quite similar to Paul Robeson's words twenty years earlier.

Inspired by Malcolm X, leaders of the Black Panther Party were careful to link peace, colonialism, and racial equality when they issued their first public statement. On May 2, 1967, party cofounder Bobby Seale, along with a group of fellow Panthers, arrived in Sacramento for a showdown with the California legislature. The goal of the trip was to present a statement written by cofounder Huey P. Newton in direct response to the legislature's decision to debate the Mulford bill.[78] As the session began, Seale and his contingent walked about thirty feet into the Capitol area. With onlookers and reporters surrounding them, Seale decided to go inside. Approaching the gate of the Assembly, the police stopped the Panthers and a struggle ensued. While reporters filled the hallway and cameras flashed, Seale found the opportunity to sneak past the police. As he made his way to the Assembly, a nervous doorman opened the large doors and in walked Seale.[79] After the police and Panthers separated and the commotion subsided, Seale gathered the reporters downstairs from the Assembly and read Executive Mandate Number 1. It stated:

> The Black Panther Party for Self-Defense calls upon the American people in general, and Black People in particular, to take careful note of the racist California Legislature now considering legislation aimed at keeping Black people disarmed and powerless while racist police agencies throughout the country intensify the terror, brutality, murder, and repression of Black people.
>
> At the same time that the American Government is waging a racist war of genocide in Vietnam the concentration camps in which Japanese-Americans were interned during World War II are being renovated and expanded. Since America has historically reserved its most barbaric treatment for non-White people, we are forced to conclude that these concentration camps are being prepared for Black people who are determined to gain their freedom by any means necessary. The enslavement of Black people at the very founding of this country, the genocide practiced on the American Indians and the confinement of the survivors on reservations, the savage lynching of thousands of Black men and women, the dropping of atomic bombs on Hiroshima and Nagasaki, and now the cowardly massacre in Vietnam all testify to the fact that toward people of color the racist power structure of America has but one policy: repression, genocide, terror, and the big stick.[80]

While this event is most known as the moment the Black Panther Party arrived on the public stage, rarely do scholars analyze the actual words of the statement. Newton and Seale did not simply call for violence or an end to racial injustice. They made sure to combine the black freedom struggle in America with the Vietnam War and the atomic bombings of Hiroshima and Nagasaki.

Former Panther leader Kathleen Cleaver explains: "From its inception the Black Panther Party saw the condition of blacks within an international context, for it was the same racist imperialism that people in Africa, Asia, and Latin America were fighting against that was victimizing blacks in the United States, according to their analysis."[81] In August 1968, Japanese activists invited Cleaver, and her husband Eldridge, to Japan to deliver a series of speeches in protest of the Vietnam War and nuclear weapons.[82] A year later, arguing that U.S. involvement in Vietnam was motivated by profit and colonialism, Newton issued a formal statement regarding the Panthers and the Peace Movement. The Panther leader made clear to the black community that they should "not only communicate with it [the Peace Movement], we should actually get out and support it fully in various ways including literature and demonstrations."[83] For Newton, being a successful black revolutionary meant following in the paths of those before him: Du Bois, Robeson, Malcolm, and King. With this statement, that is exactly what he did.

Chapter 5

"From Civil Rights to Human Rights"

African American Activism in the Post-Vietnam Era

> Governments throughout the world, led by our own, spend over $600 billion a year on arms, while an estimated 1 billion of the world's people live in poverty . . . where is the human commitment and political will to find the relative pittance of money needed to protect children?
>
> —Marian Wright Edelman, 1983

IN 1976, THE WAR RESISTERS LEAGUE (WRL), in a clear attempt to link social justice with nuclear disarmament, organized the Continental Walk for Disarmament. The activists called for the United States to unilaterally begin the process of ending the arms race, reduce military spending, and shift its focus to rebuilding inner cities. The plan was to unite African Americans, Third World groups, the gay and lesbian community, women's groups, and organized labor by having citizens join in a 3,600-mile walk around the country. The Walk, as it was known, consisted of three major contingents, each departing from a different location (San Francisco, New Orleans, and Boston). Throughout their journey the groups were to stop at various defense contractors, prisons, military installations, and nuclear power–related sites, and finally converge in Washington, D.C., for a massive demonstration of solidarity.[1]

Most of the black participants marched in the southern section of the Walk, which stretched across Alabama, Louisiana, and Mississippi. As part of the event, Southern Christian Leadership Conference (SCLC) members, who largely organized the southern leg, met with Mississippi governor Clifford Finch and presented him with a "Bill of Particulars." The "Bill" focused on unemployment, revenue sharing, food stamp inequity, and capital punishment. The group linked these issues with nuclear disarmament and called for a reordering of economic priorities. The Reverend James Orange, a prominent member of the SCLC, explained the relationship between disarmament and economic inequality: "Just as the South was starved to death during the Civil War, our country is killing its poor. We are now turning out one nuclear bomb in the U.S. every eight hours, while every hour eight families die of starvation. That is what the Walk is all about . . . We have to learn our rights, and teach our kids the truth: there is a difference between dying of an overdose like a dog, and dying for your freedom."[2]

Activists who marched on the southern leg of the Walk had a markedly different experience than those who marched from San Francisco and Boston. Not only were they fewer in numbers, but for black activists in particular, walking through the South was not merely a symbolic gesture. They risked physical violence and imprisonment on behalf of nuclear disarmament and economic equality.[3]

Seventy marchers of the southern leg of the Walk departed from Dillard University, the historically black college in New Orleans, with SCLC leaders, local black politicians, and Dr. Samuel Cook (president of Dillard University) leading the way. However, on the second day, after walking only a mile, the Kenner police confronted the group. The Reverend Bernard Lee negotiated with the police as men and women sang the freedom song "Ain't Gonna Let Nobody Turn Me Round." The police eventually relented. Participants continued their walk and concluded the day in St. Rose, singing "We Shall Overcome" on the lawn of the home of Gary Tyler, a black man on death row in Angola prison who was seeking a new trial.[4]

As the Walk proceeded through the South, the number of protesters fluctuated as the environment became increasingly hostile. After a two-week break to recruit and train participants, the Walk continued toward Baton Rouge with 150 marchers. Twenty-five miles north of Baton Rouge, at St. Francisville, the local police confronted twenty-five activists. The officers tear-gassed, arrested, and charged the protesters with "disruption of the flow of traffic." Following the arrest, the parish sheriff commented that he "didn't like these outsiders coming in to stir up our 'niggers.'" The walkers were released the following day and proceeded peacefully into Mississippi. However, these were not isolated incidents. Twenty-three marchers—twenty African Americans and three Japanese Buddhists—were arrested by the State Highway Department in Laurel, Mississippi, for "obstructing the flow of traffic" and "disobeying an officer." Participants were also arrested in Birmingham, Alabama, where the car of a white organizer was firebombed, followed by a telephone warning to "not house any more niggers."[5]

After twenty months of organizing and nine months of walking through thirty-three states on twenty different routes, the Continental Walk for Disarmament and Social Justice culminated at the Lincoln Memorial on October 16, 1976. All of the various groups gathered for a final three days of events, including a film festival, a political fair, and numerous workshops. Some marched to the White House and the Department of Housing and Urban Development. Others were

arrested demonstrating at the Pentagon. Rallies and vigils were held throughout
the day. Ralph Abernathy, Bernard Lee, and Dick Gregory added their voices to
the choir of those calling for an end to nuclear weapons.[6] Although the event
may not have gained the media publicity organizers had hoped for, it once again
demonstrated that many activists were still committed to fighting on multiple
fronts.

By the early 1970s, it appeared that activists had indeed put the world on a
path toward peace. The Nuclear Nonproliferation Treaty of 1968, the Strategic
Arms Limitation Treaty (SALT I) in 1972, combined with Soviet-American détente and various arms control negotiations made it seem as though the chances
of nuclear war were diminishing. On the basis of these developments, the United
Nations went so far as to label the 1970s the "Disarmament Decade."[7]

Despite all of the treaties and agreements, however, the development of
nuclear weapons actually *increased* in the 1970s. France rejected the partial test
ban treaty and along with China, Israel, India, and South Africa refused to sign
the Nuclear Nonproliferation Treaty. Moreover, the various treaties between the
United States and the U.S.S.R. focused more on negotiating a way to keep nuclear
weapons rather than eliminate them. Nuclear arms controls and détente were
beginning to lose their appeal. As a result, between 1972 and 1977, the U.S. government added 4,500 strategic nuclear warheads and bombs, bringing the total to
about 9,000. The Soviet Union increased its strategic arsenal from some 2,500 to
3,650, and an estimated ten nations moved closer to becoming nuclear powers.
None seemed willing to explore the possibility of total disarmament.[8]

The rise in worldwide nuclear weapons production coupled with the end
of the Vietnam War allowed activists to refocus and continue their antinuclear
actions with renewed vigor. At the same time, many in the black community
argued that poverty in the United States was linked to the government's nuclear
policies. African Americans questioned why their children suffered from mal-
nutrition as the administration continued to spend money on nuclear weapons.
These circumstances led to a rise in black activism in the latter half of the decade
and into the 1980s, beginning with President Jimmy Carter and the development
of the neutron bomb.

On June 6, 1977, the *Washington Post* revealed that the Carter administration
was planning to create an "enhanced radiation warhead" known as the "neutron
bomb." The idea was a carryover from the Ford presidency; most of the policy
makers in the Carter White House had never heard of the neutron bomb until

they came into office. But when a storm of protest broke, they rallied behind its development, claiming that it did not significantly alter the strategic situation. Furthermore, they said that by reducing the heat and blast produced by the explosion of tactical nuclear weapons, it would reduce civilian casualties in a war. The furor grew, however, and quickly spread to Congress, where liberals sought to block funding for the weapon.[9]

Many African Americans opposed the neutron bomb from the start. In addition to viewing the bomb as a weapon of mass murder, ordinary citizens were quick to point out that money allocated for nuclear weapons could be better spent in their communities. "I don't think that money, particularly this amount of money, should be spent on a neutron bomb . . . I don't even know that much about this bomb only that it kills people and leaves the buildings standing . . . that's all messed up," Pittsburgh resident Geneva Graham said. Gwen Harris asked, "What is President Carter trying to do? That money could do more good in other ways instead of being used to promote war." Ray Jackson commented, "Instead of creating some bomb that will only wipe out people, the government should create jobs for people who want to work and provide us with an opportunity to do so. I believe that the neutron bomb is a waste of taxpayers' money and not the best way to help the people." "I'm totally against the bomb," Karen Hampton exclaimed. "I can't say what I really want to say about this neutron bomb but I will tell you once again that I'm against it." Chris Weathers agreed: "I'm against the bomb too . . . I've been hearing the news and I'm against anything like this." Writing to the *Philadelphia Tribune*, Alfred Bailey warned that "at this crucial time in world history, only thirty years since the explosive ending of the second world war, military mania is again preparing to unleash a fiercesome [*sic*] neutron device in spite of the fact that we have reached a time in history when war must indeed, end, the survival of all flesh hinges on such an essential course."[10]

On learning of Carter's plans, Women Strike for Peace (WSP) embarked on a campaign throughout New York City to educate citizens about the dangers of the neutron bomb and a proposed change in the New York City health code, which would allow radioactive materials to be transported through the city streets. The group organized a benefit show at the Village Vanguard, which featured African American actress and activist Vinie Burrows. Burrows, a graduate of New York University, had previously performed on and off Broadway and was best known for her one-woman shows, including "Walk Together Children." Burrows explained that the Vanguard performance "grew out of a profound and dramatic sense of kinship with the 6,000 women who attended the World Congress of Women in Berlin," where Burrows served as a delegate and performer.[11]

While the administration favored the neutron bomb's development, Carter's U.N. ambassador became one of the bomb's most vociferous critics. Andrew Young, the former civil rights leader and Georgia congressman, was appointed U.N. ambassador in 1977. Young sought to avenge the history of a United States foreign policy that had hurt so many and to put America on the "right side of the moral issues in the world."[12] Young therefore opposed the neutron bomb from the beginning. While in Geneva for the U.N. Economic and Social Council meeting, Young stated that he hoped Carter would never order its development. He told reporters, "Were I still a member of Congress, I would have certainly strongly opposed and worked against that weapon . . . It doesn't make sense to spend all that money killing folks . . . The problem in the world today is learning to understand people, not destroy people." Asked about a Senate vote to give Carter funds to produce the neutron bomb, Young answered, "I would hope that maybe the meaning behind the vote in the Senate would be that it would strengthen the hand of our disarmament negotiators . . . and that it would be mainly a bargaining point but never developed."[13] Young's opposition, along with pressure from European leaders and grassroots activists, proved effective when, on April 7, 1978, the president announced that he was deferring production of the neutron bomb, in effect canceling plans for its production.[14]

For Young, the connection between nuclear disarmament and the black freedom struggle was much deeper. As U.N. ambassador, Young had taken a strong stance against South Africa's attempt to join the nuclear club. The South African government initially set out to create its nuclear program in the late 1950s, and in 1957 became the fourth nation to obtain a full-scale cooperation agreement under President Eisenhower's Atoms for Peace program. Throughout the 1960s, South Africa received assistance from the United States, including being supplied with the Safari-1 research reactor. As a result, South Africa constructed a solid nuclear infrastructure, which became crucial in its effort to obtain a nuclear weapon.[15]

By the next decade, South Africa's political situation began to drastically change. The international community instituted sanctions against the apartheid government, and South Africa's nuclear program became one of its first targets. The apartheid regime also feared Soviet expansion and was alarmed by the buildup of Cuban forces in Angola. In response, the South African government shifted its emphasis from "peaceful nuclear explosives" to "strategic deterrence."[16]

Finding itself increasingly isolated and in need of outside assistance, South Africa began to secretly collaborate with Israel to build a nuclear weapon.[17] South Africa's nuclear ambitions were among the reasons the United Nations met in 1978 for a Special Session on Disarmament.

In 1961, the nonaligned nations had proposed that the United Nations hold a special session dedicated to nuclear disarmament. Over fifteen years passed before these nations again proposed the idea in the form of a World Disarmament Conference. However, when plans collapsed in 1976, the major powers reluctantly agreed instead to hold a U.N. Special Session on Disarmament (SSD). The resolution for the special session thus passed unanimously in the General Assembly and in May 1978 the United Nations, for the first time, met to discuss a program dedicated to universal disarmament.[18]

On learning of the planned session, peace groups began organizing events and demonstrations to raise awareness of the SSD. Mobilization for Survival (MFS) was one of the main organizers of the events. Created in 1977, MFS was a coalition of peace, environmental, religious, community, labor, and women's groups that focused on four goals: Zero Nuclear Weapons, Ban Nuclear Power, Stop the Arms Race, and Fund Human Needs. The group sponsored more than a hundred public gatherings in August to commemorate the Hiroshima and Nagasaki bombings. In the fall, it organized over two hundred teach-ins across the country, and by the time of its first nationwide conference in December, MFS had established 350 affiliate groups.[19]

In the spring of 1978, Mobilization for Survival planned a series of events leading up to the demonstrations in support of the SSD, including the International Religious Convocation for Human Survival in New York City. Organizers sought to bring together people from different races, cultures, and religious traditions around the issue of nuclear disarmament.[20] Convocation representatives, including Coretta Scott King, stated:

> Thousands of nuclear missiles are aimed at our cities day and night. A hazardous nuclear energy technology readily lends itself to the proliferation of atomic weapons. Together they threaten to bring the human venture to an end. We must change this reality. The religious community must raise a passionate cry, end our complacency, and act against the threat of nuclear destruction.[21]

On May 24, at St. John the Divine Cathedral, the convocation held a Native American spirituality ceremony. The following day, the group launched "Witness for

Survival" in the South Bronx. Participants, including leaders from the Muslim, Jewish, and Native American faiths, as well as Buddhist monks from Hiroshima, evangelicals, and local African American and Hispanic clergy, visited some of the most impoverished areas in New York City to highlight the discrepancy between the elaborate sums spent on nuclear weapons and the paltry sums allocated for the poor.[22] On May 26, two thousand people of various faiths, praying in a dozen languages, descended on the United Nations in a call for universal disarmament. Demonstrators, including 502 Japanese citizens who presented seventeen million signatures protesting nuclear weapons, walked from the Roman Catholic Church of St. Paul the Apostle to the United Nations.[23]

The following day, one of the largest demonstrations since the Vietnam War took place at the United Nations. Between 15,000 and 20,000 demonstrators marched through Manhattan with signs that read, "No More Hiroshimas" and "No More Nagasakis." Standing in Dag Hammarskjold Plaza with Helen Caldicott, Daniel Ellsberg, Pete Seeger, Ossie Davis, and the a cappella group Sweet Honey in the Rock, Congressman John Conyers (D-MI) stated that the Special Session on Disarmament was an "opportunity for the world community to turn away from militarism and avert the catastrophe of nuclear war." Conyers, who served as an advisor to the U.S. delegation attending the SSD, noted that President Carter had been invited to the special session but sent Vice President Walter Mondale in his place. He pleaded, "Mr. President, come to New York and talk about the most important subject we will ever talk about: Whether we will live or die." The crowd responded with chants of "Mister President, Come to New York; Mister President, Come to New York." Conyers explained that he would pay particular attention to discussions on the control of tactical nuclear weapons, plans to investigate whether the neutron bomb was in violation of international treaties, and effects of nuclear weapons on the Third World.[24] Following Conyers' comments, Ron Kovic, a paraplegic Vietnam War veteran, joined hands with Masuto Higasaki, an eighty-three-year-old *hibakusha*. "My friend and I are symbols of living death," Kovic told the crowd. "We are here to hold the leaders of this country accountable." He then began chanting "Peace, Peace" as protesters linked hands and raised them above their heads.[25]

Andrew Young, who spoke at the special session, accepted petitions with tens of thousands of signatures and said he hoped the day's activities would mark the start of a "continued mobilization for the cause." He declared that the possibility of South Africa going nuclear was the "gravest concern" for the United States and all members of the international community. "Such a step would be a serious blow to the security situation in Africa and also to global efforts to prevent the further proliferation of nuclear weapons."[26]

The Special Session on Disarmament did not lead to a major breakthrough in public policy. However, as Catherine Foster notes, the session acknowledged by consensus that humanity faced a choice of either "disarmament or annihilation." Moreover, by setting forth an unprecedented program of action toward disarmament, the session helped create a climate in which controlling the nuclear arms race was for the first time seen as an achievable goal.[27] For black activists, the SSD, South Africa's attempts to develop a nuclear weapon, and the United States' insistence on building more nuclear weapons while black children starved solidified the notion that the black freedom movement, the bomb, and colonialism remained links in the same chain.

Bombs over Babies

In 1980, to commemorate the twenty-sixth anniversary of *Brown v. Board of Education*, Jesse Jackson and his organization, Operation PUSH, planned a rally under the banner, "National Youth Pilgrimage for Jobs, Peace, and Justice." On May 17, about ten thousand protesters, including six hundred black youth from Gary, Indiana, two hundred jobless autoworkers from Cleveland, Ohio, and steelworkers from Chicago and Baltimore, marched past the White House to protest the Carter administration's decision to increase military spending and cut funds for the poor. Richard Hatcher, mayor of Gary and chair of the National Conference of Black Mayors, told the crowd, "The nation's poor and unemployed are out of work, out of hope, and out of cash. We are poorer, sicker, and hungrier than we were ten years ago." Hatcher railed against Carter and Congress for announcing that the U.S. Treasury was "empty" of funds for jobs, food stamps, Social Security, education, and health care and then spending an additional $10 billion on the "arms race." He accused the president of seeking "nuclear superiority" over the Soviet Union and "menacing humanity with all out war." "They care more about housing missiles than they do about housing people," Hatcher complained. Following the mayor's powerful remarks, the crowd heard from a number of prominent speakers, including Camille Cosby, the wife of Bill Cosby, Bobby Dandridge, a professional basketball player for the Washington Bullets, Jesse Jackson, Stevie Wonder, Roberta Flack, and Gladys Knight.[28]

The beginning of the 1980s, however, appeared strikingly similar to the 1950s. African Americans who were alarmed by the Carter administration's policies saw any hope of racial equality and nuclear disarmament vanish with the election of Ronald Reagan. The newly sworn-in president referred to antinuclear activists as "communist sympathizers" and "foreign agents," who wanted to "weaken America." The threat of nuclear war seemed to increase as the administration adopted a jingoistic foreign policy and set out on a course to build more nuclear weapons, at the expense of the nation's poor. Tad Daley describes Reagan as perhaps "the fiercest military and nuclear hawk ever to occupy the Oval Office." He opposed every single nuclear arms control agreement negotiated since the dawn of the nuclear age, Daley writes. The president called for a substantial strategic nuclear buildup to "regain and sustain a military superiority over the Soviet Union," which included the MX missile, Strategic Defense Initiative, neutron bomb, and Trident submarine. To finance these new weapons, Reagan made clear his plans to dramatically cut spending on social programs that largely benefited poor and black communities. From 1981 through 1984, the administration cut $140 billion in social programs while increasing military spending by $181 billion.[29]

Reagan's focus on building up his nuclear arsenal had a dramatic effect on children. His administration significantly reduced spending on the Aid to Families with Dependent Children program, food stamps, child nutrition programs, maternal and child health programs, and family planning. Federal funds for day care were sharply cut back as were training and employment programs such as the Comprehensive Employment and Training Act, which was eliminated. In the early 1980s, 24 percent of children under the age of six lived in poverty. Free school lunches were eliminated for more than one million poor children, who depended on the meal for as much as half of their daily nutrition. Over twelve million children entered the ranks of the officially declared "poor." Black children were four times as likely as white children to grow up on welfare, which was reduced to $500–$700 a month, leaving them well below the poverty level of about $900 per month. In Michigan, where the unemployment rate was the highest in the country, the infant death rate began to rise in 1981. In parts of Detroit, one third of the children were dying before their first birthday.[30] As a result, black politicians, athletes, Hollywood celebrities, and ordinary citizens all became motivated to join the fight for peace and equality.

Inspired by the attention the 1980 U.S.–Russian Olympic hockey game received, Bob Swan, Bob Beamon, Mark Scott, and other athletes formed Athletes United for Peace (AUP), an organization composed of prominent athletes who supported nuclear disarmament. Relating the arms race to sports, AUP argued that competition between countries was both positive and necessary. However, "the rules of the game," it explained, "should prevent any player from being seriously injured or—worse yet—killed. In the U.S.-U.S.S.R. nuclear arms race, the opposite teams have enormous competitive skills. If the two should ever clash head-on, the rules of this deadly game would be tragically inadequate." The group maintained that it had a "moral obligation to prevent nuclear war and to provide sensible alternatives." AUP formally supported a nuclear freeze between the two superpowers, the creation of a joint Crisis Consultation Center to speed information exchanges between the countries, a national campaign stressing the dangers of nuclear weapons, a cost-effective national defense program, and an educational program designed to promote better understanding between the United States and the Soviet Union.[31]

Athletes United for Peace garnered significant black support and members came from a wide range of sports. Jo-Jo White, former professional basketball player for the Boston Celtics, gold medalist on the U.S. Olympic basketball team, and member of the National AUP Advisory Board, stated, "I'm concerned for the future of my family, my children. As athletes we believe in competition—but we know the rules and the limits. Because of the very real danger facing all of us, because of nuclear weapons, we have to speak out. Others will listen—here and in other countries." Marian Washington, the women's basketball and track and field coach at the University of Kansas, joined White on the advisory board. As the first African American woman to play for the Women's National Basketball team, Washington had played in the Soviet Union in 1975. "As one who has competed in the U.S.S.R., I know how influential Soviet athletes are. And as one who has coached in our own country, I know how popular American athletes are. If both American and Soviet athletes worked to promote peaceful competition between both nations, they might help save us all from the nightmare of a nuclear war," Washington said. Other notable AUP supporters included Gene Upshaw, former professional football player and executive director of the National Football Players Association, and professional football players Todd Christensen (Los Angeles Raiders), Rick Sanford (New England Patriots), and Joe Delaney (Kansas City Chiefs).[32]

Athletes United for Peace produced public service announcements for radio and television, which featured prominent athletes discussing the dangers of the nuclear arms race. It organized antinuclear conferences, and participated in marathons, bike-a-thons, and various sports-related peace trips between the United States and the Soviet Union. One of AUP's most notable actions included a trip in which the Baltimore Orioles visited Hiroshima. Orioles pitcher Mike Boddicker said, "You can't fathom what has happened here. It should be a lesson on what war can do. This was awful." Referring to the Japanese people he met in Hiroshima, John Lowenstein of the Orioles said, "The significant thing is that these people realize the absolute necessity of peace."[33]

At the same time athletes were fighting for peace, an African American librarian at Georgetown University and his wife, a part-time telephone operator, founded Blacks Against Nukes (BAN)—a group dedicated to educating the black community about the dangers of nuclear weapons. Influenced by Dr. King, James Lawson, Nelson Mandela, and Steve Biko, Greg Johnson was active in the anti-apartheid movement as a student at Ohio State University. However, he never thought his activism would lead to founding BAN. The idea for BAN originated when the Johnsons were continuously told "African Americans were not concerned about nuclear proliferation because they were too busy trying to get food on the table." The Johnsons argued that "the nuclear issue had not been addressed from a black perspective and the established peace groups did not make an effort to go into the black community." Rather than wait for traditional peace groups to act, they formed Blacks Against Nukes.[34]

The Johnsons felt that African Americans needed to understand the links between increased military spending and cutbacks for housing, education, and jobs. "Black and poor people in this country are suffering in the name of national security, which has to do with people who are educated, fed, and clothed, not with how many weapons you have in your arsenal," Greg argued. "We saw a pattern of colonialism to subjugate nonwhites. And the bomb was part of it. It was all connected," he said.[35]

Working out of their home, the Johnsons created a one-page flyer with a picture of an MX missile next to people standing in an unemployment line. They distributed the flyer to radio stations, churches, schools, and local community centers. Soon after, Greg appeared on a local radio show. With that appearance and the distribution of a newsletter, Blacks Against Nukes was launched. BAN did not, however, find success merging with the larger Peace Movement, especially in the Washington, D.C., area. Rather than take part in the planning for such out-reach, the Johnsons felt they were asked to act as "go betweens" for other peace groups and the black community. The attitude was, "What can you do for us, not how can we help you. We tried that route and it didn't work," Brenda Johnson said. Greg explained that groups like SANE hired "token folks" to go into the black community to discuss the nuclear issue. "At least they recognized a need and I was thankful for that," Johnson said. But he also made clear that for the mostly white, middle-class antinuclear groups, African Americans were never allowed in leadership positions. When it came to African Americans working in the anti-nuclear movement, "many whites still thought blacks should only work on civil rights. The attitude for many was 'stay in your place,'" Johnson said.[36]

The Johnsons refused to accept this role and took their message straight to the black community. "I always said that nuclear weapons are equal opportunity destroyers," Greg Johnson explained. From September 1981 to March 1990, the Johnsons lectured at schools, college campuses, including a number of histori-cally black college and universities, churches, and various community events. As a means of educating high school students, BAN sponsored an annual essay con-test on nuclear disarmament. "Hiroshima—What It Means to Me" was the topic for one year.[37] Letters began pouring in from ordinary black citizens requesting information, thanking the Johnsons for finally educating their community on nuclear proliferation, and asking to join their group. The Johnsons started receiv-ing donations from individuals in small increments to help cover the cost of their bimonthly newsletter.[38]

None of this was surprising to Greg: "I expected the response. I knew African Americans cared about this issue. The problem was no one ever cared about us or bothered to talk about it in the black community. African Americans were simply left out and we wanted to change all that."[39]

With little resources and mostly through word of mouth, BAN acquired a membership of over four hundred activists and established relationships with the Green Party in Germany and peace organizations in Japan, South Africa, and India. In 1983, Greg Johnson was a featured speaker at the "World Conference Against A&H Bombs" in Japan. The Johnsons were profiled in *Essence, JET*, the *Washington Post*, and numerous college newspapers. After nine years, the John-sons dissolved BAN. When asked why, Greg responded, "Our goal was to educate the black community about the dangers of the bomb. By 1990 we felt people were getting it. We did our job."[40]

The resistance the Johnsons faced from mostly white antinuclear organizations was certainly not new. Just as many white members of the Women's International League for Peace and Freedom (WILPF) and Women Strike for Peace had been reluctant to work with black female activists decades earlier, black activists still faced racism within the Peace Movement during the 1980s. Some white members held firm to the belief that peace and freedom were separate issues. Others, as the Johnsons point out, resisted having African Americans in leadership or decision-making roles. Once again black activists had to consider their effectiveness in working in predominately white peace organizations.

James Haughton, a 1951 graduate of City College of New York, was active in the Negro American Labor Council and in 1964 founded Harlem Fight Back— an organization focused on improving job opportunities for African Americans, Hispanics, Asians, and women. Harlem Fight Back also supported nuclear disarmament, a passion of Haughton's.[41] Haughton was troubled by the racism inside the Peace Movement. Peace and antinuclear organizations "dodge the racism issue" and lean more "to the Right," he argued.[42] When asked if the disproportionate number of white leaders in these groups was a problem, he responded:

> It has been up until this point. And I think that there are fairly deep reasons for that. I think that the people who are trying to put this movement together evolved out of a racist history. They may not be conscious of it—this is not to say that they are consciously racist. But they have certainly not been attuned or made aware of the profound historical importance of dealing with the question of racism as an integral part of dealing with the fight against nuclear weapons. I think it is really a failure based on a lack of understanding . . . Well they [predominately white antinuclear groups] do not make a serious effort to involve the black community. I'm not saying that it is easy either. Just as we are an organization [Harlem Fight Back] that is deeply concerned about the threats posed by nuclear militarism and technology, so there are other black organizations and Hispanic organizations with people who are equally concerned. But they have not been reached; they have not been involved; they have not been organized into the antinuclear movement. That requires a great conscience and serious reaching out into those communities to develop that kind of rapport and interest.[43]

Haughton remained hopeful that blacks and whites would unite around the nuclear issue:

The ruling class has always strived to keep workers divided along the lines of race, sex, and religion in order to weaken and therefore control them. So it is very ironic that through their proliferation of nuclear power, which exploits all people, especially workers, the ruling class has provided the workers with the very issue that will force them to unite. And under the issue of nuclear power many other issues are brought together—ecology, jobs, energy, monopoly capitalism, big government, racism, sexism, and classism. That's why I say it embraces the totality of society.[44]

Haughton's wishes would soon be fulfilled when perhaps as many as one million people gathered in New York City to demand an end to the nuclear arms race in the summer of 1982.

June 12, 1982

By 1981, the Reagan administration had continued to perpetuate the nuclear arms race by cutting programs that most benefited the poor. Around the world, countries that already possessed nuclear weapons were adding to their arsenals and more nations were seeking to join the nuclear club. At the same time, life-long activists and concerned citizens mobilized into what was known as the "Nuclear Freeze" campaign. The goal was not to propose any new, elaborate solution to the Cold War. They simply called for a "freeze" on the production, testing, and deployment of all nuclear weapons and delivery vehicles. As the campaign gained momentum, the U.N. General Assembly announced plans to hold its second Special Session on Disarmament (SSD II) in June 1982. This was the moment Haughton and other black activists had been anticipating.[45]

Organizers planned multiple events to drum up support for the June protest at the United Nations. In May, Performing Artists for Nuclear Disarmament (PAND) organized a rally that brought about six hundred children and parents to Delacorte Theater in Central Park. PAND, which several artists (Jules Feiffer, Robert Altman, Harry Belafonte, Eliot Feld, and Harold Prince) formed in 1982, included musicians, dancers, actors, playwrights, composers, screenwriters, choreographers, producers, directors, designers, critics, technicians, and administrators. The group wrote letters to Congress, appeared on talk shows, and engaged in civil disobedience.[46]

The Central Park rally included performances by such artists as Chaka Kahn, Richie Havens, and James Taylor. Former U.S. Representative Bella Abzug (D-NY) told the children about growing up with the message of her father's store, "The

Live and Let Live Meat Market," and how they should take the peace effort to heart. Havens wailed on his guitar as he sang about the next world war: "Goodbye Jerusalem, Grand Canyon, Parthenon, 'cause this one's going to be the last one."[47] In the same month, Harlem Fight Back organized a "Survival Festival" at Marcus Garvey Park, which featured numerous black artists, including Abiodun Oyewole and Gylan Yeyitos, formerly of the Last Poets, poet and writer Sonja Sanchez, Gil Scott-Heron, reggae musicians Breadnut and Bunny and the Dominos, and African drummers Los Yeyitos.[48]

On the West Coast, a massive "We Have a Dream" rally was held in Pasadena. The event was sponsored by the Alliance for Survival, the Interfaith Committee for the Year of Shalom, and the SCLC, among others. African American mayor of Pasadena Loretta Glickman, actors LaVar Burton, Mike Farrell, and Donna Mills, James Lawson, and President Reagan's daughter Patti Davis addressed the crowd. Stevie Wonder, Bob Dylan, Joan Baez, Joe Walsh, Linda Ronstadt, Jackson Browne, and Graham Nash performed. Addressing the 100,000 in attendance, Jesse Jackson declared, "We shall march until there is no more war and no more weapons. The world faces a critical choice—to freeze weapons or burn the people. We're not the only nation who ever made an atomic bomb, but we're the only nation that ever dropped one. We must wake up and tell the world, we must have peace now." Jackson urged the crowd to "choose life and choose a new president."[49]

Organizers called the June 12 demonstration "the disarmament rally to end all disarmament rallies." The official goals of the march were to show support for the United Nations Special Session ont Disarmament, to call for a freeze and reduction of all nuclear weapons, and a transfer of military budgets to human needs. This link between defense spending and cuts in social programs caused many minority groups to join the rally.[50]

Minority participants included the Reverend Herbert Daughtry's National Black United Front (BUF), the Asian American Caucus for Disarmament, Hispanics for Survival and Disarmament, and the African American Coordinating Committee. The latter served as an umbrella for groups like Harlem Fight Back, the National Alliance Against Racist and Political Repression, Women for Racial and Economic Equality, the National Conference of Black Lawyers, the National Tenants Organization, Black Veterans for Social Justice, the National Conference of Black Pastors, and many others. Led largely by BUF, the minority groups formed the Third World and Progressive People's Coalition. The coalition also included numerous small leftist organizations whose memberships were primarily white. The group called for unilateral nuclear disarmament, an end to U.S. military aggression in Central America, and an end to racism in the United States. The Third World and Progressive People's Coalition, however, did not represent the entire black or Third World community. Although some minority organizations like the Coalition of Black Trade Unionists and the Hispanic Labor Committee expressed concern over the treatment of minority groups, they hesitated to work within the Third World and Progressive People's Coalition because of its radical reputation and their desire to prevent any further splits. Simultaneously, the main rally committee had garnered some black support, and a few of the more radical organizations within the rally committee, like Mobilization for Survival, were coalitions themselves and already included minority groups like the All African Peoples Revolutionary Party.[51]

In addition to the increase in minority participation, some black leaders wanted a stronger voice in the planning process. African American Coordinating Committee member Jitu Weusi explains, "In the past, participation of blacks had been token in these activities." However, the Third World and Progressive People's Coalition was determined to shed light on how nuclear weapons affected minority communities.[52] This did not sit well with leaders of traditional peace groups, who balked at the idea of the coalition having a large role in the planning process. As a result, the coalition split off to form its own committee.[53]

The rift occurred over the message of the rally. The June 12 Rally Committee vehemently disagreed with the minority groups' proposals to link the arms race with other issues.[54] Mark Roberts, national campaign director for Greenpeace, said, "There were problems with BUF's wanting to move more to the left, which made us and other mainstream groups less apt to work with them." In short, leaders did not want to deviate from their slogan, "End the Arms Race, and Shift the Budget to Fund Human Needs." However, minority groups, who were accused of "moving to the left," thought it necessary to include U.S. intervention in the Third World and links between racism and nuclear weapons in the platform.[55] John Collins of Clergy and Laity Concerned (CALC), a group that was a founding member of the June 12 Rally Committee, argued that a lot of the difficulties arose out of the fact that "the peace and environmental movements tended to be white and middle class and to a certain degree racist." "Not in the sense of the KKK or that kind of thing," he said. "It's just that a lot people in white groups don't know how to relate to and work with Third World groups."[56]

War Resisters League leader David McReynolds became critical of the inclusiveness of the June 12 march. In January, McReynolds wrote to organizers, arguing that the Peace Movement's biggest mistake was inviting other groups into the decision-making process:

> If the women's movement plans a major demonstration they pull together women's organizations. If labor wants a Solidarity march, they begin by getting the political line clear with labor groups. If Blacks march, they do not approach whites or Marxist-Leninist sects to help them plan the basic politics. Only the peace movement seems again and again to begin at the wrong point. We—the FOR, SANE, AFSC, WRL, CALC, WISP, WILPF, the Riverside program and the U.S. Peace Council should have met, should have hammered out a political agreement, a general outline, and then asked others to come in and join us at a functional level. The SSD II is a disarmament meeting. For better or worse, it is not on energy, or civil rights, or monopoly capital, or the violation of human rights in the Soviet Bloc, or the persistent brutalization of poor Americans. It is a four-week session about disarmament. From the beginning the disarmament groups had the responsibility to take charge.[57]

McReynolds also made clear that the march was not an "anti-Reagan" rally:

> I urge those who want such a rally to get down to Washington and hold it where it makes sense . . . I do blame the Soviets as well as the Americans for the arms race. I do not want a "respectable" demonstration—I want us to raise hell, to express the anger people feel at being ripped off, but that anger needs to be a universal anger against the institution of war, not just the Republican Party. (I wish liberals would keep in mind that it was their Party, the Democrats, which began the arms race escalation, and had resumed military aid to Central America just before Reagan came into power).[58]

Addressing the "radical" faction of the demonstration, McReynolds said:

> We are not struggling just with individuals, but systems, and institutions. One of our problems is capitalism—I have no hesitation in naming it—but it wasn't capitalism that drove Vietnam into Cambodia, or China into Vietnam, or put Soviet and Chinese troops on the border of each other. I really think that those here who feel the Russians (or Chinese) never make mistakes, or must be supported at all times, are working on the wrong rally. Either that, or I'm working on the wrong rally.[59]

There was, however, an alternative position. The Third World and Progressive People's Coalition stated:

> Our view is that the political level of the disarmament movement must be raised and that Third World people must be involved in the leadership process. Many of us were involved in the movements of the '60s and we remember all too well the attempts of the most conservative leadership, usually backed by large sums of foundation money, to limit the political slogans to the most basic, to refuse to link one issue with another, and in the most treacherous fashion, to make the movement "safe" for politicians to come in and lead it.[60]

Discussing the importance of minority groups' participation, Charlene Mitchell, executive secretary of the National Alliance Against Racist and Political Repression, argued that the nuclear arms buildup "affects first and foremost, black people and black youth in particular." She noted that industries where blacks have made inroads, including steel and auto, were being hit the hardest, because "less steel was being used for civilian consumption and more was going to the making of weapons. This reduced the number of jobs available outside the military industrial complex." Mitchell was convinced that the unification of "Black, white, Native American Indian, Hispanic and all other nationally-oppressed people" would result in "the biggest demonstration for peace."[61] Jack O'Dell of Operation PUSH maintained that

> There can be no survival for the human race if the arms race continues. This is the first time the peace movement has added, as a demand, the transference of resources from the military to social and job creating programs . . . Dr. King and the Poor People's Campaign were saying this during Vietnam, but the peace movement as a whole wasn't. That's why the movement didn't go past the ending of the Vietnam War. Today's connections are bringing whole new constituencies into the movement.[62]

Frank Brown of the June 12 Rally Committee agreed. Brown described "high unemployment, poor housing, educational and recreational facilities and discrimination" as "bombs that are dropped on our communities every day." "Peace issues can seem sort of mystical in the face of it all. But when we talk about cutting the military budget so that we can put money back into social programs the issue is real," he said.[63]

By June 12, groups from both sides had managed to resolve their differences. At a lengthy meeting in Harlem, ministers from Black United Front and some of the religious groups within the Rally Committee agreed "in principle" on two major black and Third World demands: one-third minority representation in the coalition leadership, and the addition of slogans condemning racism and super-power intervention in the Third World.[64]

When the rally finally took place, approximately one million demonstrators marched through Central Park and midtown Manhattan. Companion rallies were held at both the Rose Bowl in Pasadena (90,000 in attendance), and in San Francisco (50,000). Organizers in New York held in their hands a petition, which they presented to the American and Soviet missions at the United Nations, containing no fewer than 2.3 million signatures. "There's no way the leaders can ignore this now," said Alex Willentz, who drove overnight from Utica, New York. "It's not just hippies and crazies anymore. It's everybody." Another woman stated, "We got rid of Lyndon Johnson, we stopped the war. This movement is much bigger. It combines the issues of bread and bombs."[65] Elizabeth Holtzman, the Brooklyn district attorney and later Congresswoman, described the overall sentiment: "It was the people of this country that forced the Government to end the war in Vietnam. It was the people of this country that forced the government to remove a President who committed crimes in high places. The people of this country—yes, the people of this world—will make their governments listen."[66]

On the day of the rally, 50 percent of the leadership was black. Indeed, when one white stage manager attempted to squeeze out Third World members toward the end of the day, African American leaders had him removed and replaced by a black manager. Prominent African American participants included Dick Gregory, Chaka Kahn, Toni Morrison, Sweet Honey in the Rock, Rita Marley, and Harry Belafonte.[67] At the United Nations, Ossie Davis and Ruby Dee shared the stage with white leaders. Coretta Scott King declared:

> We have come to this great city from all across America and around the world to protest the nuclear arms race. All of our hopes for equality, for justice, economic security, for a healthy environment, depend on nuclear disarmament. Yes we have come to protest nuclear weapons. But we have also come to New York because we have a dream. An affirmative vision shared by the great masses of people of every race, religion and nation down through the ages; it is the timeless dream of a world free from fear, not only of war or its instruments, but also of hunger or of not having a roof over one's head.[68]

Dick Gregory said the demonstrators had come to write "the unwritten page of the constitution, dealing with the right to live free from nuclear terror."[69]

The Third World and Progressive People's Coalition managed to express its concerns at the march as well. The Reverend Herbert Daughtry noted the $500 billion spent in arms annually and pointed to the impact such spending had on unemployment, hospitals, schools, transportation systems, and streets inside the United States. "This is a nation with the mightiest military machine in the world and yet it cannot feed, clothe, shelter, educate, heal, and employ its people. And the same thing is happening in other countries with insatiable military machines," he said. A member of the African National Congress charged South Africa with developing nuclear weapons to use against black Africans. Rubin Zemora of the Revolutionary Democratic Front of El Salvador blamed the delivery of arms instead of food to El Salvador for killing the country.[70]

As demonstrators proceeded to the United Nations, hospital union workers, Harlem Fight Back, the New York Teachers Black Caucus, and other predominately black groups marched down to Seventh Avenue, chanting, "We're fired up; we can't take no more." On 110th Street and Lexington, they were joined by the East Harlem contingent under the banner of Hispanics for Survival. Like the groups from Central Harlem, Hispanics for Survival was against nuclear weapons, but it also protested cuts in funds for social programs, U.S. intervention in the Caribbean, and minority white oppression in South Africa.[71]

In Harlem, ministers focused on the devastating economic effects of U.S. military budgets and demanded nuclear disarmament. "When you take a look at the military budget and then at our decaying cities, you can see that we are already victims of war. Not only would New York be a major target of any nuclear attack, it is already a target of the military budget," the Reverend William James, president of the Ministerial Interfaith Association of Harlem, argued. SCLC president Joseph Lowery declared, "Here in the United States the official commitment to the development of new first-strike weapons systems along with a limited nuclear war strategy virtually assures a mirror image response from the Soviet Union and other nuclear powers. And so as the economy of our cities and rural areas fall victim to military spending, we drift closer to nuclear disaster."[72] The Coalition of Black Trade Unionists passed a resolution that called on the United States government to join other nations in renouncing the "first use of nuclear weapons." The group reiterated their commitment to educating citizens about the threats to human life posed by the nuclear arms race and to work toward "securing a just and lasting peace in a more prosperous world."[73]

Harlem Fight Back wrote a timely editorial for the *New York Amsterdam News* the day of the rally, connecting racism to colonialism and nuclear weapons:

> All sectors of society—Black, white, red, yellow, brown, young and old, male and female—are and will be affected by nuclear militarism. Two present day examples demonstrate how racism and the nuclear arms race are related. The struggle over Native American lands and the building of one of the world's major nuclear arsenals in South Africa show that nuclear militarism and nuclear technology are clear expressions of racism. Recently there has been widespread theft of Indian lands where uranium has been discovered. These attacks on Native Americans command the most forceful condemnation by Blacks, antinuclear activists and progressives in general. Yet such condemnation and active support for the Native American people has yet to emerge. It is also important to take note of apartheid, nuclear militarism and power in South Africa. That country is heavily supported and invested in by the U.S. government and transnational corporations. South Africa is one of the main sources in the world for uranium. It provides imperialism with uranium mined by Blacks. This bastion of racism poses a threat not only to Africa, but the world. Where in America do we hear the outcry? With the American ruling class intensifying its exploitation of the American people, conditions are ripe for a massive educational and political campaign to combat racism and unite workers in their class interests. There is no issue more overwhelming and all embracing than nuclear technology, militarism and power.[74]

A Call to Conscience: The Twentieth Anniversary of "I Have a Dream"

Six months after the June 12 demonstration, Coretta Scott King, along with a host of African American leaders and groups, began planning a massive demonstration to commemorate Dr. King's "March on Washington," in August 1983. Under the banner "We Still Have a Dream," the Twentieth Anniversary March (TAM) focused on mobilizing citizens to "stem the tide of rising unemployment, nuclear annihilation, and racial violence."[75] Organizers dedicated a significant portion of the platform to nuclear disarmament:

> We live in constant fear of annihilation . . . The global arms race had escaped all reason and control, and restricted the ability of governments to promote the common welfare of all people . . . Were he alive today, Dr. King would still be using the "unarmed truth" to warn that we stand at the very precipice of the hell of thermonuclear

> self-immolation . . . We must transform the dynamics of the world power struggle from the nuclear arms race to a creative contest to harness man's genius for the purpose of making peace and prosperity a reality for all . . . We call upon the American public to turn the arms race into a "peace race" utilizing the existent and evolving movements in the United States as its foundation.[76]

Ending the "disastrous arms race" in the immediate months ahead "must become public policy, not just an elusive goal," leaders argued. The Twentieth Anniversary March called on both superpowers and their allies to "radically reduce and ultimately eliminate their nuclear arsenals as well as conventional weapons; to jointly act to prevent the spread of nuclear weapons to other nations; and to reduce the record levels of military expenditures."[77]

Planning for the event began in December 1982, when King, Congressman Walter Fauntroy (D-DC), SCLC president Joseph Lowery, executive director of the NAACP Benjamin Hooks, and others called on supporters to form a "Coalition of Conscience." The new coalition urged the Reagan administration to "reverse the trend towards nuclear annihilation and record defense spending."[78] In February, the Twentieth Anniversary March joined the National Freeze Campaign for a conference in St. Louis, Missouri. A month later, it took part in the National Freeze Lobby in Washington, D.C. To formally kick off the march, in June 1983, organizers premiered *In Our Hands*, a documentary film that focused on the June 12, 1982, demonstration.[79]

In the same month, thirty African Americans joined three thousand delegates from 132 nations at the World Assembly for Peace, Life, and Against Nuclear War in Prague to protest policies that would "lead to nuclear war." The weeklong gathering focused on the role of the United Nations in disarmament, social and ethical aspects of the arms race, liberation movements, and expanding the Peace Movement. Representatives of over 1,800 national organizations, 119 nongovernmental groups, and intergovernmental bodies participated in the meeting, including noted African Americans Ralph Abernathy, columnist Ethel Payne, and Berkeley, California, mayor Gus Newport. The black delegates stressed the connection between nuclear weapons and racism and urged others to join them in Washington for the Twentieth Anniversary March. Representatives of Third World liberation movements explained that while billions of dollars went to "reactionary regimes" and weapons each year, world hunger, disease, and poverty were increasing.[80]

Delegates sang "We Shall Overcome" at the opening of the conference. The assembly criticized President Reagan for promoting the suicidal idea of a "winnable nuclear war" and for planning to install first-strike nuclear missiles in Europe. It issued an appeal stating that preparation for nuclear war was "the most serious crime against humanity, but people for peace can and must influence governments." However, the conference and subsequent rally, which drew 200,000 supporters, went largely unnoticed in the U.S. media.[81]

The most notable events of the Twentieth Anniversary March occurred in August, the same month as the atomic bombings and Dr. King's "I Have a Dream" speech. The group held a vigil to commemorate the Hiroshima and Nagasaki bombings and followed it with a demonstration. Over eight hundred human rights organizations as well as antinuclear, religious, and labor groups gathered for the rally in Washington, D.C. The 250,000 protesters came from over 310 cities. Thousands more rallied in New York City. Discussing the significance of the event, Cleveland Robinson, former secretary-treasurer of the United Auto Workers and organizer of the 1963 civil rights march, said, "This march is the beginning of a struggle of great dimensions."[82]

Although the June 12 demonstration was one of the largest and most diverse in U.S. history, one could argue that activists had little success in gaining economic equality or moving the world closer to peace. The SSD II that took place inside the United Nations produced few results. Its main achievement was the adoption of "conclusions," noting the member states' commitment to respect the priorities in disarmament negotiations and the formation of the World Disarmament Campaign.[83] However, by Reagan's second term, activists' decades of work finally paid dividends. South Africa's apartheid government fell, and with it their nuclear weapons program. In the United States, antinuclear activism forced President Reagan to change course. The president's wife, Nancy, "felt strongly" that the administration's disarmament initiatives were "not only in the interest of world peace, but the correct move politically." National Security Advisor Robert McFarlane said, "You had to have appropriations, and to get them you needed political support, and that meant you had to have an arms control policy worthy of the name." Secretary of State George Shultz agreed: "Given the political climate in the U.S., we could not keep pace in modernization, production, and deployment of these deadly weapons." Even President Reagan admitted that one of his main motivations for his shift in nuclear policy was that "from a propaganda point of view, we were on the defensive."[84]

In the latter half of the decade, the United States and the Soviet Union signed the START treaty, which contained provisions not just for freezing but for actually reducing the size of each side's respective arsenals. Reagan and Soviet general secretary Mikhail Gorbachev also negotiated and signed the Intermediate Range Nuclear Forces treaty, which banned and eliminated medium-range nuclear-tipped ballistic missiles from the arsenals of both the East and the West. The Reagan administration ceased all talk about "winning" a nuclear war. And in 1985 Reagan and Gorbachev proclaimed, "Nuclear war cannot be won and should never be fought."[85]

Since 1945, black activists had fought for racial equality, nuclear disarmament, and liberation movements around the world. These men and women, who at times were the most dispossessed, refused to separate these issues, maintaining a linkage to a global struggle for freedom and wielding their collective strength to create a more peaceful world. Indeed, because of their sacrifice, strength, and commitment to fighting on multiple fronts, the Nuclear Test Ban Treaty (1963), Civil Rights Act (1964), Voting Rights Act (1965), and the gaining of independence of various African nations became realities. Perhaps their most important victory came in 2008 with the election of Barack Obama. For many hoped that Obama would become not only the first African American president, but also the most antinuclear president in U.S. history.

Chapter 6

A New START

Nuclear Disarmament in the Age of Obama

I believe the United States has a unique responsibility to act—indeed, we have a moral obligation. I say this as a president of the only nation ever to use nuclear weapons. I say it as a commander in chief who knows that our nuclear codes are never far from my side. Most of all, I say it as a father, who wants my two daughters to grow up in a world where everything they know and love can't be instantly wiped out.

—President Barack Obama, 2012

IN MARCH 1983, AN UNDERGRADUATE AT COLUMBIA UNIVERSITY wrote a story in the campus newsmagazine, *Sundial*, about eliminating nuclear weapons. Focusing on two student groups, Arms Race Alternatives and Students Against Militarism, the young Barack Obama examined the struggles activists faced in motivating students to act on issues like nuclear disarmament, military spending, and South Africa. "Most students at Columbia do not have firsthand knowledge of war," Obama wrote. "Military violence has been a vicarious experience, channeled into our minds through television, film, and print." Obama explained that student participation had increased considerably since the June 12 rally, but he questioned their sincerity, suggesting that for at least some, nuclear disarmament was simply the cause of the day. Obama also questioned the larger "Nuclear Freeze" campaign and "academic discussions" that centered on narrow issues such as first- or second-strike capabilities. The Nuclear Freeze campaign was focused on the "symptom" rather than on the "disease," Obama argued. Nuclear weapons were "linked to economics and politics and part of a much larger problem—militarism." However, observing the activists, Obama remained optimistic about student involvement and hopeful about the possibility of one day having a "nuclear free world."[1]

Years later, Obama explained that at Columbia he was driven by two central questions: "How would the United States and the Soviet Union effectively manage their nuclear arsenals, and were there ways to dial down the dangers that humanity faced?" In his senior year, Obama enrolled in a seminar on presidential decision making, in which he wrote a paper examining how to negotiate with the Soviets to cut nuclear arsenals. Obama's professor, Dr. Barton, recalls, "His focus was the nature of the strategic talks and what kind of negotiating positions might be put forward . . . It was not a polemical paper—not arguing that the U.S. should have this or that position. It was how to get from here to there and avoid misperception and conflict. He got an A."[2]

While the future president was developing his vision of a world without nuclear weapons, a host of African American politicians was paving the way for Obama to become president and to make his vision a reality. Since Obama's election, scholars have begun to study more closely the history of African American politicians. Charles Henry explains that in many ways Obama's election can be traced to Harold Washington's "racially charged campaign" to become Chicago's first black mayor in 1983. Comparing the two, Henry writes that like Obama, "Washington was a young black lawyer from Chicago with a degree from a prestigious law school." He too had "a mixed legislative record of reform and mainstream party voting in the Illinois legislature and went on to win a historic general election after beating the Democratic Party favorite in the primary." And he also was known for his "verbal eloquence and putting people together who were really enemies of each other."[3] However, Obama and Washington shared another commonality: a commitment to nuclear disarmament. As a congressman, Washington routinely spoke out against nuclear weapons and voted against nuclear proposals, often in the face of the local Chicago "machine." Washington was especially active in debates concerning nuclear power, since at the time Illinois had more nuclear power plants than any other state in the nation. Running for reelection, Washington said:

> I want to continue the fight in the Congress and in the community against the dangerous troubling assaults upon our people. I am angered by the assaults on domestic justice, civil liberties and world peace launched by the rampant Reagan administration and its allies in Congress . . . I want to return to silence the drumbeats of war. To solve problems at home, we must stop squandering hundreds of billions of dollars on war programs, the neutron bomb and other massive weapon systems. I want to stop the secret shipments of hazardous nuclear waste on the busy highways where you and your family travel.[4]

He urged for an end to "Armageddon devices, including nuclear warheads, poison gas and biological weapons." "The export of nuclear technology and nuclear power endangers the existence of the world . . . we can be successful human beings without destroying other people," Washington said.[5] During his mayoral campaign, Washington argued that a nuclear freeze would release billions of dollars that could be used for the economic and social needs of the city.[6] Once elected, Washington continued to speak at antinuclear rallies and was honored by the Chicago Peace Council for his antinuclear efforts.[7]

Like Washington, other black politicians publicly opposed nuclear weapons, often connecting the issue with economic and racial equality. A month before the June 12 rally, the National Conference of Black Mayors gathered in Birmingham, Alabama, to discuss the nation's economy. Following the meeting, the group concluded that there was a direct link between President Reagan's cutbacks in programs for their cities and the buildup of nuclear weapons. The mayors opposed nuclear proliferation and suggested that the billions of dollars allocated for the arms race be spent on building new hospitals and schools.[8]

Since its inception, the Congressional Black Caucus (CBC) has included some of the most outspoken critics of nuclear weapons. Perhaps no congressman opposed the Reagan administration's nuclear policies more than CBC cofounder Ronald Dellums (D-CA). Indeed, Dellums made stopping the production of the MX missile, a heavyweight ICBM which carried ten nuclear warheads, his personal crusade. For Dellums the connection between nuclear weapons spending and poverty in largely black communities was clear. The Carter administration had originally proposed plans for the MX missile, and in 1980, with support from representatives Charles Rangel (D-NY), Shirley Chisholm (D-NY), and John Conyers (D-MI), all cofounders of the CBC, Dellums put forth an amendment to cut the $1.6 billion Carter was asking for MX development.[9] However, two years later, Dellums was again fighting to stop development of the MX missile, this time under the Reagan administration. Dellums introduced an alternative appropriations bill, which reduced the military budget by more than $50 billion. Since the military was planning on making Utah the headquarters for the MX missile, Dellums traveled to the state and met with Spencer Kimball, head of the Mormon Church. Following their meeting, the Mormon Church announced its decision to formally oppose the MX missile, citing many of the same reasons that Dellums had mentioned to Kimball.[10]

To combat the Reagan administration's plans to dramatically increase the number of nuclear weapons, the Congressional Black Caucus put forth an alternative budget that called for the elimination of the MX missile as well as the Trident and Trident II missiles, Pershing II missile, Cruise missiles, and antisatellite weapons.[11] While Dellums's and the CBC's proposals were soundly defeated, their efforts along with pressure from antinuclear groups resulted in Congress blocking all funding for production of the MX missile in December 1982. Lawrence Wittner argues that this was a stunning defeat—the first time in the postwar era that Congress had refused any president a major nuclear weapon. The next day, however, the House of Representatives voted by a massive margin of 346 to 68 to accept a military appropriations bill of $230 billion, which would be used in part to research and develop the MX missile. Following the vote, Dellums stated:

> It is very sexy, it is very attractive now to be for the [nuclear weapons] freeze; but how do you translate that commitment into the budget? Representatives were guilty of the most blatant form of hypocrisy when they proclaimed their support for arms reductions and then vote for all the weapons that deny the freeze—the MX, Pershing II, the Trident submarine and the B-1 bomber.[12]

The battle to stop the MX missile continued throughout the next three years, and by 1985, following multiple attempts by the Reagan administration, a measure for the production of the MX missile passed. However, the administration had to agree to cut the number of missiles from two hundred to fifty. Opponents of the MX missile regarded this as a victory. President Reagan viewed it as a defeat.[13]

Jesse Jackson's Presidential Campaign

With President Reagan as their opponent, the Democrats fighting for the 1984 presidential nomination—California senator Alan Cranston, former vice president Walter Mondale, and Colorado senator Gary Hart—made sure to offer support for a nuclear freeze.[14] It was another candidate, however, who articulated the strongest antinuclear position.

Jesse Jackson, already a well-known antinuclear activist, dedicated a substantial portion of his presidential campaign to the nuclear arms race. Stating, "We will choose the human race over the nuclear race," Jackson's platform included a pledge from the United States to never again be the first to use nuclear weapons, as well as a 20 percent cut in the military budget and a six-month moratorium on the production, testing, and deployment of all nuclear weapons. Jackson called for the withdrawal of Pershing II and Cruise missiles from Europe and establishing nuclear-free zones worldwide. He favored continued adherence to the 1967 Outer Space Treaty and the 1972 Anti-Ballistic Missile Treaty; ratification of SALT II, the Threshold Test Ban Treaty, the Peaceful Nuclear Explosion Treaty, and the Comprehensive Test Ban Treaty; and the creation of a crisis control center with the Soviet Union and other world powers to reduce tensions and avert accidental disasters.[15]

Peace activists who supported Jackson contended that he was the only candidate to effectively link peace with social justice, which they defined as "the lynchpin of a genuine and lasting peace." The National Campaign for No-First-Use of Nuclear Weapons maintained that Jackson's representatives were among the strongest advocates of a no-first-use policy.[16] Supporters hoped that Jackson's candidacy would bring in thousands of new elected officials—at state, county, and local levels—who would vote differently on matters of peace and equality.[17]

While Jackson did not win the nomination, he registered over one million new voters, received 3.5 million votes, and won five primaries and caucuses. Twenty-one percent of his vote came from those outside the black community, and he had more nonblack support than Hart or Mondale had nonwhite support.[18] Examining Jackson's candidacy, Henry asserts that while Jackson started with a campaign aimed at African Americans, he combined it with traditional liberal programs like nuclear disarmament that some argued were corporatist in nature, had little appeal in the black community, and helped garner white support. This made Jackson less of a radical and much more mainstream, Henry concludes.[19] However, Jackson did not speak out against nuclear weapons for white support or to "deracialize" his campaign. He championed nuclear disarmament for the same reasons black activists had done since 1945. As a grassroots activist, Jackson had consistently expressed the belief that peace and equality were connected. Therefore, Jackson made nuclear disarmament a central component of his campaign not in spite of but because of race. Indeed, not many presidential candidates before or after Jackson have demonstrated such a strong antinuclear platform...until Barack Obama.

Candidate Barack Obama

In 2005, on his first foreign trip as a United States senator, Barack Obama accompanied Senator Richard Lugar (R-IN) on a week-long tour of Weapons of Mass Destruction facilities in the former Soviet Union. Afterward Obama often spoke about the trip, in particular the vast amount of poorly secured lethal materials that he witnessed at the sites. A few years later, as a presidential candidate, Obama declared, "The single most serious threat to American national security is nuclear terrorism."[20]

Not since Jesse Jackson had a presidential candidate more opposed nuclear weapons. In August 2007, when asked if he would ever consider using nuclear weapons to fight terrorism, Obama stated that he would not use nuclear weapons in situations involving civilians. Going further, he said, "I think it would be a profound mistake for us to use nuclear weapons in any circumstance." Then, he clarified: "Let me scratch that. There's been no discussion of nuclear weapons. That's not on the table. That's not a hypothetical that I'm going to discuss."[21]

Two months later, speaking at DePaul University, Obama suggested the United States should begin to greatly reduce its nuclear stockpiles and proposed setting a goal of eliminating all nuclear weapons worldwide. The presidential hopeful called for pursuing vigorous diplomatic efforts aimed at a global ban on the development, production, and deployment of intermediate-range missiles. Obama pledged to end production of fissile material for nuclear weapons, not build new weapons, remove any remaining nuclear weapons from hair-trigger alert, and if elected, lead a global effort to secure nuclear weapons and material at vulnerable sites within four years. "In 2009, we will have a window of opportunity to renew our global leadership and bring our nation together," Obama said. "If we don't seize that moment, we may not get another."[22]

In July 2008, Obama reiterated his goal of ridding the world of nuclear weapons. Speaking at Purdue University, he declared: "It's time to send a clear message to the world: America seeks a world with no nuclear weapons . . . As long as nuclear weapons exist, we'll retain a strong deterrent. But we'll make the goal of eliminating all nuclear weapons a central element in our nuclear policy." Following the event, Obama distributed a fact sheet to reporters that stated he would work to eliminate all nuclear weapons but would not commit the United States to giving them up while other states retained them. He also repeated his commitment to secure all nuclear weapons materials in four years and to increase funding by $1 billion a year to make sure nuclear weapons were removed from vulnerable sites around the world. Obama promised to strengthen nonproliferation programs, reach disarmament deals with Russia, and bolster sanctions against North Korea, Iran, and other states with rogue nuclear programs. He vowed to seek a verifiable global ban on production of nuclear weapons material and to "stop the development of new nuclear weapons."[23]

While Obama had campaigned against nuclear weapons, activists were cautiously optimistic following his election. Antinuclear groups pointed to his choices of Hillary Clinton for secretary of state and Robert Gates for defense secretary, along with his willingness to explore "safe" nuclear power for energy, as signs that President Obama might move to the right once inside the White House. However, as Secretary of State Clinton reiterated, Obama's campaign positions on nuclear weapons had become administration policy. Testifying before Congress in January, Clinton made clear that the number one threat in the world was nuclear weapons. "This represents a dramatic change in U.S. national security policy," said Joseph Cirincione, president of the Ploughshares Fund and nuclear weapons expert.[24]

Gates proved especially troubling. The former defense secretary for George W. Bush had advocated on numerous occasions for the production of new nuclear weapons with the renewal of the Reliable Replacement Warhead (RRW) program. A policy paper titled "National Security and Nuclear Weapons in the 21st Century," coauthored by Gates and Bush's energy secretary Samuel Bodman, argued, "The Reliable Replacement Warhead program deserves continued study and development." They described it as a "key to sustaining confidence in the U.S. nuclear stockpile."[25] Mark Thompson in *Time* observed that while serving under Bush, Gates had repeatedly called for the RRW. "The Reliable Replacement Warhead is not about new capabilities, but about safety, reliability and security," Gates said. Activists were quick to point out that President Obama's decision on RRW would indicate his true intentions on nuclear weapons.[26]

President Obama: Making His Vision a Reality

On January 20, 2009, President Barack Obama stood in front of over two million citizens in Washington, D.C., as he delivered his inaugural address. Discussing the need for a new era of responsibility, he recalled when earlier generations "faced down fascism and communism not just with missiles and tanks, but with the sturdy alliances and enduring convictions." "They understood that our power alone cannot protect us, nor does it entitle us to do as we please," he said. "With old friends and former foes, we'll work tirelessly to lessen the nuclear threat and roll back the specter of a warming planet."[27] A month later, Obama started making good on his promises.

Shortly after taking the oath of office, President Obama declared that the new administration "will stop the development of new nuclear weapons." And in his first budget, Obama called for an end to the Reliable Replacement Warhead program. "The program is for all intents and purposes dead," said Daryl Kimball, executive director of the Arms Control Association in Washington, D.C.[28] Moreover, Obama announced his plans to establish a nonproliferation office at the White House to oversee talks between the United States and Russia, aimed at slashing each country's stockpile of nuclear weapons by 80 percent. The treaty would cut the number of nuclear warheads to one thousand each. "We are going to re-engage Russia in a more traditional, legally binding arms reduction process," the administration stated.[29] Discussing Obama's decisions, Cirincione said, "I think this administration gets it like no administration in recent memory has gotten it . . . Obama came into office with the most comprehensive, integrated, detailed nuclear policy of any candidate ever to assume the presidency."[30]

Cirincione's words rang true when, in April, Obama delivered the most antinuclear speech of any president in United States history. The decision to make what is known as the "Prague Speech," was entirely Obama's. According to Ben Rhodes, Obama's foreign policy speechwriter, "Giving the Prague speech, was essentially the president's vision . . . He decided he wanted to do all these things on nuclear weapons in the campaign, so he gave a speech saying we're going to do them. It made it an easy speech to write. The president had an agenda and he laid it out. It was our message to our government as well as a message to the world."[31]

When President Obama took the stage in the Czech Republic, he reaffirmed his commitment to create a world free of nuclear weapons. Obama reminded the crowd of the Cold War, when "generations lived with knowledge that their world could be erased in a single flash of light." Eliminating nuclear weapons linked all people together because "one nuclear weapon exploded in one city—be it New York or Moscow, Islamabad or Mumbai, Tokyo or Tel Aviv, Paris or Prague— could kill hundreds of thousands of people. And no matter where it happens, there is no end to what the consequences might be—for our global safety, our security, our society, our economy, to our ultimate survival."[32] The most powerful line of the speech came when Obama declared, "As the only nuclear power to have used a nuclear weapon, the United States has a moral responsibility to act. We cannot succeed in this endeavor alone, but we can lead it, we can start it." Discussing a litany of plans, including negotiating a new START treaty, ratifying the Comprehensive Test Ban Treaty, and reducing the number of warheads and stockpiles, Obama returned to his campaign slogan and challenged those who argued that the world would never eliminate nuclear weapons. "Yes, we can," Obama exhorted. The president announced that he would set forth on a campaign to lock down all vulnerable nuclear material around the world within four years. "Let us bridge our divisions, build upon our hopes, accept our responsibility to leave this world more prosperous and more peaceful than we found it. Together we can do it," Obama concluded.[33]

Not since John F. Kennedy's 1963 commencement address at American University had a president so forcefully called for peace and a world without nuclear weapons. Analyzing the speech, Kimball maintained that it represented "a fundamental and important transformation in U.S. thinking about nuclear weapons."[34] "Obama was not just pledging to 'pursue' nuclear disarmament—as past U.S. presidents have done—but to make it the strategic goal of U.S. policy to eliminate all the world's nuclear weapons. The cynics believe Obama's words are wishful thinking. They're wrong. The real fantasy is to expect nuclear restraint and greater commitment to nonproliferation from other states in the absence of bold U.S. action on disarmament," Kimball argued.[35]

Obama was only ten months into his presidency when, due in large part to his commitment to nuclear disarmament, he won the Nobel Peace Prize. However, instead of expressing jubilation, the administration began to debate how best to address the obvious question that was to follow: How could President Obama accept the Nobel Peace Prize as a commander in chief of a military involved in two wars? Even the president, clearly uneasy about accepting the award, told reporters he did not deserve to be in the same company as those who had won it before him.[36] While he spoke out forcefully against nuclear weapons and was planning on ending the war in Iraq, Obama was also in the process of adding troops in Afghanistan and increasing Predator drone strikes in the Middle East.

To prepare for his acceptance speech, Obama studied a three-hundred-page binder that included various historical speeches, including those of past Nobel Peace Prize winners as well as analysis and debates about war and peace. Obama read Truman's celebratory statement on dropping the atomic bomb on Hiroshima. He also examined Gandhi's condemnation of the creation of the bomb. Richard Wolffe, who has written extensively on the Obama presidency, explains that liberation theologian Reinhold Niebuhr's concept of a "just war" made the largest impact on Obama. When he delivered his acceptance speech, the president attempted to position himself between Niebuhr's theory and the nonviolent, antiwar views of Gandhi and Dr. King, using President Kennedy's vision of a "gradual evolution to peace," to justify his actions.[37]

Critics were quick to point out that when King received the Nobel Peace Prize he made sure to connect nuclear weapons, militarism, and racial equality. Moreover, at the time King won the Prize, he was risking his life for peace and equality. However, as Melissa Harris-Perry correctly states: "Obama is not the leader of a progressive social movement. He is the president. As president he is both more powerful than Dr. King and more structurally constrained. He has more institutional power at his disposal and more crosscutting constituencies demanding his attention. He has more powerful allies and more powerful opponents." Along the same lines, Michael Eric Dyson argues that "Obama is not a prophet but a president so he cannot do the same things as King or other black activists." Indeed, that is why when asked if Dr. King would support his candidacy, Obama responded, "No, Dr. King would call on the American people to hold me accountable . . . change does not happen from top down. It comes from the bottom up."[38]

Obama's "Nuclear Spring"

A year after winning the Nobel Peace Prize and conducting 150 interagency meetings, including thirty by the National Security Council, the Obama administration produced its first Nuclear Posture Review (NPR) and proposal for a new START treaty. Eight years earlier, the Bush administration had released its Nuclear Posture Review. The contrast was striking. Ignoring the U.S. commitment to eliminate nuclear weapons at the 2000 Nuclear Non-Proliferation Treaty (NPT) conference, the report described Bush's extensive plans to rebuild the United States' nuclear arsenal, including the development of new ICBMs, sea-launched ballistic missiles, nuclear warheads, smaller nuclear weapons, and a new heavy bomber. These weapons would "assure allies and friends," "dissuade competitors," "deter aggressors," and "defeat enemies." The report also suggested that although the administration planned on decreasing the number of operationally deployed weapons, it would warehouse the remainder, thus giving it the ability to deploy as many as five thousand strategic nuclear warheads within a reasonably short time. Meanwhile, it would continue to produce nuclear weapons and create plans for nuclear attacks on China, Iran, Iraq, Libya, North Korea, Russia, and Syria. Since some of these countries did not possess nuclear weapons, the Nuclear Posture Review provided a further indication of the growing willingness of U.S. officials to initiate nuclear war against nonnuclear nations.[39]

In a clear repudiation of Bush's nuclear policies, President Obama's Nuclear Posture Review stated that the United States would not design, produce, or test any new nuclear weapons.[40] It removed one whole class of nuclear weapons delivery systems—the nuclear-armed "Tomahawk, " a sea-launched land-attack cruise missile—from the arsenal. It called for further Russian and American nuclear arms reductions. The sentence that received the most attention, however, was, "The United States will not use or threaten to use nuclear weapons against non-nuclear weapons states that are party to the Nuclear Nonproliferation Treaty and in compliance with their nuclear nonproliferation obligations."

This was remarkably different from Bush, who declared the United States could use nuclear weapons if it fell victim to a biological or chemical attack.[41]

Immediately following the release of Obama's NPR, both sides of the aisle criticized the president, a process that occurred nearly every time Obama announced a policy decision. For conservatives, Obama's nuclear policies "weakened America's deterrence against attacks with non-nuclear weapons of mass destruction." For progressives, the administration left far too many loopholes that authorized the president to use nuclear weapons. Peter Feaver of the *New York Times* points out that the administration still threatened to use nuclear weapons against nuclear states that are party to the Nuclear Non-Proliferation Treaty, including Russia and China, if they hit the United States with a cyber, biological, or chemical attack. Moreover, the NPR clearly implied that the United States reserved the right to use nuclear weapons against states that are not party to the nonproliferation treaty, left open the possibility of using nuclear weapons against "non-state actors" like Al-Qaeda, and explicitly stated that the "no-nuclear weapons assurance" did not apply to states that were in violation of the treaty, a list that included Iran, North Korea, and Syria.[42]

While Washington politicians used the Nuclear Posture Review to gain political points with their core constituencies, nuclear weapons experts viewed Obama's NPR as a dramatic start to a process the president had envisioned since college. Further proof of this occurred when the administration announced that for the first time since the United States had tested the bomb, it would disclose how many nuclear weapons were in its active stockpile. Speaking before the United Nations, Secretary of State Clinton said, "For those who doubt that the United States will do its part on disarmament, this is our record, these are our commitments. And they send a clear, unmistakable signal." "You can't get anywhere towards disarmament unless you are going to be transparent about how many weapons you have," Sharon Squassoni, director of the Proliferation Prevention Program at the Center for Strategic and International Studies, told the *Associated Press*. Cirincione agreed, explaining that the action "only enhanced U.S. credibility around the world that it was serious about nuclear disarmament."[43]

Perhaps the most important short-term success of Obama's nuclear weapons policy was that it halted the erosion of the Nuclear Non-Proliferation Treaty (NPT). Scott Sagan of the *Bulletin of Atomic Scientists* explains that at the 2005 NPT Review Conference, the treaty suffered a major setback when the international community failed to reach consensus on any new steps that could strengthen the nonproliferation regime—a failure that many nations blamed on the Bush administration's displays of contempt toward multilateral negotiations, and toward the United States' NPT obligation to pursue "negotiations in good faith" on nuclear disarmament. By contrast, at the May 2010 NPT Review Conference, the 189 signatories to the treaty welcomed "the reductions announced by some nuclear weapons states in the role of nuclear weapons in their security doctrines," praised new and improved International Atomic Energy Agency safeguard inspection protocols, and underscored the importance of international discussions on multilateral control of sensitive nuclear fuel facilities. Harald Müller, a political scientist and member of the German delegation, reported that this modest but valuable outcome would not have been possible if not for Obama's open embrace of the goal of a nuclear-free world and the adoption of a nuclear posture that moved the United States slowly toward that objective. Sagan, however, pointed out that some foreign governments, chiefly China and India, still viewed the new U.S. posture with skepticism, due largely to the administration's pledge to increase nuclear spending in the next decade.[44]

The next step in Obama's goal of eliminating nuclear weapons came in April 2010, when the president brought together forty-seven nations for a historic summit that focused on locking down all vulnerable nuclear materials. "Our objective is clear: to ensure that terrorists never gain access to plutonium or highly enriched uranium—the essential ingredients of a nuclear weapon," leaders stated.[45] The summit was part of Obama's "nuclear spring," a broad initiative to revive U.S. arms-control efforts and elevate the role of international treaties in U.S. nuclear weapons policy. The idea was to enhance the standing of the United States as it tried to prevent the world's nonproliferation system from collapsing. As a result, the Ukraine, Argentina, Chile, and Mexico all committed to eliminating their nuclear materials, while Kazakhstan, Vietnam, and Canada agreed to dispose of hundreds of pounds of highly enriched uranium used in civilian facilities. The United States and Russia agreed to dispose of 68 metric tons of plutonium, enough material to build more than 17,000 nuclear weapons. India declared that it would build a center to promote nuclear security, in what experts called a significant change in its focus on the issue. This trend continued into Obama's second term when the Czech Republic, with help from the United States, eliminated its stockpile of highly enriched uranium, Japan agreed to turn over hundreds of pounds of sensitive nuclear material, and Myanmar signed a nuclear agreement with the International Atomic Energy Agency declaring all of its nuclear facilities and materials and its intention to "actively pursue nuclear disarmament and nonproliferation."[46]

The summit was where Obama's vision from the Prague speech began to become a reality. Kenneth Luongo, an expert on nuclear security and president of the Partnership for Global Security, said that Obama "put his personal prestige on the line like no other world leader has before" on the nuclear issue.[47] After the terrifying decades of MAD (Mutually Assured Destruction), in two days in April President Obama "ushered in the new era to begin to confront the ultimate threat," declared Charles Hanley of the *Associated Press*. Hanley called Obama's "new mindset" an "important first step" in keeping nuclear weapons out of the hands of terrorists and smugglers.[48] Examining Obama's "nuclear spring," Steve Clemons of *Politico* wrote that "Obama has mended the foundation and infrastructure of a global nonproliferation regime that United Nations Ambassador John Bolton, Senator Jon Kyl (R-AZ), Vice-President Dick Cheney and others of the pugnacious nationalist wing of the last administration worked hard to tear down."[49] Cirincione observed that "the process and the momentum it creates, may move us from the *Dr. Strangelove* world of massive, mutual annihilation to the Dr. Einstein world where nuclear weapons have finally changed everything— including our way of thinking . . . There are times when you can fee the hinge of history moving. This is one of them," he concluded.[50]

Obama's "nuclear spring" also ushered in a new era in U.S.–Russian relations as the two countries signed a new START treaty, which would cut nuclear warheads by 30 percent.[51] However, unlike previous negotiations, the new START treaty became a much heavier lift than the president expected. Following the lofty goals Obama had set for himself in Prague, and winning the Nobel Peace Prize just three weeks before the START treaty was set to expire, he had to deliver. Richard Wolffe contends that there were problems from the start. Obama began his presidency trying to repair the frayed relations between the United States and Russia. Bush, Wolffe writes, had started off bonding with Vladimir Putin "by looking into his eyes and getting a sense of his soul." The two leaders agreed on a brief treaty to limit their nuclear arsenals, but disagreements over missile defense plans and Putin's attempts to extend Russia's influence over former Soviet countries prevented any progress as their relationship continued to disintegrate. Obama made clear his desire to reset relations with Russia and not to repeat the mistakes of his predecessor.[52]

The original START treaty took nine years to negotiate. Obama began working on START only eight months before it was due to expire. The preceding treaty with Putin had been three pages long; Obama and Russian prime minister Dmitry Medvedev were working on an agreement that ran to 180 pages. Pressure inside the White House was intense. Chief of Staff Rahm Emmanuel pressed the team to "get the fucking treaty done." However, the deadline lapsed and the treaty expired, in large part because every time the administration thought it had secured a deal, negotiations crumbled over issues like missile defense. Wolffe explains that the Russians knew Obama was under the clock and felt pressure to live up to the Nobel Peace Prize. Moreover, Obama was suffering politically at home in the battle to reform health care and Democrats losing the Massachusetts senate race. The Russians viewed the president as weak. They thought they could roll Obama and dictate the terms of the treaty. The Russians, however, underestimated the president's commitment to nuclear disarmament. Obama held firm with Medvedev, refusing to back down, and in mid-March Medvedev called Obama and the two reached a deal. Less than a month later, almost a year to the day that he told the world of his vision to eliminate nuclear weapons, Obama returned to Prague to sign the new START treaty with Medvedev.[53] The administration knew, however, that START was not a done deal. Congress still had to ratify the treaty.

"No More Hiroshimas"

While individuals around the world welcomed the president's shift away from nuclear weapons, it was Japanese citizens that perhaps expressed the highest hopes for Obama. In a letter to the president, Funado Yasutaro wrote:

> I've read the whole of your speech at Prague . . . I do want to join your honest pursuit of peace. We must ignore the voices who tell that the world cannot change. Please come to Hiroshima and Nagasaki and let me join your voice for peace and progress: Yes, we can. We shall abolish all nuclear weapons from the earth.[54]

"I am deeply moved at the courageous and sincere declaration by you, the President of the United States," Fujiyoshi Yoshitake told Obama. Ando Takao wrote, "Mr. President: I am 76 years old. I have grandchildren, many relatives, friends, and good neighbors. For their happy safe lives, I will do my best and will continue to work for the peace of the world. I am really happy to hear your speech, which had made me feel invincible."[55]

In addition to ordinary citizens, Hiroshima's former mayor Tadatoshi Akiba became a staunch supporter of Obama. Addressing the Nuclear Non-Proliferation Treaty Preparatory Committee at the United Nations, Akiba appealed for every nation to take immediate action toward the abolition of nuclear weapons with the public's support. He pointed out that a "world without nuclear weapons, as advocated by President Obama," is also the "wish of the majority of cities and people around the world." Speaking as president of Mayors for Peace, Akiba coined a phrase to describe the growing number of people in Japan who shared the president's vision: the "Obamajority."[56]

Japanese support for Obama only increased when he sent Ambassador John Roos to Hiroshima to attend the ceremony commemorating the sixty-fifth anniversary of the atomic bombing, on August 6, 2010. Prior to Roos, no American official had ever attended the annual ceremony. As Martin Fackler of the *New York Times* explained, "Past presidents have shied away from sending representation for fear of being viewed as an apologist for the atomic bombings." Indeed, this is exactly what happened. Gene Tibbets, son of Paul Tibbets, who piloted the *Enola Gay*, immediately attacked Obama's decision as an "unsaid apology" and labeled Roos's visit an attempt to "rewrite history." "It's making the Japanese look like they're the poor people, like they didn't do anything. They hit Pearl Harbor, they struck us. We didn't slaughter the Japanese—we stopped the war," Tibbets told *Fox News*. Roos did not speak at the ceremony but said in a statement, "For the sake of future generations, we must continue to work together to realize a world without nuclear weapons."[57]

While many in Japan praised President Obama, they also comprised some of the most disappointed. Just as the world watched Obama hit the "reset" button with Russia and take concrete steps toward nuclear disarmament, the United States conducted its first subcritical nuclear test under the Obama administration. The test was the twenty-fourth since 1997 and the first one since 2006.[58]

The test, conducted in Nevada at a vault some 300 meters below the earth's surface, did not create a chain reaction that would cause a nuclear explosion. Rather, scientists bombarded plutonium with conventional explosives to see how the substance reacts, without hiking the quantity of the substance to critical mass, the point at which a self-sustaining nuclear fission reaction occurs. The Obama administration maintained that this test was the only way to ensure the reliability and safety of the U.S. nuclear arsenal and since the test did not create a nuclear explosion, it was not banned under the Comprehensive Nuclear

Test Ban Treaty.[59] To the Japanese, the administration's explanation sounded like semantics. "I deeply deplore it because I had expected President Obama to take leadership in eliminating nuclear weapons," Nagasaki governor Hodo Nakamura said. Nagasaki mayor Tomihisa Taue commented, "I fear and am concerned that the test, which runs counter to a march toward a world free from nuclear weapons, will adversely affect the international situation." About fifty people, including members of the Hiroshima Council of A-Bomb Sufferers Organization, took part in a sit-in at Hiroshima Peace Memorial Park. "We cannot tolerate the U.S. action that betrayed the president's promise to pursue a world without nuclear weapons," the council's deputy director general Yukio Yoshioka declared following the sit-in.[60] Former Hiroshima mayor Tadatoshi Akiba, the individual responsible for creating the "Obamajority" campaign, wrote to Obama: "I am outraged by your trampling on the expectations and hopes of the A-bomb survivors and the vast majority of Earth's inhabitants, and, on behalf of the A-bombed city of Hiroshima, I vehemently protest."[61]

The *hibakusha*, many of whom had publicly supported President Obama, also felt a sense of betrayal. "It is extremely disappointing," said Toshiko Tanaka, a seventy-one-year-old *hibakusha* from Hiroshima. Tanaka, who felt the world was "moving forwards a half a step" toward eliminating nuclear weapons, now felt "anger that we have moved back to where we were." Koji Hosokawa, eighty-two, whose younger sister was killed by the atomic bomb in Hiroshima, "believed Obama to be a president with a totally different nuclear philosophy." However, "I have to question what the Prague speech was all about," he said. Nevertheless, Hosokawa now hoped even more that Obama would make a point of visiting Hiroshima. "I would like to tell him that young girls the same age as his daughters died along with their dreams and aspirations, and have him feel the horror of nuclear weapons for himself," Hosokawa said. Sumiteru Taniguchi, an eighty-one-year-old *hibakusha* from Nagasaki, called the test a "major betrayal against global society and A-bomb devastated cities." However, Hideo Tsuchiyama, former president of Nagasaki University, attempted to put the subcritical test in proper context. Tsuchiyama argued that Obama and the Democrats were facing tough midterm elections and the president was simply appeasing the "hawks of the U.S. military and Republicans" who opposed sharp reductions of nuclear weapons. While Obama had lifted the hopes of countless people around the world with his Prague speech, "the President maintained that eliminating nuclear weapons would not be reached quickly—perhaps not in his lifetime," Tsuchiyama said.[62]

Ratifying START

While some questioned President Obama's commitment to nuclear disarmament, Republicans in Congress made it strikingly clear where they stood on the issue, and on the president. Since Obama's first day in office, conservatives began to plan his demise.[63] Indeed, in December 2010, Senate minority leader Mitch McConnell (R-KY) made their intentions public when he declared, "The single most important thing we want to achieve is for President Obama to be a one-term president."[64] Congressional Republicans obstructed the president in an unprecedented fashion to prevent him from racking up legislative victories and to embarrass the president on a world stage. Opposing ratification of the new START treaty would achieve both. Republicans unified in their opposition to the treaty.

In his first year in office, Obama had been able to overcome Republican obstructionism since Democrats controlled both houses of Congress. However, in November 2010, Republicans handed Democrats a "shellacking" in the midterm elections and took control of the House of Representatives.[65] As a result, Obama knew he had only a few months left to pass his agenda, including ratification of the new START treaty.

The administration originally viewed ratification as a "speed bump." However, as David Sanger of the *New York Times* explains, "it became a mountain."[66] At the start, Obama enlisted Senator Jon Kyl (R-AZ) to gather the necessary number of Republican votes for ratification. However, Kyl backed out at the last minute refusing to give the administration anything that would resemble a victory. Some of Obama's aides advised the president to stand down and avoid "a huge loss." Obama refused and pushed even harder. The president decided he would settle on "nothing short of full Senate ratification," said a White House official. "We've just got to go ahead," Obama told aides. Peter Baker of the *New York Times* describes this as the "moment Obama decided to fight." The nuclear issue was just too important to him.[67] The president mounted a five-week campaign that included public pressure and private suasion. He enlisted the likes of Henry Kissinger and German chancellor Angela Merkel. Vice President Joseph Biden held at least fifty meetings or phone calls with senators. "The president made a gutsy decision that he was willing to lose it, and that was a gutsy decision. Everybody said it wasn't going to happen. Even colleagues on our side said it wasn't going to happen," commented then Senator John Kerry (D-MA).[68]

By the final weeks of 2010, President Obama was fighting for three major pieces of legislation: repealing "Don't Ask, Don't Tell," passing the Dream Act, and ratifying START. He won repeal of DADT. Refusing to give Obama any more victories, Republicans unified against the Dream Act and START. While the GOP was successful in killing the Dream Act, Obama was able to garner enough votes for START, and the Senate ratified the treaty 71–26, the smallest-ever margin of victory in the history of Russian-American arms treaties. However, Obama's accomplishment stands in contrast to President Jimmy Carter's failure to win passage of the SALT II treaty, which was negotiated in 1979 but never ratified after the Soviets invaded Afghanistan. Two decades later, the Senate rejected President Bill Clinton's treaty to ban all underground nuclear testing, in a 51–48 vote.[69]

Sunao Tsuboi, chair of the Hiroshima Prefectural Confederation of A-bomb Sufferers Organizations, said, "Though the contents of the treaty differ from the wish of the *hibakusha*, the failure to ratify it would have had a detrimental effect on the antinuclear movement. I would like to regard as a positive the effort made by the Obama administration." Akiba agreed: "This is a step forward in terms of the treaty coming into force and a great impetus for the realization of the world without nuclear weapons that President Obama seeks." Others were more cautious in their praise. "Ratification could lead to the expansion of nuclear arms rather than nuclear disarmament," said Haruko Moritaki, cochair of the Hiroshima Alliance for Nuclear Weapons Abolition. Kazumi Mizumoto, vice president of the Hiroshima Peace Institute at Hiroshima City University, viewed the ratification differently: "Now that the United States has ratified the treaty, it can move on to other goals, including ratification of the Comprehensive Nuclear Test Ban Treaty and further reductions in nuclear weapons. To achieve such goals, more efforts by Hiroshima and the international community are essential."[70]

Two years after his Prague speech, President Obama continued his march toward nuclear disarmament. In October 2011, the United States destroyed the country's most powerful nuclear bomb, as the final parts of a massive B53 bomb were dismantled at a plant in Texas. The 10,000-pound, minivan-sized weapon was considered six hundred times more powerful than the atomic bomb used in Hiroshima and was put together during the Cold War.[71] Assessing the administration two years after the Prague speech, Kimball contends that Obama had made "significant progress" toward a nuclear weapons–free world. The new START treaty, a more diplomatic approach to Iran and North Korea than Bush's, and the nuclear summit among other things would not have come about if "not for Obama's persistent commitment to these issues," Kimball explained.[72] Sagan argues that while Obama's critics called his vision a "utopian fantasy," evidence suggests otherwise. "Foreign governments' response to Obama's Nuclear Posture Review shows that the President's actions significantly influenced a number of countries' nuclear doctrines and diplomatic postures," Sagan writes. Contrary to the critics' belief, Obama's NPR produced "considerable progress toward a safer nuclear world." Indeed, Russia's nuclear doctrine, which was being rewritten to include prompt use of nuclear weapons in many regional and local conflict scenarios, was instead revised in the opposite direction—to include nuclear options only in response to attacks that "threaten the very existence of the state." In addition, many of the NATO allies without nuclear weapons—such as Germany, Norway, and Belgium—were encouraged by the new U.S. posture to push for the removal of the small number of "substrategic" or tactical nuclear bombs remaining on U.S. bases inside NATO territories. In 2011, at the NATO summit in Lisbon, NATO governments agreed to address that concern by offering to negotiate with the Russian government for reductions or elimination of substrategic nuclear weapons in a future arms-control agreement.[73]

By 2012, the Obama administration was in the middle of a once-in-a-decade study of its nuclear arsenal and nuclear war plans. START would cut the number of deployed long-range nuclear weapons to 1,550 each, from 2,200, by February 2018. However, the treaty said nothing about the estimated 11,000 nuclear weapons that the United States and Russia kept as backups. Nor did it address America's five hundred short-range nuclear weapons, which were considered safely guarded, or Russia's three thousand or more, which may be vulnerable to theft.[74] Moreover, Republicans, specifically Jon Kyl, held Obama hostage during the START negotiations. Therefore, Obama agreed to invest an extra $85 billion over ten years for nuclear labs to maintain and modernize the arsenal, including overhauling thousands of older bombs that should be retired. He proposed spending $125 billion over the next decade for a new fleet of nuclear-armed submarines, one hundred new bombers, a new land-based intercontinental ballistic missile, and two other missiles. The entire budget for nuclear weapons and related programs could cost $600 billion or more over the next decade.[75]

While Obama appeared to appease Republicans to ratify START, he had no intention of changing course. In February, he delayed funding for a new plutonium facility and for a new class of nuclear submarines. In addition, the administration prepared a new warhead ceiling, considering alternatives of 1,000–1,100 warheads, 700–800, or 300–400. A level of three hundred deployed strategic nuclear weapons would take the United States back to levels not seen since 1950. However, as word spread that Obama may be taking the nuclear arsenal to historic lows, thus making good on his lifelong mission of a world without nuclear weapons, many Republicans went into hysteria. Senator James Inhofe (R-OK) accused Obama of "catering to his liberal base," which he said wants to "unilaterally disarm." Congressman Trent Franks (R-AZ) called the plans "reckless lunacy." "I just want to go on record as saying that there are many of us that are going to do everything we possibly can to make sure that this preposterous notion does not gain any real traction," declared Franks.[76] A group of Republicans, almost all members of the House Armed Services Committee that helps oversee how the nation spends its massive defense budget, sent a letter to the president stating, "At a time when every other nuclear weapons state has an active nuclear weapons modernization program and many are growing their stockpiles and capabilities, it is inconceivable to us that you would lead the United States down such a dangerous path." However, campaign finance records suggest these Republicans may have been motivated by something more than national security. Indeed, over the past three years alone, the signers had received $1.2 million from the employees and political action committees of the four largest defense contractors that have a major stake in the government's decision making about new bombers, missiles, and submarines.[77]

Keeping his promise to meet with leaders two years after the first nuclear summit, Obama traveled to Seoul, South Korea, in March for what he called a "progress report." While the initial agreements of the forty-seven countries were nonbinding and had no enforcement, 80 percent of the commitments had been fulfilled. This was driven, according to Micah Zenko, a fellow at the Council on Foreign Relations, not by economic sanctions or diplomatic pressure but by fear of embarrassment that they could not deliver on their promises, combined with U.S. technical and financial assistance. While serious progress had been made, it was also clear that Obama would fall short of his goal of securing all loose nuclear material in four years. Speaking at Hankuk University, Obama declared:

> Three years ago, I traveled to Prague and I declared America's commitment to stopping the spread of nuclear weapons and to seeking a world without them. I said I knew that this goal would not be reached quickly, perhaps not in my lifetime, but I knew we had to begin, with concrete steps. And in your generation, I see the spirit we need in this endeavor—an optimism that beats in the hearts of so many young people around the world. It's that refusal to accept the world as it is, the imagination to see that world as it ought to be, and the courage to turn that vision into reality.[78]

Obama's Second Term

Upon his reelection, many of Obama's critics viewed the president as someone who was big on delivering speeches but little when it came to actual policy. Moreover, Obama's dramatic increase of Predator drone strikes, targeted assassinations, and the United States' military buildup in Asia did little to bring the world any closer to peace or disarmament. Adding validity to the criticism, the administration repeated throughout election season that "all options were on the table" to prevent Iran from obtaining a nuclear weapon.[79] Even with all of this, Obama's supporters, many who also favored nuclear disarmament, were relieved that the president was returning for another four years. No longer having to worry about reelection, Obama, they hoped, would perhaps finally take the left turn Kennedy made in 1963. However, Obama appeared to do just the opposite, especially when it came to nuclear weapons, which left many of his most ardent supporters perplexed and disappointed.

At the heart of their anger were the proposed upgrades to the United States' nuclear arsenal, specifically the two hundred B61 gravity bombs stockpiled in Belgium, the Netherlands, Germany, Italy, and Turkey. The plans called for outfitting the Cold War–era bombs with new tail fins that would turn them into guided weapons, which could be delivered by stealth F-35 fighter-bombers. Various reports put the cost of this project into the tens of billions of dollars. The Obama administration argued that the B61 was "essential to U.S. national security." However, the B61 represents less than 10 percent of the 5,113 bombs and missiles that make up the U.S. nuclear arsenal. Examining the B61 proposal, Cirincione said, "I'm convinced the president wants to continue his efforts to reform U.S. nuclear policy, but the administration had a schizoid approach on this issue. They believe they have to buy off legislators with billions of dollars in expenditure in their states in order to get votes for arms control measures later. The billions of dollars we are lavishing on the B61 is criminal. This is billions of dollars spent on a weapon whose mission evaporated at the end of the cold war. It's clearly aimed at buying senators' votes."[80]

Put simply, Obama's budget appeared to run contrary to the positive steps he had taken in his first term to eliminate nuclear weapons. In 2012, the administration put forth plans to spend $640 billion on nuclear weapons and related programs over the next decade. The numbers continued to balloon. Obama's proposed budget for 2014 increased funding for nuclear weapons to $7.9 billion, nearly 30 percent more than when he took office. Some reports estimated the

United States would spend $1 trillion over the next thirty years to maintain and modernize the nuclear arsenal.[81] If increased spending on nuclear weapons was not alarming enough, activists were even more troubled when they discovered that the same budget called for a $400 million cut to nonproliferation programs. Just as supporters were trying to digest the proposed budget numbers, the administration carried out yet another subcritical nuclear test. "I just can't stop being angry," Hiroshima mayor Kazumi Matsui said. Nagasaki mayor Tomihisa Taue sent a letter to the president saying that the test "let down a lot of people and hurt the sentiment of the bomb places."[82]

Not everyone, however, was convinced that Obama had abandoned his antinuclear position. Indeed, one could argue that Obama, at the start of his second term, finally started the shift to the left, as many had hoped. Assembling his new cabinet, Obama appointed officials much more in favor of nuclear disarmament than those in his first term. Susan Rice was named national security advisor. While Rice rarely speaks out publicly against nuclear weapons, Cirincione, who reported to Rice on nuclear policy issues for Obama's 2008 campaign, argues that she played a major role in shaping Obama's nuclear weapons positions as a presidential candidate. Rice supported the new START treaty, ratification of the Comprehensive Test Ban Treaty, and cutting the number of deployed nuclear weapons down to one thousand. Following Rice's appointment, Obama went even further, nominating Senator John Kerry (D-MA) for secretary of state and former senator Chuck Hagel (R-NE) for secretary of defense. Hagel was especially pleasing to antinuclear activists. A supporter of the nuclear disarmament organization Global Zero, Hagel had called for "the U.S. and other NPT nuclear weapons states to commit themselves to the goal of a world without nuclear weapons and to pursuing practical steps that would lay the groundwork for moving towards that goal." Moreover, Hagel cowrote a report with former vice chairman of the Joint Chiefs of Staff General James Cartwright and others, making the case for the United States to decrease deployment to nine hundred nuclear weapons. Rounding out Obama's antinuclear cabinet, in December Caroline Kennedy began her post as ambassador to Japan. It came as no surprise that one of her first stops was to the Nagasaki Atom Bomb museum followed by a meeting with a group of *hibakusha*.[83]

In June 2013, Obama returned to Berlin to deliver a speech that many assumed would pay tribute to President Kennedy's "Ich bin ein Berliner" address in 1963. While Obama did echo Kennedy, it was an echo of the speech Kennedy had given ten days earlier at American University. Calling for reducing the number of deployed U.S. strategic nuclear warheads by one third, Obama told the crowd of 4,500 that "peace with justice means pursuing the security of a world without nuclear weapons, no matter how distant the dream may be." Announcing he would host a 2016 summit on nuclear materials worldwide and calling for a treaty to end production of fissile material, Obama said, "We may no longer live in fear of global annihilation, but so long as nuclear weapons exist, we are not truly safe."[84]

Obama's shift appeared more obvious with his refusal to invade Syria, Iran, or Ukraine at the end of his fifth year in the White House. Following the diplomatic path, the administration was able to destroy Syria's chemical weapons stockpile and temporarily halt Iran's nuclear program. The president appeared to return to his roots as someone who had consistently argued for diplomacy when dealing with foreign crisis, and military force as a last resort.[85]

While pundits and experts have unsuccessfully tried to pin down Obama's foreign policy doctrine, Michael Crowley of *Time* argues that the one unifying theme throughout the Obama presidency is his drive to eliminate nuclear weapons. Citing Obama's official national security strategy, speeches, and focus on Iran's nuclear program, Crowley is convinced that nuclear disarmament remains a constant for Obama. David Kenner of *Foreign Policy* agrees. Kenner contends that Obama is "fixated on ridding the world of nuclear weapons" and this desire has been a "central thread of Obama's foreign policy views for his entire adult life." However, many questions remain for Obama's final years in office. Republicans in Congress added amendments to the 2014 Defense Authorization Bill aimed at halting the progress of START, while senators on both sides of the aisle continue to advocate for war in the Middle East. All of these issues, along with a failed "reset" with Russia, make it unclear as to how much progress Obama can make on his vision of a nuclear weapons–free world in his remaining time in office. The answer to that question, however, may depend on how much concerned citizens are willing to fight for nuclear abolition. Obama never said, "Yes I can." It has always been, "Yes *we* can."[86]

Conclusion

While nuclear disarmament has been a common thread throughout Obama's presidency, so too has race. Since his run for president, some in the black community have consistently and vocally called into question Obama's commitment to African Americans. From publicly speaking out about the death of Trayvon

Martin to creating such initiatives as "My Brother's Keeper" and "Educational Excellence for African Americans," one could argue that Obama has focused more on the black community in his second term. This, however, has not stopped numerous pundits, journalists, and scholars from asking, "Is Obama Black Enough?" suggesting the president has not fought for African Americans as much as other groups, like the LGBT community. Others criticize the adverse effects of Obama's economic policies, citing the unemployment rate for African Americans, which is considerably higher than the national average. Those like Tavis Smiley and Cornel West have gone so far as to call the president "another black mascot" for "Wall Street oligarchs."[87] This debate has only intensified, as the Reverend Al Sharpton, Melissa Harris-Perry, Michael Eric Dyson, and others have publicly refuted many of these critics and remained largely supportive of the president. However, many of these scholars and activists have ignored President Obama's most significant achievements in regards to the black community.[88]

Obama, like Du Bois, Robeson, Rustin, King, and so many others before him, understands that stopping the process Harry Truman put into place is not only the most important thing he can do for African Americans, but for all human beings. The right to live without fear of nuclear war is not only a black issue but a human issue, which is why, since 1945, many African Americans have fought so vehemently for peace and equality. They knew that colonialism, the black freedom movement, and the bomb were connected. Perhaps the most convincing evidence of this is Obama himself. And as Malcolm X, possibly the one who best understood these links, said in 1964: "My purpose here is to remind the African heads of state that there are 22 million of us in America who are also of African descent, and to remind them also that we are the victims of America's colonialism or American imperialism, and that our problem is not an American problem, it's a human problem. It's not a Negro problem, it's a problem of humanity. It's not a problem of civil rights, but a problem of human rights."[89]

Notes

Introduction

1. St. Luke was the first independent black Episcopal church in Washington, D.C. "Clergy Calls Atomic Bomb Both Blessing and Curse," *Washington Afro-American*, August 18, 1945, p. 3.

2. Martin Luther King, Jr., "Vietnam Is Upon Us," February 6, 1968, reprinted in *Speeches by the Reverend Dr. Martin Luther King, Jr. About the War in Vietnam*, 1968, Homer Jack Papers, Series 6, Box 7, SCPC.

3. King, "Vietnam Is Upon Us."

4. Milton S. Katz, *Ban the Bomb: A History of SANE, the Committee for a Sane Nuclear Policy, 1957–1985* (New York: Greenwood Press, 1986), 150.

5. Simon Anekwe, "Colors Finally Blended in Giant Peace Protest," *New York Amsterdam News*, June 19, 1982, p. 1; Pamela Mincey, "Afro-Americans Get Set for June 12," *Daily World*, February 25, 1982, p. 3.

6. Langston Hughes, "Here to Yonder: Simple and the Atom Bomb," *Chicago Defender*, August 18, 1945, p. 14; Eric F. Sundquist, "Who Was Langston Hughes?" *Commentary* 102, no. 6 (December 1996): 58; Phillis R. Klotman, "Langston Hughes's Jess B. Semple and the Blues," *Phylon* 36 (1st qtr., 1975): 68.

7. Mary L. Dudziak, *Cold War, Civil Rights: Race and the Image of American Democracy* (Princeton: Princeton University Press, 2000); Brenda Gayle Plummer, *Rising Wind: Black Americans and U.S. Foreign Affairs, 1935–1960* (Chapel Hill: University of North Carolina Press, 1996); James Roark "American Black Leaders: The Response to Colonialism and the Cold War, 1943–1953," *African Historical Studies* 4, no. 2 (1971): 253–70; Penny M. Von Eschen, *Race Against Empire: Black Americans and Anticolonialism, 1937–1957* (Ithaca: Cornell University Press, 1997); Carol Anderson, *Eyes Off the Prize: The United Nations and the African American Struggle for Human Rights, 1944–1955* (Cambridge: Cambridge University Press, 2003); Robin D.G. Kelley, *Hammer and Hoe: Alabama Communists During the Great Depression* (Chapel Hill: University of North Carolina Press, 1990); Mark Naison, *Communists in Harlem During the Great Depression* (Urbana: University of Illinois Press, 1983); Bill Mullen, *Popular Fronts: Chicago and African-American Cultural Politics, 1935–1946* (Urbana: University of Illinois Press, 1999); Gerald Horne, *Black and Red: W.E.B. Du Bois and the Afro-American Response to the Cold War, 1944–1963* (Albany: State University

of New York Press, 1986); Jacquelyn Dowd Hall, "The Long Civil Rights Movement and the Political Use of the Past," *Journal of American History* 91 (March 2005): 1233–1336; Timothy B. Tyson, *Radio Free Dixie: Robert F. Williams and the Roots of Black Power* (Chapel Hill: University of North Carolina Press, 1999); Robert O. Self, "The Black Panther Party and the Long Civil Rights Era," in *In Search of the Black Panther Party: New Perspectives on a Revolutionary Movement*, ed. Jama Lazerow and Yohuru Williams (Durham: Duke University Press, 2006); Peniel E. Joseph, *Waiting 'til the Midnight Hour: A Narrative History of Black Power in America* (New York: Holt, 2006); Glenda Gilmore, *Defying Dixie: The Radical Roots of Civil Rights, 1919–1950* (New York: Norton, 2008); Martha Biondi, *To Stand and Fight: The Struggle for Civil Rights in Postwar New York* (Cambridge: Harvard University Press, 2003); Robbie Lieberman and Clarence Lang, eds., *Anticommunism and the African American Freedom Movement: Another Side of the Story* (New York: Palgrave Macmillan, 2009).

8. Jason C. Parker, "'Made-in-America Revolutions'? The 'Black University' and the American Role in the Decolonization of the Black Atlantic," *Journal of American History* 96, no. 3 (December 2009): 727.

9. Robbie Lieberman, "'Another Side of the Story': African American Intellectuals Speak Out for Peace and Freedom During the Early Cold War Years," in Lieberman and Lang, *Anticommunism and the African American Freedom Movement*.

10. Brenda Gayle Plummer, *In Search of Power: African Americans in the Era of Decolonization, 1956–1974* (Cambridge: Cambridge University Press, 2013), 5–6.

11. Parker, "'Made-in-America Revolutions'?"; Dudziak, *Cold War, Civil Rights;* Anderson, *Eyes Off the Prize*; Carol Anderson, "International Conscience, the Cold War, and Apartheid: The NAACP's Alliance with the Reverend Michael Scott for South West Africa's Liberation, 1946–1951," *Journal of World History* 19, no. 3 (September 2008): 297–325.

Chapter 1

1. "American Hails End of War!" *Chicago Defender*, August 18, 1945, p. 1; Toki Schalk, "'The Prayers of the Righteous Bear Rich Fruit!' Pittsburghers Alternate Prayer with Hilarity as News of the End of World War II Is Broadcast," *Pittsburgh Courier*, August 18, 1945, p. 8; S. W. Garlington, "V-J Explosion of Excitement Blasts Harlem," *New York Amsterdam News*, August 18, 1945, p. 1; "Washington Marks V-J Day After 3-1/2 Years of Struggle," *Washington Afro-American*, August 18, 1945, p. 1; "New York Goes Wild on V-J Day," *New York Amsterdam News*, August 18, 1945, p. 1; "Early Victory Seen as Russia Joins Jap War," *Norfolk Journal and Guide*, August 11, 1945, p. C1; "Russia Declares War on Japan," *Atlanta Daily World*, August 9, 1945, p. 1; "Russians Sweep into Manchuria," *Atlanta Daily World*, August 10, 1945, p. 1.

2. Samuel A. Stouffer, *The American Soldier: Adjustment During Army Life, Volume 1* (Princeton: Princeton University Press, 1949), 513–20.

3. "Negro Scientists Played Important Role in Atomic Bomb Development," *Pittsburgh Courier*, August 18, 1945, p. 1; "Negro Scientists Help Produce 1st Atom Bomb," *Chi-*

cago Defender, August 18, 1945, p. 1; "7,000 Employed at Atomic Bomb Plant," *Washington Afro-American*, August 18, 1945, p. 1; "7000 Negroes Work in Atom Bomb Plant," *New York Amsterdam News*, August 18, 1945, p. 2; "Negro Scientists Assisted in Developing Atomic Bomb," *Norfolk Journal and Guide*, August 18, 1945, p. 1.

4. Ted Coleman, "Chicago Men in Spotlight," *Pittsburgh Courier*, August 18, 1945, p. 17; George Schuyler, "Negro Scientists Played Important Role in Development of Atomic Bomb," *Pittsburgh Courier*, August 18, 1945, p. 17; John C. Wright, "From My Study Window," *Atlanta Daily World*, September 2, 1945, p. 4; "12 Race Scientists Contributed to Development of Atomic Bomb," *Atlanta Daily World*, August 23, 1946, p. 1; "Math Expert," *Chicago Defender*, August 18, 1945, p. 1; "Atom Scientist," *Chicago Defender*, August 25, 1945, p. 9C; "Helped Develop Atomic Bomb," *Norfolk Journal and Guide*, August 18, 1945, p. B1; "Negro Scientists Assisted in Developing Atomic Bomb," *Norfolk Journal and Guide*, August 18, 1945, p. 1; "Norfolk Scientist Assisted in Developing New Atomic Bomb," *Norfolk Journal and Guide,* August 18, 1945, p. B1; George Schuyler, "Dr. William J. Knox Headed Group at Columbia University," *Pittsburgh Courier*, August 18, 1945, p. 1; Ted Coleman, "Young Dr. Wilkins Among Chicago U. Laboratory Heroes," *Pittsburgh Courier*, August 18, 1945, p. 1.

5. Jimmy Williams, "Atom Bomb in the Hands of the Negro," *Chicago Defender*, October 20, 1945, p. 14.

6. Alvin A. Webb, "World's Greatest Secret! Negroes Guard Atomic Files," *Pittsburgh Courier*, October 18, 1947, p. 1.

7. John Dower, *War Without Mercy: Race and Power in the Pacific War* (New York: Pantheon Books, 1986); Ronald Takaki, *Hiroshima: Why America Dropped the Atomic Bomb* (Boston: Little, Brown, 1995), 69–76; John Dower, "Triumphal and Tragic Narratives of the War in Asia," in *Living With the Bomb: American and Japanese Cultural Conflicts in the Nuclear Age*, ed. Laura Hein and Mark Selden (New York: Sharpe, 1997), 42; Yui Daizaburo, "Between Pearl Harbor and Hiroshima/Nagasaki: Nationalism and Memory in Japan and the United States," in Hein and Selden, *Living With the Bomb*, 55.

8. Dower, *War Without Mercy*, 9; Takaki, *Hiroshima*, 69–76.

9. Among those interviewed, support for the two milder courses was highest among African Americans. Sadao Asada, "The Mushroom Cloud and National Psyches: Japanese and American Perceptions of the Atomic-Bomb Decision, 1945–1995," in Hein and Selden, *Living With the Bomb*, 177; Paul Boyer, *By the Bombs Early Light: American Thought and Culture at the Dawn of the Atomic Age* (New York: Pantheon Books, 1985), 22, 182–83; Lawrence S. Wittner, *Rebels Against War: The American Peace Movement, 1933–1983* (Philadelphia: Temple University Press, 1984), 106.

10. Lawrence S. Wittner, *One World or None: A History of the World Nuclear Disarmament Movement Through 1953* (Stanford: Stanford University Press, 1993), 56–58.

11. Leaders of the atomic scientist movement—Albert Einstein, Linus Pauling, Leo Szilard, Harold Urey, Eugene Rabinowitch, Harrison Brown—supported the idea of a world government. Moreover, in January 1946, a poll of the Association of Oak Ridge Engineers and Scientists, one of the most active FAS affiliates, found that 90 percent of the

members supported the formation of a world government. Wittner, *One World or None*, 60–64, 71–74.

12. "Scientists Speak on Peaceful Use of Bomb," *Norfolk Journal and Guide*, April 19, 1947, p. A12.

13. Kuznick's apocalyptic narrative argues that U.S. actions have even a greater relevance to citizens living in the aftermath of the atomic bombings, who must continually grapple with the long-term ramifications, particularly the threat of extinction. Peter J. Kuznick, "The Decision to Risk the Future: Harry Truman, the Atomic Bomb, and the Apocalyptic Narrative," *Japan Focus*, July 30, 2007, http://www.japanfocus.org /products/ details/2479.

14. Gordon B. Hancock, "The Science of Destruction," *Atlanta Daily World*, August 26, 1945, p. 4.

15. William A. Fowlkes, "That Bomb!" *Atlanta Daily World*, August 12, 1945, p. 4; "Atomic Bomb Revolutionizes War," *Norfolk Journal and Guide*, August 11, 1945, p. C1.

16. "Splitting the Atom of Race Hate," *Chicago Defender*, August 18, 1945, p. 12.

17. "Are We Prepared for Peace?" *Washington Afro-American*, August 18, 1945, p. 4.

18. "Atomic Bomb Brings Fear of Cave Life, Joblessness," *Baltimore Afro-American*, August 18, 1945, p. 17.

19. J. Andrew Bowler, "The Inquiring Reporter," *Norfolk Journal and Guide*, August 18, 1945, p. B10.

20. George Schuyler, "Views and Reviews," *Pittsburgh Courier*, August 18, 1945, p. 7.

21. Schuyler, "Views and Reviews," *Pittsburgh Courier*, August 18, 1945, p. 7; George Schuyler, "Views and Reviews," *Pittsburgh Courier*, December 15, 1945, p. 7; George Schuyler, "The World Today," *Pittsburgh Courier*, August 18, 1945, p. 13.

22. "Clergy Calls Atomic Bomb Both Blessing and Curse," *Washington Afro-American*, August 18, 1945. The few pastors who were less critical of the decision appeared grateful for the war's end, but concerned about the future.

23. "Atomic Seen as Force to Mankind," *Atlanta Daily World*, August 31, 1945, p. 1.

24. Langston Hughes, "Here to Yonder: Simple and the Atom Bomb," *Chicago Defender*, August 18, 1945, p. 14; Eric F. Sundquist, "Who Was Langston Hughes?" *Commentary* 102, no. 6 (December 1996): 58; Phillis R. Klotman, "Langston Hughes's Jess B. Semple and the Blues," *Phylon* 36 (1st qtr., 1975): 68.

25. Zora Neale Hurston, letter to Claude Barnett, July 21, 1946, reprinted in *Zora Neale Hurston: A Life in Letters*, ed. Carla Kaplan (New York: Doubleday, 2002), 545–46.

26. The listing of the NAACP's areas of focus read (a) Segregation, (b) O.P.A. (Office of Price Administration), and (c) Atomic energy. "Resolutions Adopted by the 37th Annual Conference of the National Association for the Advancement of Colored People Statement of Policy," June 29, 1946, NAACP Papers, Part II, Box A30, LOC.

27. Archibald J. Carey Jr., keynote address, 37th Annual Conference of the NAACP, June 1946, NAACP Papers, Part II, Box A31, LOC.

28. Walter White, "Atom Bomb and Lasting Peace," *Chicago Defender*, September 8, 1945, p. 15.

29. National Committee on Atomic Information to Walter White, March 15, 1946; Donald Nelson to Walter White, March 23, 1946; Albert Cahn to Walter White, April 4, 1946; Herbert Bayard Swope to Walter White, April 11, 1946; Daniel Melcher to Walter White, April 22, 1946, NAACP Papers, Part II, Box A84, LOC.

30. Following Truman's appointments, elder statesman Bernard Baruch presented the Acheson-Lilienthal plan for the gradual assumption of international control of atomic energy by the United Nations. In short, the plan called for the creation of an international body that would control all nuclear processing plants and all stocks of uranium and thorium in the world. In contrast, the Soviets proposed immediately halting all production of nuclear weapons and destroying all stockpiles within three months. The United Nations debated the two proposals for several years, but could never reach an agreement. Michael Uhl and Tod Ensign, *GI Guinea Pigs: How the Pentagon Exposed Our Troops to Dangers More Deadly than War* (New York: Wideview Books, 1980), 32–33.

31. "Young to Cover Atomic Bomb Pacific Tests," *Atlanta Daily World*, May 14, 1946, p. 6; Uhl and Ensign, *GI Guinea Pigs*, 33–34.

32. For more on *Hiroshima*'s impact on Americans' attitudes toward the atomic bomb see Boyer, *By the Bomb's Early Light*, 203–10; Robert Jay Lifton and Greg Mitchell, *Hiroshima in America: Fifty Years of Denial* (New York: Putnam's, 1995), 86–92.

33. Uhl and Ensign, *GI Guinea Pigs*, 37.

34. "Young to Cover Atomic Bomb Pacific Tests," p. 6; P. Bernard Young Jr., "Report on Atom Bomb Damage," *Norfolk Journal and Guide*, July 6, 1946, p. B1; P. Bernard Young Jr., "Second Atom Blast July 20," *Norfolk Journal and Guide*, July 6, 1946, p. 1; P. Bernard Young Jr., "Destruction Wrought by Atomic Bomb: 'Terrible to Behold,'" *Norfolk Journal and Guide*, July 13, 1946, p. A2.

35. Sutherland quoted in Tracy, *Direct Action*, 18–19.

36. Tracy, *Direct Action*, 20–22.

37. Of the six founders—George Houser, James Robinson, Joe Guinn, Homer Jack, James Farmer, and Bernice Fisher—four were white, two were black, and all were pacifists. Scott H. Bennett, *Radical Pacifism: The War Resisters League and Gandhian Nonviolence in America, 1915–1963* (Syracuse: Syracuse University Press, 2003), 96; Tracy, *Direct Action*, 22; See also August Meier and Elliot Rudwick, *CORE: A Study in the Civil Rights Movement* (New York: Oxford University Press, 1973).

38. Wittner, *Rebels Against War*, 66–67; Tracy, *Direct Action*, 28–31.

39. John D'Emilio, *Lost Prophet: The Life and Times of Bayard Rustin* (Chicago: University of Chicago Press, 2003), 34.

40. Born in 1885, Muste started out as a minister in the Dutch Reformed Church. In 1914, Muste took a pastorship in a Congregational church, where he embraced absolute pacifism. This led him in 1915 to organize the first American branch of the Fellowship of Reconciliation (FOR), which had been established by British pacifists the previous year. When the United States entered the First World War, Muste's congregation forced him out for continuing to preach against war. In 1919, he began working with the International Workers of the World (IWW) and other unions in the labor movement. After converting

to Marxism, Muste helped found the American Workers Party in 1933. However, by 1940 Muste had rediscovered Christianity and became the leader of the FOR. Tracy, *Direct Action*, 23.

41. D'Emilio, *Lost Prophet*, 37, 44–45.

42. Bayard Rustin, "In Apprehension How Like a God!" 1948, http://pamphlets. quaker.org/wp1194 8a.html.

43. Rustin, "In Apprehension How Like a God!"

44. D'Emilio, *Lost Prophet*, 128–29; Wittner, *Rebels Against War*, 156–57.

45. D'Emilio, *Lost Prophet*, 128–29; Tracy, *Direct Action*, 60–62; Wittner, *Rebels Against War*, 165; Jervis Anderson, *Bayard Rustin: Troubles I've Seen* (Berkeley: University of California Press, 1998), 136–37.

46. Paul Robeson, "American Negroes in the War," speech at the Twelfth Annual Herald Tribune Forum, November 16, 1943, in *Paul Robeson Speaks: Writings, Speeches, and Interviews, 1918–1974*, ed. Philip Foner (New York: Brunner/Mazel, 1978), 147.

47. Nnamdi Azikiwe, Jomo Kenyatta, Kwame Nkrumah, and C.L.R. James were some of the African leaders Robeson met during the trip. Martin Bauml Duberman, *Paul Robeson* (New York: Knopf, 1988), 170–71.

48. Max Yergan, Paul Robeson, Ralph Bunche, Channing Tobias, and Hubert T. Delaney were among the black members. The white members included Raymond Leslie Buell, a member of the Foreign Policy Association and a noted Harvard political scientist, and sociologist Mary Van Kleek, a Russell Sage Foundation official. Solomon, "Black Critics of Colonialism and the Cold War," 207–8; James Meriwether, *Proudly We Can Be Africans* (Chapel Hill: University of North Carolina Press, 2002), 59–61; Plummer, *Rising Wind*, 79–80; Von Eschen, *Race Against Empire*, 16–20, 40.

49. Solomon, "Black Critics of Colonialism and the Cold War," 207–8; Paul Robeson, "The Negro People and the Soviet Union," address at banquet sponsored by the National Council of American-Soviet Friendship, November 10, 1949, in *Paul Robeson Speaks*, 236–37.

50. In 1942, the CAA, chaired by Robeson, went through a revival. The group made clear that the fight for black equality in the United States was connected to the liberation movements around the world, and it adopted a variety of goals, including the political liberation of the colonized African nations and improved economic and social conditions on the African continent. Plummer, *Rising Wind*, 190; Von Eschen, *Race Against Empire*, 18–21.

51. Jacqueline Castledine, *Cold War Progressives: Women's International Organizing for Peace and Freedom* (Urbana: University of Illinois Press, 2012), 17.

52. W.E.B. Du Bois, "Negro's War Gains and Losses," *Chicago Defender*, September 15, 1945, p. 15; W.E.B. Du Bois, "Atom Bomb and the Colored World," *Chicago Defender*, January 12, 1946, reprinted in *Newspaper Columns by W.E.B. Du Bois, Volume 2, 1945–1961*, ed. Herbert Aptheker (White Plains: Kraus-Thomson, 1986), 670; W.E.B. Du Bois, "Reasoning Deficiency," *Chicago Defender*, July 6, 1946, reprinted in Aptheker, *Newspaper Columns by W.E.B. Du Bois, Volume 2*, 687; Zhang Juguo, *W.E.B. Du Bois: The Quest for Abolition of the Color Line* (New York: Routledge, 2001), 149–51; Gerald Horne, *Black and Red*, 277;

W.E.B. Du Bois, "The Atom Bomb," *Chicago Defender*, July 5, 1947, reprinted in Aptheker, *Newspaper Columns by W.E.B. Du Bois, Volume 2*, 723.

53. Von Eschen, *Race Against Empire*, 103–4; Jean Allman, "Nuclear Imperialism and the Pan-African Struggle for Peace and Freedom: Ghana, 1959–1962," *Souls* 10, no. 2 (2008): 85.

54. Murali Balaji, *Professor and the Pupil: The Politics and Friendship of W.E.B. Du Bois and Paul Robeson* (New York: Nation Books, 2007), xxiv.

55. Paul Robeson, "Anti-Imperialists Must Defend Africa," address at Big Three Unity Rally, June 6, 1946, reprinted in Foner, *Paul Robeson Speaks*, 169.

56. Greg Robinson, "Paul Robeson and Japanese Americans," *Nichi Bei Times* (San Francisco), March 13, 2008, http://www.blackpast.org/?q=perspectives/paul-robeson-and -japanese-americans-1942-1949.

57. Robeson, "Anti-Imperialists Must Defend Africa," 169.

58. President Harry S. Truman, "Address Before a Joint Session of Congress," March 12, 1947, http://www.yale.edu/lawweb/avalon/trudoc.htm.

59. Dudziak, *Cold War Civil Rights*, 27–28; Von Eschen, *Race Against Empire*, 107; Meriwether, *Proudly We Can Be Africans*, 70–71.

60. Lieberman, *Strangest Dream*, 57–58.

61. Lieberman, *Strangest Dream*, 58.

62. In 1946, Joliot-Curie became the high commissioner of the French Atomic Energy Commission and then the director of France's nuclear research program. He was an antinuclear activist and communist. Wittner, *One World or None*, 175–82; Lieberman, *Strangest Dream*, 58.

63. P. L. Prattis, "Robeson, Du Bois Cause Uproar at Paris Meet," *Pittsburgh Courier*, April 30, 1949, p. 3; Meriwether, *Proudly We Can Be Africans*, 81; Lieberman, *Strangest Dream*, 58.

64. Lieberman, *Strangest Dream*, 33; Anderson, *Eyes Off the Prize*, 120–21.

65. "10,000 in N.Y. Hear Wallace," *Philadelphia Tribune*, February 17, 1948, p. 1; Julius J. Adams, "Politics and People," *New York Amsterdam News*, February 21, 1948, p. 12.

66. Manning Marable, *W.E.B. Du Bois: Black Radical Democrat* (Boston: Twayne, 1986), 173–74.

67. Marable, *W.E.B. Du Bois*, 173–74.

68. Paul Robeson, "For Freedom and Peace," address at Welcome Home Rally, June 19, 1949, reprinted in Foner, *Paul Robeson Speaks*, 204–5.

69. Jacqueline Castledine, "Quieting the Chorus: Progressive Women's Race and Peace Politics in Postwar New York," in *Anticommunism and the African American Freedom Movement*, ed. Robbie Lieberman and Clarence Lang (New York: Palgrave Macmillan, 2009), 53–58.

70. Barbara Ransby, *Eslanda: The Large and Unconventional Life of Mrs. Paul Robeson* (New Haven: Yale University Press, 2013), 143–45, 186–89, 194, 206.

71. Castledine, "Quieting the Chorus," 53–58; *Cold War Progressives*, 87–88.

72. Castledine, "Quieting the Chorus," 53–58.

73. Von Eschen, *Race Against Empire*, 109–10.

74. Anderson, *Eyes Off the Prize*, 119, 126–29.

75. Truman routinely used racist language when discussing African Americans, most notably in letters to Bess, his wife. In 1911, Truman wrote to Bess:

> I think one man is just as good as another so long as he's not a nigger or a Chinaman. Uncle Will says that the Lord made a white man from dust, a nigger from mud, then threw up what was left and it came down a Chinaman. He does hate Chinese and Japs. So do I. It is race prejudice I guess. But I am strongly of the opinion negroes ought to be in Africa, yellow men in Asia and white men in Europe and America.

Biographer Merle Miller notes that "privately Truman always used the word 'nigger'" when he talked to him about African Americans. For more on Truman's racism, see Takaki, *Hiroshima*, 93–97; and Merle Miller, *Plain Speaking: An Oral Biography of Harry S. Truman* (Berkeley: Berkeley Medallion, 1974). "Truman Asks Congress for FEPC Anti-Lynching, Anti-Poll Tax Laws," *Norfolk Journal and Guide*, February 7, 1948, p. A1; "Truman Offers Civil Rights Program," *Los Angeles Sentinel*, February 5, 1948, p. 1; "President Intends to Push Rights—White," *Atlanta Daily World*, December 1, 1948, p. 1; "Truman Proclamation Splits Negro Leaders," *Los Angeles Sentinel*, July 29, 1948, p. 1; Anderson, *Eyes Off the Prize*, 116.

76. Channing H. Tobias, "Truman's Civil Rights Message Praised as Sincere," *Atlanta Daily World*, February 20, 1948, p. 1; "Civil Rights Speech Praised by NAACP," *Norfolk Journal and Guide*, February 14, 1948, p. 9; "We Need Only the Will," *Norfolk Journal and Guide*, February 7, 1948, p. A10; P. L. Prattis, "The Horizon," *Pittsburgh Courier*, February 14, 1948, p. 7; "Walter White in Hopes President Moves Forward," *Norfolk Journal and Guide*, August 7, 1948, p. C2; "NAACP Lauds Truman, Blasts GOP for Failure of Congress to Act on Civil Rights," *Pittsburgh Courier*, July 3, 1948, p. 14.

77. "President Intends to Push Rights—White," *Atlanta Daily World*, December 1, 1948, p. 1; Dudziak, *Cold War Civil Rights*, 26; Marable, *Race, Reform, and Rebellion*, 24–25; Thomas Borstelmann, *The Cold War and the Color Line: American Race Relations in the Global Arena* (Cambridge: Harvard University Press, 2001), 60.

78. Marable, *Race, Reform, and Rebellion*, 27.

79. See Robbie Lieberman, "'Another Side of the Story': African American Intellectuals Speak Out for Peace and Freedom During the Early Cold War Years," in Lieberman and Lang, *Anticommunism and the African American Freedom Movement*; Susan Lynn, *Progressive Women in Conservative Times: Racial Justice, Peace, and Feminism, 1945–1960s* (New Brunswick: Rutgers University Press, 1992).

Chapter 2

1. Wittner, *Rebels Against War*, 182; Mary Helen Washington, "Alice Childress, Lorraine Hansberry, and Claudia Jones: Black Women Write the Popular Front," in *Left of the Color Line*, ed. Bill V. Mullen and James Smethurst (Chapel Hill: University of North Carolina Press, 2003), 184.

2. William Stueck, *The Korean War: An International History* (Princeton: Princeton University Press, 1995), 62–63; Conrad Crane, *American Airpower Strategy in Korea, 1950–1953* (Lawrence: University Press of Kansas, 2000), 58; James Chace, *Acheson: The Secretary*

of State Who Created the American World (New York: Simon & Schuster, 1998), 308; Joseph Gerson, *Empire and the Bomb: How the US Uses Nuclear Weapons to Dominate the World* (London: Pluto Press, 2007), 81–82.

3. Pierre J. Huss, "US Must Consult Other Nations Before Using Atom in Korean War," *Atlanta Daily World*, July 18, 1953, p. 1; Dean Acheson, *The Korean War* (New York: Norton, 1971), 84; Lawrence S. Wittner, *Cold War America: From Hiroshima to Watergate* (New York: Holt, Rinehart and Winston, 1978), 77; Stueck, *Korean War*, 131–32.

4. Stueck, *Korean War*, 131–32.

5. "Use of Atomic Weapons in Korea Under Discussion," *Atlanta Daily World*, October 13, 1951, p. 1; "May Use Atom in Korean War," *Atlanta Daily World*, July 18, 1953, p. 5.

6. Michael Cullen Green, *Black Yanks in the Pacific: Race in the Making of American Military Empire After World War II* (Ithaca: Cornell University Press, 2010), 109–10,119–22; Paul Robeson, speech at "Civil Rights Congress Rally," June 29, 1950, reprinted in Foner, *Paul Robeson Speaks*, 252.

7. Langston Hughes, "Colored Asia Makes Highly Colored News These Days," *Chicago Defender*, August 15, 1953, p. 11.

8. *Peacegram* 1, no. 4 (Mid-Summer 1950): 1; PIC, press release, July 13, 1950, PIC Papers, CDGA Collective Box, SCPC; Plummer, *Rising Wind*, 206–9.

9. Charles A. Hill, president of Wilberforce University, the Reverend E. R. Artist, editor of *New York Messenger*, Ralph Matthews, editor of *Afro-American*, W.E.B. Du Bois, and Paul Robeson were among the over one hundred black leaders who signed the statement. "A Protest and a Plea," in "Voices for Peace: The Negro People Speak Out for Peace," August 28, 1950, PIC Papers, CDGA Collective Box, SCPC.

10. Wittner, *One World or None*, 182.

11. "The People of the World Want Peace," PIC, brochure, 1950, PIC Papers, CDGA Collective Box, SCPC.

12. James Aronson, C. B. Baldwin, Dr. Edward Barsky, Cedric Belfrage, Howard Fast, Mike Gold, Albert Kahn, Rockwell Kent, John Howard Lawson, Elizabeth Moos, Richard Morford, Anton Refregier, Joseph Starobin, Louis Weinstock, and Gene Weltfish were among those in attendance. "'World Peace' Plea Is Circulated Here," *New York Times*, July 14, 1950, p. 7; Horne, *Black and Red*, 126; "The People of the World Want Peace," PIC, brochure, 1950, PIC Papers, CDGA Collective Box, SCPC.

13. "Prominent Americans Call for Outlawing Atomic Warfare," PIC, press release, August 10, 1950, PIC Papers, CDGA Collective Box, SCPC.

14. "Partial List of Prominent Americans Endorsing the World Peace Appeal," PIC, press release, August 14, 1950; "Voices for Peace: The Negro People Speak Out for Peace," August 28, 1950, PIC Papers, CDGA Collective Box, SCPC.

15. Paul Robeson, "Forge Negro-Labor Unity for Peace and Jobs," speech delivered at meeting of the National Labor Conference for Negro Rights," June 10, 1950, reprinted in Foner, *Paul Robeson Speaks*, 245, 251.

16. The Department Store Locals and Local 65 in the garment workers area pledged to collect 15,000 signatures and the United Electrical Workers initiated a campaign to

collect 50,000 signatures. *Peacegram* 1, no. 2 (May 31, 1950): 2–3; *Peacegram* 1, no. 3 (June 1950): 2–3; "Peace Activists in the U.S.A.," June 1950, PIC Papers, CDGA Collective Box, SCPC; "145,000 Have Signed Peace Pledge," *New York Amsterdam News*, July 8, 1945, p. 9; see also Horne, *Black and Red*, 127.

17. Paul Robeson, "Here's My Story," *Freedom*, January 1951, reprinted in Foner, *Paul Robeson Speaks*, 265.

18. Paul Robeson, "Voting for Peace," address at National Convention of the Progressive Party, July 4, 1952, reprinted in Foner, *Paul Robeson Speaks*, 319.

19. Paul Robeson Sr., FBI files, Part 9, Section 6; Paul Robeson Sr., FBI files, Part 17, Section 12.

20. *Peacegram* 1, no. 1 (May 12, 1950): 6; *Peacegram* 1, no. 2 (May 31, 1950): 1; *Peacegram* 1, no. 4 (Mid-Summer 1950): 5, PIC Papers, CDGA Collective Box, SCPC; "600 More 'Peace' Signers," *New York Times*, August 14, 1950, p. 15; see also Horne, *Black and Red*, 128.

21. *Peacegram* 1, no. 1 (May 12, 1950): 6; *Peacegram* 1, no. 2 (May 31, 1950): 1; *Peacegram* 1, no. 4 (Mid-Summer 1950): 5, PIC Papers, CDGA Collective Box, SCPC.

22. "Leaders of 3 Faiths Denounce 'Deceptive' Red Peace Appeal," *New York Amsterdam News*, September 2, 1950, p. 13; George Dugan, "Protestants Told to Shun Atom Plea," *New York Times*, July 6, 1950, p. 19; "Vienna Red Rally Draws Slim Crowd," *New York Times*, June 11, 1950, p. 28; Horne, *Black and Red*, 134.

23. Wittner, *One World or None*, 188.

24. The WRL worked on producing an alternative to the Peace Appeal and organized an effort to obtain signatures from prominent individuals and media coverage to counter the communist-led peace campaign. WRL Interim Administrative Committee, meeting minutes, June 26, 1950, WRL Papers, Series B, Box 1, SCPC; Wittner, *One World or None*, 203. See also Bennett, *Radical Pacifism*, 200.

25. Duke Ellington and Emily Balch of WILPF were among those who reversed their earlier position. "Ellington Warns Reds in 'Peace' Movement," *New York Amsterdam News*, September 30, 1950, p. 2; "Socialists Assail Reds' Atomic Plea," *New York Times*, June 4, 1950, p. 20; George Dugan, "Protestants Told to Shun Atom Plea," *New York Times*, July 6, 1950, p. 19; "Vienna Red Rally Draws Slim Crowd," *New York Times*, June 11, 1950, p. 28; Wittner, *One World or None*, 203.

26. "Fight On Reds Urged," *New York Times*, July 16, 1950, p. 38; "Peace Plea Pinned to 'Red Chicanery,'" *New York Times*, July 14, 1950, p. 7.

27. George Schuyler, "Views and Reviews," *Pittsburgh Courier*, March 17, 1951, p. 6.

28. "Sell Democracy, Porters Urge U.S.," *New York Times*, September 15, 1950, p. 18.

29. Walter H. Waggoner, "Acheson Derides Soviet Peace Bids," *New York Times*, July 13, 1950, p. 1.

30. Part of Du Bois's letter to Dean Acheson on July 14, 1950, was published in the *New York Times*, July 17, 1950, p. 5, with the headline: "Dr. Du Bois Calls on Acheson to Promise U.S. Will 'Never Be First to Use Bomb.'" The full text of the letter can be found in *The Correspondence of W.E.B. Du Bois, Volume II Selections, 1944–1963*, ed. Herbert Aptheker

(Amherst: University of Massachusetts Press, 1978), 303–6, and *Peacegram* 1, no. 4 (Mid-Summer 1950): 5, PIC Papers, CDGA Collective Box, SCPC.

31. "Peace Proponent Asks Atom Pledge," *New York Times*, July 17, 1950, p. 5.

32. W.E.B. Du Bois, *In Battle for Peace* (Millwood: Kraus-Thomson, 1976), 37.

33. Russell Porter, "Red 'Peace' Rally Defies Court; Routed by Police; 14 Held, 3 Hurt," *New York Times*, August 3, 1950, p. 1; "4 Seized in 'Peace' Drive," *New York Times*, July 15, 1950, p. 5; "Judge's Son Wins Jury Trial to Test Order Prohibiting the 'Stockholm' Peace Petition," *New York Times*, August 24, 1950, p. 39; "'Peace' Advocate Freed," *New York Times*, September 15, 1950, p. 21; "Peace Pleaders Menaced," *New York Times*, August 8, 1950, p. 13.

34. "Shipping News and Notes," *New York Times*, August 31, 1951, p. 31; "2 Churches Dismiss Pastor as a Leftist," *New York Times*, August 25, 1950, p. 5; Lieberman, *Strangest Dream*, 91.

35. "Noted Scholar Denies Charges," *Chicago Defender*, February 11, 1951, p. 1; "U.S. Indicts Dr. Du Bois," *Baltimore Afro-American*, February 17, 1951, p. 1; "'Not Guilty-Du Bois,'" *Baltimore Afro-American*, February 24, 1951, pp. 1–2; "5 of 'Peace' Group Here Indicted; All Sponsors of Stockholm Plea," *New York Times*, February 10, 1951, p. 1.

36. "Du Bois Is 'Shocked'" *New York Times*, February 10, 1951, p. 6; "U.S. Indicts Dr. Du Bois," *Baltimore Afro-American*, February 17, 1951, p. 2; Lieberman, "Another Side of the Story," 22.

37. Du Bois, *In Battle for Peace*, 74–80.

38. "The Case of Dr. Du Bois," *Baltimore Afro-American*, February 24, 1957, p. 4.

39. P. L. Prattis, "The Horizon: Handcuffs on Dr. Du Bois Is Evidence of 'The Terror' Used to Victimize Us," *Pittsburgh Courier*, March 3, 1951, p. 22.

40. "What People Think: Prattis' Column on Dr. Du Bois Prompts Many Courier Readers to Pen Letters," *Pittsburgh Courier*, March 24, 1951, p. 11; "What People Think," *Pittsburgh Courier*, April 7, 1951, p. 11.

41. Arnold Rampersad, *The Life of Langston Hughes, Volume II: 1941–1967, I Dream a World* (New York: Oxford University Press, 2002), 190.

42. The NAACP purged suspected communists, rigged the elections in the San Francisco branch to oust its left-leaning president, and limited support for the victims of the government's loyalty program to those whose patriotism had been questioned solely because of race or membership in the NAACP. Anderson, *Eyes Off the Prize*, 167, 173–74.

43. Even the government's main witness, O. John Rogge, could produce no documentation of a connection between the PIC and the U.S.S.R. Anderson, *Eyes Off the Prize*, 174.

44. Horne, *Black and Red*, 177–79.

45. Wittner, *One World or None*, 171, 183.

46. Wittner, *One World or None*, 182–83, 203, 209. Allan Taylor, "Story of the Stockholm Petition," *New York Times*, August 13, 1950, p. E6.

47. Lieberman, *Strangest Dream*, 81–96.

48. "Signers Reaffirm Support of World Peace Appeal," PIC Papers, CDGA Collective Box, SCPC.

49. "Signers Reaffirm Support of World Peace Appeal," PIC Papers, CDGA Collective Box, SCPC.

50. "Peace Plea Pinned to 'Red Chicanery,'" *New York Times*, July 14, 1950, p. 7.

51. Horne, *Black and Red*, 137–38.

52. W.E.B. Du Bois, "I Speak for Peace," September 24, 1950, reprinted in *Pamphlets and Leaflets by W.E.B. Du Bois*, ed. Herbert Aptheker (White Plains: Kraus-Thomson, 1986): 287–89.

53. Du Bois held major rallies at the Golden Gate Ballroom and in Madison Square Garden, and he wrote for the *Chicago Globe*. "U.S. Needs No More Cowards," *National Guardian*, October 25, 1950, reprinted in Aptheker, *Newspaper Columns by W.E.B. Du Bois, Volume 2, 1945–1961*, 878; Horne, *Black and Red*, 142.

54. Horne, *Black and Red*, 144–45.

55. Horne, *Black and Red*, 146.

56. Bayard Rustin to A. J. Muste, February 2, 1950, FOR Papers, Series C, Box 3, SCPC; see also Lieberman, *Strangest Dream*, 83.

57. Connie Muste to Bayard Rustin, February 3, 1950; George Houser to Bayard Rustin, February 3, 1950; Roy Kepler to Bayard Rustin, February 7, 1950; Al Hassler to Bayard Rustin, February 13, 1950, FOR Papers, Series D, Box 52, SCPC.

58. "Support Grows for Fast for Peace," press release; "Open Letter to American Christians"; "The Stones Will Cry Out!" 1950, Bayard Rustin Papers, Fast for Peace.

59. "Support Grows for Fast for Peace," press release; "Record of Parallel Action," 1950, Bayard Rustin Papers, Fast for Peace.

60. Fast for Peace Committee to Sumner Pike, April 6, 1950; Fast for Peace Committee to Willard E. Givens, April 6, 1950; Fast for Peace Committee to Alexander S. Panyushkin, April 4, 1950; Fast for Peace Committee to President Truman, April 3, 1950; Fast for Peace Committee to President Truman, April 5, 1950, Bayard Rustin Papers, Fast for Peace; Bayard Rustin to Charles Livermore, April 27, 1950; Bayard Rustin to Lillian and Bob Pope, March 1, 1950; Lillian and Bob Pope to Bayard Rustin, March 6, 1950; Bayard Rustin to Lillian and Bob Pope, March 14, 1950, FOR Papers, Series D, Box 51, SCPC.

61. Caravans for Peace, pamphlet, June 1950, FOR Papers, Series D, Box 52, SCPC.

62. Caravans for Peace New York, minutes, July 20, 1950, in Caravans for Peace New York/Lancaster binder; Caravans for Peace New York, minutes, July 25, 1950, in Caravans for Peace New York/Lancaster binder; "Group Here Marks Date of Hiroshima," *New York Times*, August 7, 1950, in Caravans for Peace New York/Lancaster binder, FOR Papers, Series D, Box 52, SCPC.

63. Rustin's involvement with the FOR ended in 1953 when he was arrested in Los Angeles for having sex in a parked car with another man. Upon finding out, Muste immediately kicked Rustin out of the FOR. Muste claimed that Rustin's arrest could damage "the cause of radical pacifism," Bill Sutherland said. However, Sutherland suspected Muste's hostility also stemmed from his puritanical views on sexuality. Indeed, within a week of Rustin's arrest, the FOR released an official statement that portrayed Rustin's

sexual orientation as a moral failing. Nonetheless, Rustin rebounded with positions at the WRL and CNVA, where he continued his antinuclear activities. Tracy, *Direct Action*, 82–83.

Chapter 3

1. Toshihiro Higuchi, "An Environmental Origin of Antinuclear Activism in Japan, 1954–1963: The Government, the Grassroots Movement, and the Politics of Risk," *Peace and Change* 33, no. 3 (July 2008): 334; http://www.bikiniatoll.com.

2. Dudziak, *Cold War, Civil Rights*, 105–6.

3. Dudziak, *Cold War, Civil Rights*, 105–6.

4. *Adam by Adam: The Autobiography of Adam Clayton Powell, Jr.* (New York: Dial Press, 1971), 102; "Rep. Powell Rips U.S. Snub of Afro-Asians," *Los Angeles Sentinel*, April 21, 1955, p. A1; Lieberman, *Strangest Dream*, 138; Cary Fraser, "An American Dilemma: Race and Realpolitik in the American Response to the Bandung Conference, 1955," in Plummer, *Window of Freedom*, 115; Castledine, "Quieting the Chorus," 51.

5. *Spotlight on Africa: Review of the Asian-African Conference* 14, no. 5 (May 1955): 11, NAACP Papers, Part II, Box A97, LOC.

6. Castledine, "Quieting the Chorus," 51.

7. Robeson, *Here I Stand*, 45–46; "Bandung Meeting Replies to Greetings from NAACP," May 5, 1955, NAACP Papers, Part II, Box A97, LOC; Fraser, "American Dilemma," 116.

8. *Spotlight on Africa: Review of the Asian-African Conference* 14, no. 5 (May 1955): 17, NAACP Papers, Part II, Box A97, LOC.

9. Lieberman, *Anticommunism and the African American Freedom Movement*, 9.

10. Lieberman, "Another Side of the Story," 17, 30.

11. Lawrence S. Wittner, *Resisting the Bomb: A History of the World Nuclear Disarmament Movement, 1954–1970* (Stanford: Stanford University Press, 1997) 1–13, 29; D'Emilio, *Lost Prophet*, 253.

12. Scott had previously worked on civil rights and antiwar issues with James Farmer and CORE as well as Peacemakers. Bennett, *Radical Pacifism*, 227; Tracy, *Direct Action*, 101.

13. "What Is CNVA?" CNVA Papers, Series 2, Box 2, SCPC; Tracy, *Direct Action*, 101.

14. D'Emilio, *Lost Prophet*, 253.

15. "Highlights of WRI Conference," *WRL News*, September–October 1957, p. 2; D'Emilio, *Lost Prophet*, 254–55.

16. "First Protest at Test Site," *WRL News*, September–October 1957, pp. 1–2.

17. Just before departing for Europe, Rustin helped launch a peace walk in New York, in which several hundred pacifists converged on the United Nations. CNVA, press release, February 17, 1958, CNVA Papers, Series 3, Box 3, SCPC; D'Emilio, *Lost Prophet*, 254–56.

18. CNVA, press release, February 17, 1958, CNVA Papers, Series 3, Box 3, SCPC. Albert S. Bigelow, "Why I Am Sailing into the Pacific Bomb-Test Area," *Liberation*, February 1958, pp. 4–6; Bennett, *Radical Pacifism*, 228. The "Hiroshima maidens" were a group of twenty-five *hibakusha* who were brought to the United States for reconstructive surgery.

19. CNVA, press release, May 7, 1958, CNVA Papers, Series 3, Box 3, SCPC; Bennett, *Radical Pacifism*, 229.

20. CNVA, press release, May 7, 1958, CNVA Papers, Series 3, Box 3, SCPC; Bennett, *Radical Pacifism*, 229.

21. Plummer, *Window of Freedom*, 1; Anderson, *Bayard Rustin*, 215; Wittner, *Resisting the Bomb*, 48.

22. Plummer, *Window of Freedom*, 1.

23. Wittner, *Resisting the Bomb*, 48–49.

24. "Summary Information on the Sahara Nuclear Bomb Protest Team," December 22, 1959, CNVA Papers, Series 2, Box 2, SCPC; Thomas J. Hamilton, "French Insist on Atom Test Unless Others Yield Arms," *New York Times*, November 5, 1959, p. 1; "France to Proceed with A-Bomb Plans," *Daily Defender*, November 4, 1959, p. 4; "Africa Against A-Bomb Tests," *Daily Defender*, September 16, 1959, p. 10; "Ghana Against French Nuclear Tests in Sahara," *Daily Defender*, September 13, 1958, p. 10; Anderson, *Bayard Rustin*, 219–20.

25. "Sahara Protest Team Fact Sheet," December 4, 1959, Bayard Rustin Papers, Africa Files of Bayard Rustin, 1959; April Carter, "The Sahara Protest Team," in *Liberation Without Violence: A Third-Party Approach*, ed. A. Paul Hare and Herbert H. Blumberg (Totowa: Rowman & Littlefield, 1977), 126; Richard Taylor, *Against the Bomb: The British Peace Movement 1958–1965* (Oxford: Clarendon Press, 1988), 158.

26. Anderson, *Bayard Rustin*, 220; D'Emilio, *Lost Prophet*, 279–80.

27. Tracy, *Direct Action*, 14, 18–19; Bennett, *Radical Pacifism*, 232; Carter, "Sahara Protest Team," 128; D'Emilio, *Lost Prophet*, 280.

28. Carter, "Sahara Protest Team," 128.

29. Plummer, *In Search of Power*, 69.

30. Bill Sutherland and Matt Meyer, *Guns and Gandhi in Africa: Pan African Insights on Nonviolence, Armed Struggle, and Liberation in Africa* (Trenton: Africa World Press, 2000), 36–37; Carter, "Sahara Protest Team," 128.

31. "Report from Bayard Rustin on the Sahara Project," October 24, 1959, CNVA Papers, Series 6, Box 13, SCPC. For more on Collins and the CND, see Taylor, *Against the Bomb*.

32. "Report from Bayard Rustin on the Sahara Project," October 24, 1959, CNVA Papers, Series 6, Box 13, SCPC; Bayard Rustin, "Report No. 3," November 24, 1959, CNVA Papers, Series 6, Box 13, SCPC; D'Emilio, *Lost Prophet*, 282; Carter, "Sahara Protest Team," 130; "Ghana Aids Sahara Protest," *New York Times*, November 20, 1959, p. 16.

33. "Report from Bayard Rustin on the Sahara Project," George Willoughby to CNVA Members and Consultants, October 24, 1959, CNVA Papers, Series 6, Box 13, SCPC; D'Emilio, *Lost Prophet*, 281.

34. James H. Meriwether, "'Worth a Lot of Negro Votes': Black Voters, Africa, and the 1960 Presidential Campaign," *Journal of American History* 95, no. 3 (December 2008): 745–47.

35. "Committee for Protest Action Draft Statement," 1960, WRL Papers, Series B, Box 13, SCPC; Bayard Rustin to George Willoughby, A. J. Muste, Stanley Levison, Ralph di Gia, and Tom Marcel, November 5, 1959, CNVA Papers, Series 6, Box 13, SCPC.

36. Bayard Rustin to George Willoughby, A. J. Muste, Stanley Levison, Ralph di Gia, and Tom Marcel, November 5, 1959, CNVA Papers, Series 6, Box 13, SCPC.

37. Jim Peck to Bayard Rustin, November 17, 1959, CNVA Papers, Series 6, Box 13, SCPC. Bayard Rustin, "Report No. 3," George Willoughby to CNVA Members of Committee and Advisors, November 24, 1959, CNVA Papers, Series 6, Box 13, SCPC.

38. Bayard Rustin, "Report No. 3," George Willoughby to CNVA Members of Committee and Advisors, November 24, 1959, CNVA Papers, Series 6, Box 13, SCPC; George Willoughby to CNVA Committee Members and Consultants, December 3, 1959, CNVA Papers, Series 6, Box 13, SCPC; Bennett, *Radical Pacifism*, 233.

39. Bayard Rustin, "Report No. 3," George Willoughby to CNVA Members of Committee and Advisors, November 24, 1959, CNVA Papers, Series 6, Box 13, SCPC; George Willoughby to CNVA Committee Members and Consultants, December 3, 1959, CNVA Papers, Series 6, Box 13, SCPC; D'Emilio, *Lost Prophet*, 286.

40. Allman, "Nuclear Imperialism and the Pan-African Struggle for Peace and Freedom," 90.

41. There were eighteen men and one woman on the team, including Rustin and Sutherland, three Britons, a Frenchwoman, eleven Ghanaians, and various other Africans, among them the president of the Basutoland National Congress. A. J. Muste, "Africa Against the Bomb," *Liberation*, January 1960, pp. 4–5; "Summary Information on the Sahara Nuclear Bomb Protest Team," December 22, 1959, CNVA Papers, Series 2, Box 2, SCPC; Sahara Protest–Bulletin I, November 10, 1959, CNVA Papers, Series 6, Box 13, SCPC.

42. Muste, "Africa Against the Bomb," 4–5.

43. Muste, "Africa Against the Bomb," 4–5; "Summary Information on the Sahara Nuclear Bomb Protest Team," December 22, 1959, CNVA Papers, Series 2, Box 2, SCPC; *WRL News*, January–February 1960, p. 1.

44. Thomas J. Hamilton, "French Insist on Atom Test Unless Others Yield Arms," *New York Times*, November 5, 1959, p. 1; "Ghana Aids Sahara Protest," *New York Times*, November 20, 1959, p. 16; "A-Test Opponents Ousted," *New York Times*, January 5, 1960, p. 14; "Ghanaians Protest," *New York Times*, January 31, 1960, p. 13; "French Shops Looted," *New York Times*, February 10, 1960, p. 8; Benjamin Welles, "Moroccans Protest French Atom Blast by Canceling Pact," *New York Times*, February 16, 1960, p. 1; Muste, "Africa Against the Bomb," 7; Bennett, *Radical Pacifism*, 234.

45. "French Shops Looted," *New York Times*, February 10, 1960, p. 8; "Ghanaians Protest," *New York Times*, January 31, 1960, p. 13; Benjamin Welles, "Moroccans Protest French Atom Blast by Canceling Pact," *New York Times*, February 16, 1960, p. 1; "Ghana Explains Anti-French Act," *Chicago Defender*, April 2, 1960, p. 11; "Ghana Freezes French Assets," *Daily Defender*, February 16, 1960, p. 4; Taylor, *Against the Bomb*, 161; Carter, "Sahara Protest Team," 140; Bennett, *Radical Pacifism*, 234.

46. Sutherland, *Guns and Gandhi in Africa*, 40; Taylor, *Against the Bomb*, 165–66; Bayard Rustin, "The Significance of the Sahara Project," *WRL News*, January–February 1960, pp. 2–3.

47. George Willoughby to CNVA supporters, 1960, CNVA Papers, Series 2, Box 2, SCPC; Carter, "Sahara Protest Team," 140; Lawrence S. Wittner, "The Forgotten Alliance of African Nationalists and Western Pacifists," March 19, 2007, http://www.zmag.org/znet/viewArticle/1798.

48. Allman, "Nuclear Imperialism and the Pan-African Struggle for Peace and Freedom," 93–94.

49. Allman, "Nuclear Imperialism and the Pan-African Struggle for Peace and Freedom," 93–94; Carter, "Sahara Protest Team," 140; Wittner, "Forgotten Alliance of African Nationalists and Western Pacifists."

50. Accra Assembly, press release, August 28, 1963, SANE Papers, Series B5, Box 33, SCPC.

51. "Attended Ban Bomb Confab," New York Amsterdam News, July 28, 1962, p. 4; Wittner, Resisting the Bomb, 270–71.

52. Lieberman, "Another Side of the Story," 24–25.

53. "Selassie, Nkrumah Protest Soviet Superbomb Testing," Daily Defender, October 24, 1961, p. 8.

54. "Nigerian Warns JFK on Nuclear Annihilation," Chicago Defender, July 14, 1962, p. 7.

55. Wittner, Rebels Against War, 273; Cold War America, 199.

56. Wittner, Cold War America, 199; Katz, Ban the Bomb, 30; "No Contamination Without Representation," New York Herald Tribune, March 24, 1958; "To the Men at Geneva," New York Times, October 31, 1958, p. 21; "Mr. Eisenhower … Mr. Khrushchev … Mr. Macmillan—The Time Is Now!" New York Times, February 13, 1959, p. 15, SANE Papers, Series A, Box 12, SCPC.

57. "We Are Facing a Danger Unlike Any Danger That Has Ever Existed," New York Times, November 15, 1957, p. 54; see also SANE Papers, Series A, Box 12, SCPC.

58. "To the Men at Geneva," New York Times, October 31, 1958, p. 21, SANE Papers, Series A, Box 12, SCPC; see also Katz, Ban the Bomb, 35–36.

59. Donald Keys to SANE supporters, March 25, 1960, SANE Papers, Series A, Box 11, SCPC; "5,000 March Here After Atom Rally," New York Times, May 20, 1960, p. 1; Katz, Ban the Bomb, 45–46.

60. Jules Witcover, "SANE: Moderation," Long Island Star-Journal, July 25, 1963, p.13; Hollywood for SANE, brochure; "An Evening with Belafonte," program, June 10, 1960; "6500 Attend Belafonte Performance for SANE," Bulletin of the National Committee for a Sane Nuclear Policy, June 1960, p. 389; SANE, television short, n.d., SANE Papers, Series B4, Box 19, SCPC.

61. "Hollywood Stars Request Ban on All Nuclear Tests," n.d.; "Actors Seek Demo Plank to Ban H-Tests," n.d.; "Actors Ask for Banishment of Nuclear Tests," Evansville Courier, June 18, 1960; "Actors Ask Halt to Nuclear Tests," Omaha World-Herald, June 18, 1960; "Actors Ask Banning of U.S. Nuclear Tests," Wisconsin State Journal, June 18, 1960; "Entertainers Request Ban on Nuclear Tests," Raleigh, N.C. News and Observer, June 18, 1960; "Actors Seek Bomb as 'Plank,'" Glendale, California News-Press, June 18, 1960; "$52,000 Raised by Harry

Belafonte," *Pittsburgh Courier*, June 25, 1960; "Actors Ask 'SANE' Policy on H-Tests," *Oklahoman*, June 18, 1960; "Belafonte, Allen, Ryan Seek A-Ban," *Northern Virginia Sun*, June 20, 1960; "Actors Allen, Belafonte, and Ryan Ask A-Test Bans," *Sun-Star* [Merced, Calif.], June 18, 1960; "Actors Urge A-Ban Plank," *Spokane Chronicle*, June 18, 1960, reprinted in SANE Papers, Series B4, Box 19, SCPC.

Chapter 4

1. Terry Wallace, "Novelist Baldwin Links Civil Rights and Peace," *Washington Post*, April 1, 1961; "James Baldwin to Talk at 'Witness for Peace,'" *Afro-American*, March 28, 1961; "Peace Rally Scheduled by Non-Violent Groups," *Afro-American*, April 1, 1961; "Plan Record Peace Actions Throughout U.S. and Europe," *Survival* 2, no. 4 (March 27, 1961): 1, 4, reprinted in SANE Papers, Series B5, Box 37, SCPC.

2. Martin Luther King, Jr., "Beyond Vietnam," April 4, 1967, Homer Jack Papers, Series 6, Box 7, SCPC; Lieberman and Lang, *Anticommunism and the African American Freedom Movement*, 10; see also Michael Eric Dyson, *I May Not Get There With You: The True Martin Luther King, Jr.* (New York: Free Press, 2000); Michael Eric Dyson, *April 4, 1968: Martin Luther King, Jr.'s Death and How It Changed America* (New York: Basic Civitas Books, 2008); Gerald D. McKnight, *The Last Crusade: Martin Luther King, Jr., the FBI, and the Poor People's Campaign* (Boulder: Westview Press, 1988); David J. Garrow, *Bearing the Cross: Martin Luther King, Jr., and the Southern Christian Leadership Conference* (New York: HarperCollins, 1986); Thomas F. Jackson, *From Civil Rights to Human Rights: Martin Luther King, Jr., and the Struggle for Economic Justice* (Philadelphia: University of Pennsylvania Press, 2006).

3. Martin Luther King, Jr., "Advice for Living," *Ebony*, December 1957, reprinted in *The Papers of Martin Luther King, Jr., Volume IV: Symbol of the Movement, January 1957–December 1958*, ed. Clayborne Carson (Berkeley: University of California Press, 2000), 327.

4. Martin Luther King, Jr., "Advice for Living," *Ebony*, September 1958, reprinted in Carson, *Papers of Martin Luther King, Jr., Volume IV*, 471.

5. Martin Luther King, Jr., "Address at the Thirty-sixth Annual Dinner of the War Resister's League," February 2, 1959, reprinted in *The Papers of Martin Luther King, Jr., Volume V: Threshold of a New Decade, January 1959–December 1960*, ed. Clayborne Carson (Berkeley: University of California Press, 2005), 122.

6. Martin Luther King, Jr., "Farewell Statement for All India Radio," March 9, 1959, reprinted in Carson, *Papers of Martin Luther King, Jr., Volume V*, 135–36.

7. Robert F. Williams, *Negroes with Guns* (Detroit: Wayne State University Press, 1962); Carson, *Papers of Martin Luther King, Jr., Volume V*, 17–18; Marable, *Race, Reform, and Rebellion*, 62–63.

8. Carson, *Papers of Martin Luther King, Jr., Volume V*, 17–18, 300; "Can Negroes Afford to Be Pacifists?" *Liberation*, October 1959, pp. 5–7; Plummer, *In Search of Power*, 70.

9. Martin Luther King, Jr., "A Walk Through the Holy Land," Easter Sunday sermon delivered at Dexter Avenue Baptist Church, March 29, 1959, reprinted in Carson, *Papers of Martin Luther King, Jr., Volume V*, 173.

10. Martin Luther King, Jr., "Pilgrimage to Nonviolence," April 13, 1960, reprinted in Caron, *Papers of Martin Luther King, Jr., Volume V*, 424.

11. Marin Luther King, Jr., "Keep Moving from This Mountain," address at Spelman College, April 10, 1960, reprinted in Carson, *Papers of Martin Luther King, Jr., Volume V*, 416.

12. "Will 'Blush with Shame' over Bigotry, King Says," *Daily Defender*, January 2, 1962, p. 3.

13. Martin Luther King, Jr., *Strength to Love* (Philadelphia: Fortress Press, 1963), 58–59.

14. King, *Strength to Love*, 58–59.

15. King, *Strength to Love*, 116.

16. King, *Strength to Love*, 120.

17. Martin Luther King, Jr., "New Year Hopes," January 5, 1963, SCLC Records, Part 1, Series II, Subseries 1.

18. Martin Luther King, Jr., "Nobel Peace Prize Speech," 1964, http://nobelprize.org/nobel_prizes/peace/laureates/1964/king-lecture.html.

19. Steven R. Carter, "Commitment Amid Complexity: Lorraine Hansberry's Life in Action," *MELUS* 7, no. 3, Ethnic Women Writers I (Autumn 1980): 48–49; Lieberman, "Another Side of the Story," 31–32; Washington, "Alice Childress, Lorraine Hansberry, and Claudia Jones: Black Women Write the Popular Front," 194.

20. Margaret B. Wilkerson, "The Sighted Eyes and Feeling Heart of Lorraine Hansberry," *Black American Literature Forum* 17, no. 1, Black Theatre Issue (Spring 1983): 12–13; Lieberman, "Another Side of the Story," 32; *To Be Young, Gifted, and Black: Lorraine Hansberry in Her Own Words*, adapted by Robert Nemiroff (Englewood Cliffs: Prentice-Hall, 1969), 149–64.

21. Catherine Foster, *Women for All Seasons: The Story of the Women's International League for Peace and Freedom* (Athens: University of Georgia Press, 1989), 7.

22. Blackwell notes that because officials did not maintain membership records by race or ethnicity no one is quite sure how many black women were involved in WILPF. National WILPF workers in the Philadelphia administration records office have estimated that less than one percent of its membership was African American. Joyce Blackwell, *No Peace Without Freedom: Race and the Women's International League for Peace and Freedom 1915–1975* (Carbondale: Southern Illinois University Press, 2004), 6–7; Joyce Blackwell-Johnson, "African American Activists in the Women's International League for Peace and Freedom, 1920s–1950s," *Peace and Change* 23, no. 4 (October 1998): 468.

23. Bertha McNeill, Addie Hunton, Mary Talbert, Dr. Mary Waring, Lucy Diggs Slowe, Charlotte Atwood, Helen Curtis, Mayme Williams, Mary Church Terrell, and Alice Dunbar-Nelson were among the black women who joined WILPF before World War II. Blackwell, *No Peace Without Freedom*, 7–8.

24. Work in the early 1950s centered on the Korean War and the use of atomic weapons. In 1953, WILPF appealed for a "World Truce," which called for a two-year pledge by nations not to produce or use armaments and to prepare for a "Disarmament Conference" during the pause. WILPF members also worked with the United Nations to get the World

Health Organization to investigate the radiation effects of atomic tests beginning in 1956. Foster, *Women for All Seasons*, 27.

25. "Harris Lived an Independent Life," *Wichita State University Alumni News* 3, no. 6 (May/June 1995); Larry Dougherty, "Activist Harris Recalls Her Life Fighting Racism," *Daily Californian*, February 26, 1986; Statement by Erna P. Harris, n.d., WILPF/Erna P. Harris Papers, Part III, Series A1, Box 4A, SCPC.

26. "Erna Harris Mourned, *The Post*, Oakland, Calif., May 10, 1995; Ronald V. Dellums, "A Tribute to Erna P. Harris," *Congressional Record* 136, no. 50 (April 30, 1990); Erna P. Harris, resume, WILPF/Erna P. Harris Papers, Part III, Series A2, Part 3B, Box 1, SCPC; "Harris Lived an Independent Life," *Wichita State University Alumni News* 3, no. 6 (May/June 1995); Larry Dougherty, "Activist Harris Recalls Her Life Fighting Racism," *Daily Californian*, February 26, 1986; Statement by Erna P. Harris, n.d., WILPF/Erna P. Harris Papers, Part III, Series A1, Box 4A, SCPC.

27. Claire H. Walsh, WILPF, press release, 1961; WILPF, "Conference of Russian and American Women," list of sponsors, delegates, and agenda, November 1961; "Russian, U.S. Women Join in Call for Peace," n.d., reprinted in WILPF/Erna P. Harris Papers, Part III, Series A4, Part II, Box 3, SCPC. The U.S. section of WILPF also organized the first meeting, which took place in Bryn Mawr, Pennsylvania, in November 1961.

28. Dorothy Hutchinson, "Soviet-American Women's Conference," 1964; "Final Agenda for Conference of Soviet and U.S. Women in Moscow," March 26, 1964; Erna P. Harris to Dorothy Hutchinson, March 21, 1964; Joan McCoy, "Long Talks Pay Off in Global Relations," *Rocky Mountain News*, May 15, 1964; Henry Bussey, "Peace Worker Finds Small Chink in Russ Public Relations Front, *Portland Reporter*, May 21, 1964, p. 32, WILPF/Erna P. Harris Papers, Part III, Series A2, Part 3B, Box 1, SCPC.

29. Wittner, *Resisting the Bomb*, 251–52.

30. Amy Swerdlow, *Women Strike for Peace: Traditional Motherhood and Radical Politics in the 1960s* (Chicago: University of Chicago Press, 1993), 90–91.

31. Dyson, *I May Not Get There With You,* 64; Phyl Garland, "In Her Husband's Footsteps," *Ebony*, September 1968, p. 156.

32. "Geneva Statement," April 1962, WSP Papers, Series A4, Box 1, SCPC; "List of Delegates to Geneva Conference," April 1, 1962, WSP Papers, Series A4, Box 1, SCPC; "Press Release," April 11, 1962, WSP Papers, Series A4, Box 1, SCPC; "Negro Proving Desire for Freedom, Says Mrs. King," *Daily Defender*, May 21, 1962.

33. "Viet Policy Raked Mrs. King: Peace Warrior," *Detroit Free Press*, November 29, 1965, p. 3; Coretta Scott King, FBI files, Part 1.

34. Swerdlow, *Women Strike for Peace*, 91–92.

35. Swerdlow, *Women Strike for Peace*, 92–93.

36. Harvey originally formed WU to assist Freedom Riders who were arrested and held in the Hinds County jail in Jackson, Mississippi. Cosmetic dealer A.N.E. Logan and millinery shop owner Thelma Sanders cofounded WU with Harvey. "List of Delegates to Geneva Conference," April 1, 1962, WSP Papers, Series A4, Box 1, SCPC; "Women for Peace Pilgrimage to

Rome," 1963, WSP Papers, Series A4, Box 1, SCPC; "Accra Assembly Press Release," August 28, 1963, SANE Papers, Series B5, Box 33, SCPC; "Attended Ban Bomb Confab," *New York Amsterdam News*, July 28, 1962, p. 4; Myrlie Evers-Williams and Manning Marable, eds., *The Autobiography of Medgar Evers: A Hero's Life and Legacy Revealed Through His Writings, Letters, and Speeches* (New York: Basic Civitas Books, 2005), 239; John Dittmer, *Local People: The Struggle for Civil Rights in Mississippi* (Urbana: University of Illinois Press, 1995), 98.

37. Oliver Stone and Peter Kuznick, "Barack's Betrayal," *New Statesman*, April 11, 2011, pp. 40–41; James W. Douglass, *JFK and the Unspeakable: Why He Died and Why It Matters* (New York: Simon & Schuster, 2008), 31–36.

38. WSP Press Release," March 6, 1965, WSP Papers, Series B1, Box 1, SCPC; Swerdlow, *Women Strike for Peace*, 92–93; Marjorie Hunter, "Women Besiege Capitol, Demanding Test Ban," *New York Times*, May 8, 1963, p. 17.

39. Martin Luther King, Jr., to Carl Keith Jr., October 14, 1963, SCLC Records, Part 1, Series 1, Subseries 1.

40. Douglass, *JFK and the Unspeakable,* 50–54.

41. Lifton and Mitchell, *Hiroshima in America*, 337–40; Wittner, *Resisting the Bomb*, 444, 451–55; Boyer, *By the Bomb's Early Light*, 358–59.

42. Gerson, *Empire and the Bomb*, 130–31.

43. "1,000 Here Mark Hiroshima Bomb," *New York Times*, August 7, 1965, p. 3.

44. Simon Hall, *Peace and Freedom: The Civil Rights and Antiwar Movements in the 1960s* (Philadelphia: University of Pennsylvania Press, 2005), 24–26.

45. Hall, *Peace and Freedom*, 24–26.

46. Sanford Gottlieb to Norman Thomas, Homer Jack, Arthur Waskow, and Seymour Melman, June 11, 1963, SANE Papers, Series B6, Box 55, SCPC.

47. "The Struggle for Freedom and a World Without War," SANE policy statement, June 17, 1963, SANE Papers, Series B6, Box 55, SCPC. Homer Jack sent this statement to King, Farmer, and Baldwin on June 21, 1963.

48. "Emergency Rally on Vietnam," flyer and program, June 8, 1965, SANE Papers, Series A, Box 11A, SCPC; Katz, *Ban the Bomb*, 96; Hall, *Peace and Freedom*, 26.

49. Edith Evans Asbury, "Protests Today to Mark Hiroshima Anniversary," *New York Times*, August 6, 1966, p. 4; Douglas Robinson, "5,000 in Times Square," *New York Times*, August 7, 1966, pp. 1, 3.

50. "Viet' Protest March Aimed at Washington," *Daily Defender*, October 19, 1965, p. 6; "March on Washington for Peace in Vietnam: A Call to Mobilize the Conscience of America," flyer, November 27, 1965; "March on Washington for Peace in Vietnam," flyer, November 27, 1965; Benjamin Spock to supporters, November 18, 1965, SANE Papers, Series A, Box 11A, SCPC; Hall, *Peace and Freedom*, 26–27; Meier and Rudwick, *CORE*, 376, 404.

51. "King Urges Peaceful U.S.-Viet Negotiations," *Daily Defender*, March 4, 1965, p. 8; Hall, *Peace and Freedom*, 26; Dyson, *I May Not Get There With You*, 54.

52. King's first speech dedicated solely to Vietnam was titled "Casualties of the War in Vietnam" at a conference sponsored by the *Nation* magazine on February 25, 1967. Dyson, *I May Not Get There With You*, 59.

53. Martin Luther King, Jr., "The Casualties of the War in Vietnam," February 25, 1967, reprinted in *Dr. Martin Luther King, Jr., Dr. John C. Bennett, Dr. Henry Steele Commager, Rabbi Abraham Heschel Speak on the War in Vietnam* (1967), 8, FOR Papers, Series E, Box 17, SCPC.

54. Martin Luther King, Jr., "Beyond Vietnam," April 4, 1967, Homer Jack Papers, Series 6, Box 7, SCPC.

55. "HHH Hits Dr. King on Viet," *Chicago Daily Defender*, April 17, 1967, p. 3; Garrow, *Bearing the Cross,* 554; Dyson, *I May Not Get There With You,* 61–62; Hall, *Peace and Freedom*, 80–81; Henry E. Darby and Margaret N. Bowley, "King on Vietnam and Beyond," *Phylon* 47, no. 1 (1986): 49.

56. "Wilkins in Bitter Attack on Dr. King's Peace Stand," *Chicago Daily Defender*, April 20, 1967, p. 2.

57. "Leaders Rap King on Viet," *Chicago Daily Defender*, April 8, 1967, p. 1; Dyson, *I May Not Get There With You,* 61; Hall, *Peace and Freedom*, 84.

58. Bayard Rustin, "Dr. King's Painful Dilemma," *New York Amsterdam News*, April 22, 1967, p. 14.

59. Dyson, *I May Not Get There With You,* 69.

60. Martin Luther King, Jr., "Comments on NAACP Resolution," April 12, 1967, reprinted in *Dr. Martin Luther King, Jr., Dr. John C. Bennett, Dr. Henry Steele Commager, Rabbi Abraham Heschel Speak on the War in Vietnam* (1967): 28, FOR Papers, Series E, Box 17, SCPC.

61. William B. Hixon Jr., "To the Editor," *New York Times*, April 10, 1967, reprinted in *Dr. Martin Luther King, Jr., Dr. John C. Bennett, Dr. Henry Steele Commager, Rabbi Abraham Heschel Speak on the War in Vietnam* (1967): 29, FOR Papers, Series E, Box 17, SCPC.

62. John P.C. Matthews, "To the Editor," *New York Times*, April 8, 1967, reprinted in *Dr. Martin Luther King, Jr., Dr. John C. Bennett, Dr. Henry Steele Commager, Rabbi Abraham Heschel Speak on the War in Vietnam* (1967): 30, FOR Papers, Series E, Box 17, SCPC.

63. Benjamin Spock, "To the Editor," *New York Times*, April 10, 1967, reprinted in *Dr. Martin Luther King, Jr., Dr. John C. Bennett, Dr. Henry Steele Commager, Rabbi Abraham Heschel Speak on the War in Vietnam* (1967): 30, FOR Papers, Series E, Box 17, SCPC.

64. "Peace, Rights Coalition," *Chicago Defender*, April 15, 1967, p. 11.

65. Darby and Bowley, "King on Vietnam and Beyond," 47–48; Garrow, *Bearing the Cross,* 546; Hall, *Peace and Freedom*, 105–6.

66. In January 1967, Mobe asked James Bevel to become its national director. Bevel, a thirty-year-old Baptist preacher had built his reputation on his civil rights activism throughout the South, including working with the Nashville sit-ins in 1960 and Freedom Riders in 1961. As a prominent member of the SCLC, Bevel worked closely with King. "Biographical Sketch of James Bevel," 1967; Douglas Robinson, "Scattered Peace Activists Seek to Unify Movement," *New York Times*, February 26, 1967, p. 3, FOR Papers Series E, Box 18, SCPC; Garrow, *Bearing the Cross,* 543; Hall, *Peace and Freedom*, 106–8.

67. Martin Luther King, Jr., "Vietnam Is Upon Us," February 6, 1968, reprinted in *Speeches by the Reverend Dr. Martin Luther King, Jr. About the War in Vietnam*, 1968, Homer Jack Papers, Series 6, Box 7, SCPC.

68. King, "Vietnam Is Upon Us."

69. David R. Colburn and George E. Pozzetta, "Race, Ethnicity, and the Evolution of Political Legitimacy," in *The Sixties: From Memory to History*, ed. David Farber (Chapel Hill: University of North Carolina Press, 1994), 130; Charles DeBenedetti, *An American Ordeal: The Antiwar Movement of the Vietnam Era* (Syracuse: Syracuse University Press, 1990), 158; David Burner, *Making Peace with the Sixties* (Princeton: Princeton University Press, 1996), 73; Hall, *Peace and Freedom*, 59–60.

70. Plummer, *In Search of Power*, 14–15; see also Joseph, *Waiting 'til the Midnight Hour*; Gilmore, *Defying Dixie*.

71. Yuri Kochiyama, *Passing It On—A Memoir* (Los Angeles: UCLA Asian American Studies Center Press, 2004), 67; "Yuri Kochiyama: With Justice in Her Heart," *Revolutionary Worker*, December 13, 1998, http://rwor.org/a/v20/980-89/986/yuri.htm; Annie Nakao, "Inspired by Malcolm X, Asian American Activist Makes Her Own History," *SFGate*, September 9, 2005, http://www.sfgate.com; Diane C. Fujino, *Heartbeat of Struggle: The Revolutionary Life of Yuri Kochiyama* (Minneapolis: University of Minnesota Press, 2005), 140–43.

72. The "World's Worst Fair" was taking place while the regular tourist-attraction fair was held at Flushing Meadows in Queens. Harlem activists thought of the idea of opening up a "Fair" in one of the most impoverished blocks in Harlem so that tourists could see how some people in Harlem had to live under the supervision of uncaring landlords and the sanitation department. The "World's Worst Fair" highlighted living quarters with broken windows, broken-down staircases, toilets that would not flush, clogged-up bathtubs, and garbage piled high on the streets. Kochiyama, *Passing It On*, 67.

73. Kochiyama, *Passing It On*, 69–70; Fujino, *Heartbeat of Struggle*, 140–43.

74. "Gregory: Fight for Freedom Just Begun," *Daily Defender*, June 22, 1964, p. 3; Erna P. Harris, letter, June 26, 1964, WILPF/Erna Harris Papers, Part III, Series A2, Part 3B, Box 1, SCPC.

75. Manning Marable, *Malcolm X: A Life of Reinvention* (New York: Viking Press, 2011), 305, 336.

76. Marable, *Malcolm X*, 316.

77. Marable, *Malcolm X*, 395.

78. If passed, the Mulford Bill, named after Donald Mulford, a conservative Republican state assembly member, would have made it illegal for the Black Panthers to engage in any armed patrols of their neighborhoods. The bill would ban any ordinary citizen from having a loaded firearm on his or her person or inside a vehicle. David Hilliard with Keith and Kent Zimmerman, *Huey: Spirit of the Panther* (New York: Thunder's Mouth Press, 2006), 63.

79. Hilliard, *Huey*, 68.

80. Toni Morrison, ed., *To Die For the People: The Writings of Huey P. Newton* (New York: Writers and Readers Publishing, 1995), 7.

81. Kathleen Cleaver, quoted in Michael L. Clemons and Charles E. Jones, "Global Solidarity: The Black Panther Party in the International Arena," in *Liberation, Imagination,*

and the Black Panther Party: A New Look at the Panthers and Their Legacy, ed. Kathleen Cleaver and George Katsiaficas (New York: Routledge, 2001), 27.

82. Clemons and Jones, "Global Solidarity," 33; Huey P. Newton, *Revolutionary Suicide* (New York: Writers and Readers Publishing, 1973), 193.

83. Morrison, *To Die For the People,* 149.

Chapter 5

1. Steve Ladd and Scott Ullman, "Walk to Begin January 31," *WRL News*, November–December 1975, p. 1, SCPC; Ed Hedemann, "1000 Set Out from San Francisco," *WRL News*, January–February 1976, p. 1, SCPC; "The Continental Walk for Disarmament and Social Justice," flyer, n.d., WSP Papers, ACC 96A-040, Box 1, SCPC.

2. Rosa Parks, the Southern Conference of Black Mayors, the Reverend Bernard Lee, Ralph Abernathy, the SCLC, Dick Gregory, James Orange, and various black clergy formally endorsed the Walk. Continental Walk for Disarmament and Social Justice Coordinating Committee, meeting minutes, March 29, 1976; *The Continental Walk News*, June 15, 1976, p. 1, WSP Papers, ACC 96A-040, Box 1, SCPC; "25 Walkers Arrested in Mississippi," *The Continental Walk News*, May 24, 1976, p. 1, WSP Papers, ACC 96A-040, Box 1, SCPC; Mike Jendrzejczyk, "Southern Route on the Road Again," *The Continental Walk News*, July 1, 1976, pp. 1–2, WSP Papers, ACC 96A-040, Box 1, SCPC.

3. Jim Peck, "Southern Walk Hits the Road," *WRL News*, May–June 1976, pp. 1–2, SCPC.

4. Peck, "Southern Walk Hits the Road," pp. 1–2.

5. Peck, "Southern Walk Hits the Road," pp. 1–2; Peck, "15 Years After the Freedom Rides," *WRL News*, November–December 1976, p. 5; Jendrzejczyk, "Southern Route on the Road Again," pp. 1–2; "25 Walkers Arrested in Mississippi," *The Continental Walk News*, May 24, 1976, p. 1, WSP Papers, ACC 96A-040, Box 1, SCPC.

6. Ed Hedemann, "Dramatic End to Walk in DC," *WRL News*, November–December 1976, pp. 1–2, SCPC; "The Continental Walk—the Pentagon, October 18, 1976," *The Continental Walk News*, October 30, 1976, pp. 1–6, WSP Papers, ACC 96A-040, Box 1, SCPC.

7. SALT I limited the deployment of intercontinental and sea-launched ballistic missiles and the deployment of antiballistic missile systems (ABM). In May 1972, Richard Nixon and Leonid Brezhnev signed an agreement, "Basic Principles in Relations," in which the United States and Soviet Union pledged to do "their utmost to avoid military confrontation and to prevent the outbreak of nuclear war." A little over a year later, the two governments signed the "Prevention of Nuclear War" agreement, which bound them to "act in such a manner as to exclude the outbreak of nuclear war between them and between either of the Parties and other countries." In November 1974, the Vladivostok Accord was signed, which set additional nuclear limits. Lawrence S. Wittner, *Toward Nuclear Abolition: A History of the World Nuclear Disarmament Movement, 1971 to the Present* (Stanford: Stanford University Press, 2003), 1–3.

8. Wittner, *Toward Nuclear Abolition*, 3, 7–8.

9. Wittner, *Toward Nuclear Abolition*, 47–48.

10. "Pittsburghers' Views Split on New Neutron Bomb," *Pittsburgh Courier*, July 30, 1977, p. 7; Alfred Bailey, "To the Editor," *Philadelphia Tribune*, July 23, 1977, p. 6.

11. "Sister! Sister!" flyer for WSP; "Salute to Women," press release, October 30, 1977, WSP Papers, ACC 96A-040, Box 2, SCPC.

12. Carl Gershman, "The World According to Andrew Young," *Commentary*, August 1978, http://www.commentarymagazine.com/article/the-world-according-to-andrew-young/.

13. Carter has stated that he could not recall any attempts made by Young to persuade him one way or the other on the neutron bomb. Scholars have concluded that while Young seldom criticized Carter directly, his public outspokenness on the neutron bomb embarrassed the White House and forced Carter to reevaluate his position. "Young Criticized Neutron Bomb," *Washington Post*, July 16, 1977, p. A13; Bartlet C. Jones, *Flawed Triumphs: Andy Young and the United Nations* (Lanham: University Press of American, 1996), 46; Gershman, "World According to Andrew Young"; John Dumbrell, *The Carter Presidency: A Re-Evaluation* (Manchester: Manchester University Press, 1993), 102.

14. Wittner, *Toward Nuclear Abolition*, 47–48.

15. David Albright, "South Africa and the Affordable Bomb," *Bulletin of the Atomic Scientists* 50, no. 4 (July/August 1994), http://www.thebulletin.org; Tami Hultman and Reed Kramer, "South Africans Have a Nuclear Trump Card Yet to Play," *Baltimore Sun*, August 28, 1977, p. K1, reprinted in *Current News*, Part 2, August 29, 1977, SANE Papers, Series G, Box 53, SCPC.

16. There is some disagreement about when officials adopted a military justification for South Africa's nuclear explosive program. President de Klerk said in March 1993 that the decision to develop a limited nuclear deterrent capability was taken as early as 1974. Philippe de Villiers agreed. In contrast, Waldo Stumpf stated that the program was not military in nature until 1977. Armscor (Armaments Corporation of South Africa), which largely agreed with Stumpf, maintained that the formal shift occurred in 1978. David Albright, "South Africa and the Affordable Bomb," *Bulletin of the Atomic Scientists* 50, no. 4 (July/August 1994), http://www.thebulletin.org.

17. Both countries repeatedly denied the relationship, but rumors persisted of secret agreements to exchange Israel's advanced nuclear knowledge for an assured supply of South African uranium. According to one U.S. official, Pretoria resisted disclosure of its nuclear activities, in part to prevent revelations about its dealings with Israel. The Central Intelligence Agency reported that "Israelis have not only participated in certain South African nuclear research activities over the last few years, but they have also offered and transferred various sorts of advanced non-nuclear weapons technology to South Africa." Moreover, in 1976, South African prime minister John Vorster and Israeli officials signed an agreement which increased economic and scientific cooperation and established a joint ministerial committee to annually review Israeli–South African relations. Vorster's visit also produced an agreement to work on multiple military projects in addition to the missile and patrol boats Israel was already supplying to South Africa. By 1977, bilateral trade stood at more than $100 million a year. Jeffrey Antevil, "Israel and South Africa: A

Nuclear Family?" *New York News*, August 28, 1977, p. 69, reprinted in *Current News*, Part 2, August 29, 1977, SANE Papers, Series G, Box 53, SCPC; David Albright and Mark Hibbs, "South Africa: The ANC and the Atom Bomb," *Bulletin of the Atomic Scientists* 49, no. 3 (April 1993): 33–34, http://www.thebulletin.org.

18. WILPF United Nations Special Session on Disarmament Bulletin, no. 1, January 12, 1978, WILPF Papers, Part III, Series A5, Box 14, SCPC; Rally for Disarmament, brochure, WILPF Papers, Part III, Series A4, Part 1, Box 10, SCPC.

19. Wittner, *Toward Nuclear Abolition*, 30; Rally for Disarmament, brochure, WILPF Papers, Part 3, U.S. Section, Series A4, Part 1, Box 10, SCPC.

20. International Religious Convocation for Human Survival, program, May 25–26, 1978, FOR Papers, Programs, Series J, Box 1, SCPC.

21. International Religious Convocation for Human Survival, press release, n.d., FOR Papers, Programs, Series J, Box 1, SCPC.

22. "Witness for Survival, South Bronx," flyer, n.d., FOR Papers, Programs, Series J, Box 1, SCPC.

23. George Vecsey, "UN Rally by 2,000 Backs Disarmament," *New York Times*, May 27, 1978, p. 23, reprinted in FOR Papers, Series J, Box 1, SCPC.

24. "Conyers at U.N. on Disarmament," *Baltimore Afro-American*, June 10, 1978, p. 8.

25. "Ban-the-Bomb Rally," *Washington Post*, May 28, 1978, p. A9; "Conyers at UN on Disarmament," *Baltimore Afro-American*, June 10, 1978, p. 8; "Disarmament Rally Draws 10,000 at UN," *New York Times*, May 28, 1978, p. 29, reprinted in FOR Papers, Series J, Box 1, SCPC; Connie Hogarth to WILPF Members, May 10, 1978, WILPF Papers, Part 3, U.S. Section, Series A4, Part 1, Box 10, SCPC; "Rally for Disarmament May 27," *The Mobilizer*, n.d., WILPF Papers, Part 3, U.S. Section, Series A4, Part 1, Box 10, SCPC.

26. Jones, *Flawed Triumphs*, 43–46; "Ban-the-Bomb Rally," *Washington Post*, May 28, 1978, p. A9.

27. Foster, *Women for All Seasons*, 77; Wittner, *Toward Nuclear Abolition*, 29.

28. Tim Wheeler, "Thousands Bring Jobs Demand to Carter," SANE Papers, Series G, Box 63, SCPC; National Youth Pilgrimage for Jobs, Peace, and Justice, program schedule, 1980, SANE Papers, Series G, Box 63, SCPC.

29. Tad Daley, "How Reagan Brought the World to the Brink of Nuclear Destruction," *Alternet*, February 7, 2011, http://www.alternet.org/module/printversion/149821; Howard Zinn, "Reagan's Economic Policies Favored the Rich," in *Ronald Reagan*, ed. James D. Torr (San Diego: Greenhaven Press, 2001), 69; Wittner, *Toward Nuclear Abolition*, 113–14, 170–71, 321.

30. Ruth Sidel, *Keeping Women and Children Last: America's War on the Poor* (New York: Penguin Books, 1996), xii–xiv; Zinn, "Reagan's Economic Policies Favored the Rich," 69–70; see also Ralph de Costa Nunez, *A Shelter Is Not a Home or Is It? Lessons from Family Homelessness in New York City* (New York: White Tiger Press, 2004); Manning Marable, *How Capitalism Underdeveloped Black America* (Cambridge: South End Press, 2000); Kevin Phillips, *The Politics of Rich and Poor: Wealth and the American Electorate in the Reagan Aftermath* (New York: Random House, 1990).

31. John Thomas was AUP's international director and Phil Shinnick was AUP's executive director. Athletes for Peace, brochure, n.d.; *Athletes United for Peace*, 1983; *Athletes United for Peace*, Winter 1984; "Who Supports Athletes United for Peace," AUP, brochure; "AUP Advisory Board Members," Athletes United for Peace Papers, CDGA Collective Box, SCPC.

32. Athletes for Peace, brochure, n.d.; *Athletes United for Peace*, 1983; *Athletes United for Peace*, Winter 1984; "Who Supports Athletes United for Peace," AUP, brochure; "AUP Advisory Board Members," Athletes United for Peace Papers, CDGA Collective Box, SCPC.

33. *Athletes United for Peace*, Winter–Spring 1985, Athletes United for Peace Papers, CDGA Collective Box, SCPC.

34. Greg Johnson, interview by author, December 30, 2013, Silver Spring, Md.; Dolores Jackson Richards, "Blacks Against Nukes Making the Connections," n.d., Blacks Against Nukes Papers, CDGA Collective Box, SCPC.

35. Greg Johnson, interview by author, December 30, 2013, Silver Spring, Md.

36. Greg Johnson, interview by author, December 30, 2013, Silver Spring, Md.; Richards, "Blacks Against Nukes Making the Connections."

37. Richards, "Blacks Against Nukes Making the Connections."

38. Greg Johnson, interview by author, December 30, 2013, Silver Spring, Md.; Stephanie Whyche, "Blacks Against Nukes Want to Ban the Bomb," *Pace Morning News*, November 20, 1982, p. D1; Sheila Smith, "BAN Urges More Blacks to Join Anti-Nuclear Fight," *Hilltop*, April 9, 1982, p.3.

39. Greg Johnson, interview by author, December 30, 2013, Silver Spring, Md.

40. Greg Johnson, interview by author, December 30, 2013, Silver Spring, Md.; Richards, "Blacks Against Nukes Making the Connections"; "Blacks Urged to Boycott War Toys This Christmas," *JET*, December 6, 1982; Kenneth M. Jones, "Blacks Against the Bomb," *Essence*, January, 1985, p. 46; Whyche, "Blacks Against Nukes Want to Ban the Bomb"; Smith, "BAN Urges More Blacks to Join Anti-Nuclear Fight"; Crispin Y. Campbell, "District Antinuclear Group Calls for Boycott of War Toys," *Washington Post*, December 15, 1982, p. 3; Patrice Gaines-Carter, "Making Nuclear Power of Concern to All," *National Leader*, October 28, 1982, pp. 12–13.

41. Dawn Cavrell, "Haughton Says Blacks Must Join Anti-Nukers," *The Campus*, September 26, 1979, pp. 7–9, James Haughton Papers, Box 13, SCRBC.

42. Minutes of antinuclear/anti-racism meeting, April 27, 1980, James Haughton Papers, Box 13, SCRBC.

43. Cavrell, "Haughton Says Blacks Must Join Anti-Nukers," pp. 7, 9.

44. Cavrell, "Haughton Says Blacks Must Join Anti-Nukers," pp. 7, 9.

45. Daley, "How Reagan Brought the World to the Brink of Nuclear Destruction."

46. Florence Falk, "Performing Artists for Nuclear Disarmament," *Performing Arts Journal* 6, no. 2 (1982): 110; "Performing-Arts Group for Atom Curb Formed," *New York Times*, April 4, 1982, p. 55.

47. Robin Herman, "Children Stage Nuclear Protest in Central Park," *New York Times*, May 17, 1982, p. B4; Robin Herman, "Anti-Nuclear Groups Are Using Professions as Rallying Points," *New York Times*, June 5, 1982, p. 26.

48. "Survival Festival," flyer, May 30, 1982, James Haughton Papers, Box 13, SCRBC.

49. "Peace Sunday Draws Crowd of 100,000," *Los Angeles Sentinel*, June 10, 1982, p. A4. LaVar Burton, who played Kunta Kinte in "Roots," was the keynote speaker at multiple events in July for the California Nuclear Weapons Freeze Campaign. "'Roots' Star Speaks for Nuke Freeze," *Los Angeles Sentinel*, July 8, 1982, p. C12.

50. James Feron, "Momentum Gains on Nuclear-Limit Rally," *New York Times*, June 6, 1982, p. WC1; Robin Herman, "Protesters Old and New Forge Alliance for Antinuclear Rally," *New York Times*, June 4, 1982, p. B6.

51. "National Sponsors of the June 12th Rally," April 19, 1982, SANE Papers, Series G, Box 67, SCPC; David Lindorff, "War in Peace: The Fight for Position in New York's June 12 Disarmament Rally," *Village Voice*, April 20, 1982, p. 12; Pamela Mincey, "Afro-Americans Get Set for June 12," *Daily World*, February 25, 1982, p. 3.

52. Lindorff, "War in Peace," p. 12; Mincey, "Afro-Americans Get Set for June 12," p. 3.

53. At one point the split became so wide that Gordon J. Davis, the city's parks commissioner, was given two separate applications for a rally permit. Mincey, "Afro-Americans Get Set for June 12," pp. 3, 7; Herman, "Protesters Old and New Forge Alliance for Antinuclear Rally," p. B6; "Summation of the June 12 Executive Committee Meeting," March 30, 1982, SANE Papers, Series G, Box 67, SCPC.

54. The June 12 Rally Committee was run primarily by the Riverside Church Disarmament Program, Greenpeace USA, the AFSC, and SANE and had the endorsements of eighty national organizations and 150 local groups. June 12 Rally Committee, minutes, February 26, 1982, SANE Papers, Series G, Box 67, SCPC; David Cortight to Richard Bowers, June 7, 1982, SANE Papers, Series G, Box 67, SCPC; Lindorff, "War in Peace," p. 12.

55. Lindorff, "War in Peace," p. 13.

56. Lindorff, "War in Peace," pp. 13–14.

57. David McReynolds, "Memo on the Events in June," January 30, 1982, SANE Papers, Series G, Box 67, SCPC.

58. McReynolds, "Memo on the Events in June."

59. McReynolds, Memo on the Events in June."

60. Lindorff, "War in Peace," p. 13.

61. Mincey, "Afro-Americans Get Set for June 12," p. 7.

62. De Nitto, "June 12 Buildup Gaining Support," p. 2.

63. De Nitto, "June 12 Buildup Gaining Support," p.10.

64. Lindorff, "War in Peace," p. 12.

65. Paul L. Montgomery, "Throngs Fill Manhattan to Protest Nuclear Weapons," *New York Times*, June 13, 1982, p. 1; Robert D. McFadden, "A Spectrum of Humanity Represented at the Rally," *New York Times*, June 13, 1982, p. 42.

66. June 12 Rally Committee, program schedule, SANE Papers, Series G, Box 67, SCPC; Robin Herman, "Rally Speakers Decry Cost of Nuclear Arms Race," *New York Times*, June 13, 1982, p. 43; Daley, "How Reagan Brought the World to the Brink of Nuclear Destruction."

67. Simon Anekwe, "Colors Finally Blended in Giant Peace Protest," *New York Amsterdam News*, June 19, 1982, p. 1.

68. Montgomery, "Throngs Fill Manhattan to Protest Nuclear Weapons," p. 1; June 12 Rally Committee, program schedule, SANE Papers, Series G, Box 67, SCPC; Anekwe, "Colors Finally Blended in Giant Peace Protest," p. 1.

69. Anekwe, "Colors Finally Blended in Giant Peace Protest," p. 1.

70. Anekwe, "Colors Finally Blended in Giant Peace Protest," p. 1; Herman, "Rally Speakers Decry Cost of Nuclear Arms Race," p. 43.

71. June 12 Rally Committee, logistics fact sheet, SANE Papers, Series G, Box 67; Anekwe, "Colors Finally Blended in Giant Peace Protest," p. 1.

72. June 12 Rally Committee, logistics fact sheet, SANE Papers, Series G, Box 67; Simon Anekwe, "Nuke Protest," *New York Amsterdam News*, June 12, 1982, p. 1.

73. "Resolution on Nuclear Disarmament," *New York Amsterdam News*, June 12, 1982, p. 33.

74. "Militarism and Racism: A Harlem Fight Back Statement," *New York Amsterdam News*, June 12, 1982, p. 32.

75. Stevie Wonder, Joseph Lowery, Harry Belafonte, Jesse Jackson, Ossie Davis, Ruby Dee, Andrew Young, Dorothy Height, Dick Gregory, Julian Bond, Shirley Chisholm, James Lawson, Ronald Dellums, Harold Washington, Marion Barry, James Orange, Ronald Walters, Manning Marable, John Conyers, Walter Fauntroy, and Donna Brazile were among the main organizers of the march. Support also came from the Congressional Black Caucus, Congress of National Black Churches, National Black Student Congress, National Council of Negro Women, FOR, AFSC, SANE, NAACP, and SCLC, among others. TAM, minutes of the National Planning Council meeting, May 1, 1983; TAM, list of endorsers, 1982; TAM, program, August 27, 1983; TAM, financial support list; Ernest B. Furgurson, "Rekindling of the Spirit of the '60s Sought," *Washington Post*, August 12, 1982, pp. A1, A8, SANE Papers, Series G, Box 62, SCPC; "310 Cities to Join Washington March," *Philadelphia Tribune*, August 12, 1983, p. 21.

76. TAM, "Peace/Foreign Policy Statement of Purpose," 1983, pp. 1–4, SANE Papers, Series G, Box 62, SCPC.

77. TAM, program, August 27, 1983, SANE Papers, Series G, Box 62, SCPC.

78. TAM, list of endorsers, 1982; TAM, "Christmas Call to the Nation from National Black Leaders," 1982; TAM, "Background of the Twentieth Anniversary Call," 1982, SANE Papers, Series G, Box 62, SCPC; "Fauntroy Calls Meeting to Commemorate March on Washington; New March Planned," *Atlanta Daily World*, January 13, 1983, p. 1; William Rasberry, "March to Stress Jobs and Rights," *New York Amsterdam News*, January 1, 1983, p. 13; "To Commemorate March on Washington; New March Planned," *Atlanta Daily World*, January 13, 1983, p. 1.

79. 20th Anniversary Celebration for Jobs, Peace, and Freedom, program, June 11, 1983, SANE Papers, Series G, Box 62, SCPC.

80. "Prague Peace Meet Pulls Thirty Black Delegates," *Baltimore Afro-American*, August 27, 1983, p. 7.

81. "Prague Peace Meet Pulls Thirty Black Delegates," p. 7.

82. TAM, timetable, n.d., SANE Papers, Series G, Box 62, SCPC; "310 Cities to Join Washington March," *Philadelphia Tribune*, August 12, 1983, p. 21; Pamela Newkirk, "10,000 N.Yorkers to Join DC March," *New York Amsterdam News*, August 6, 1983, p.4.

83. William Epstein, "Uncertain Prospects for UNSSOD III," *Peace* 4, no. 3 (June–July 1988): 14, http://archive.peacemagazine.org/v04n3p14.htm.

84. Daley, "How Reagan Brought the World to the Brink of Nuclear Destruction."

85. Daley, "How Reagan Brought the World to the Brink of Nuclear Destruction."

Chapter 6

1. Barack Obama, "Breaking the War Mentality," *Sundial*, March 10, 1983, pp. 2 –5; William J. Broad and David E. Sanger, "Obama's Youth Shaped His Nuclear-Free Vision," *New York Times*, July 5, 2009, http://www.nytimes.com/2009/07/05/world/05nuclear.html ?pagewanted=all.

2. Broad and Sanger, "Obama's Youth Shaped His Nuclear-Free Vision."

3. Charles P. Henry, "Toward a Multiracial Democracy: The Jackson and Obama Contributions," in *The Obama Phenomenon: Toward a Multiracial Democracy*, ed. Charles P. Henry, Robert L. Allen, and Robert Chrisman (Urbana: University of Illinois Press, 2011), 15.

4. Washington served in the Illinois House of Representatives from 1965 to 1976, the State Senate from 1977 to 1980, and in the U.S. House of Representatives from January 1981 until his resignation on April 30, 1983. He was elected to mayor of Chicago on April 12, 1983, reelected in 1987, and served until his death in November 1987. Florence Hamlish Levinsohn, *Harold Washington: A Political Biography* (Chicago: Chicago Review Press, 1983), 173–74.

5. Harold Washington, "The Black Vote: The New Power in Politics," *Ebony*, November 1983, pp. 108–10.

6. Thelma Murphy, "For a Freeze on Nuclear Weapons," *Chicago Tribune*, February 22, 1983, p. 12.

7. Levinsohn, *Harold Washington*, 173–74.

8. "Black Mayors Converge, Discuss Nation's Economy," *Pittsburgh Courier*, May 15, 1982, p. 1.

9. SANE, action memo, April 17, 1981, SANE Papers, Series G, Box 27, SCPC. "The MX Missile Is in Big Trouble, But It's Not Dead Yet!" SANE, action memo, May 7, 1980; SANE, action memo, April 2, 1980, SANE Papers, Series G, Box 27, SCPC.

10. Manning Marable, "The Politics of the Arms Race," *New York Amsterdam News*, April 2, 1983, p. 13; SANE, action memo, April 17, 1981, SANE Papers, Series G, Box 27, SCPC. "The MX Missile Is in Big Trouble, But It's Not Dead Yet!" SANE, action memo, May 7, 1980; SANE, action memo, April 2, 1980, SANE Papers, Series G, Box 27, SCPC; Harry Kreisler, "Legislating for the People: Conversation with Ronald V. Dellums," February 10, 2000, http://globetrotter.berkeley.edu/people/Dellums/dellums-con0.html.

11. The Dellums amendment was defeated by a margin of 55 yes, 348 no, 31 not voting. The CBC budget was also defeated: 86 yes, 322 no, and 24 not voting. "Support the

Congressional Black Caucus Budget Alternative," Marable, "Politics of the Arms Race," p. 13; SANE, action memo, April 17, 1981, SANE Papers, Series G, Box 27, SCPC. "The MX Missile Is in Big Trouble, But It's Not Dead Yet!" SANE, action memo, May 7, 1980; SANE, action memo, April 2, 1980, SANE Papers, Series G, Box 27, SCPC; Wittner, *Toward Nuclear Abolition*, 322.

12. Marable, "Politics of the Arms Race," p. 13.

13. Wittner, *Toward Nuclear Abolition*, 322–25.

14. Wittner, *Toward Nuclear Abolition*, 185.

15. "Jesse Jackson: Study War No More," presidential campaign brochure, 1984; Jesse Jackson for President Committee: New Direction Platform of the Jesse Jackson Campaign for President, 1984, SANE Papers, Series G, Box 77, SCPC.

16. Dr. John Somerville, "Democratic Convention Put No-First-Use on National Map," July 23, 1984, National Campaign for No-First-Use of Nuclear Weapons Papers, CDGA Collective Box, SCPC.

17. Among those who actively supported Jackson were the Reverend William Sloane Coffin (Riverside Church), Richard Deats (executive secretary, FOR), Howard Morland (disarmament coordinator, Coalition for a New Foreign and Military Policy), the Reverend John Collins (codirector, Clergy and Laity Concerned), Molly Rush (Ploughshares), Marjorie Tulte (director, Citizen Action, Church of Women United), the Reverend William Howard (former president, National Council of Churches), Dr. Jonathan King (Jobs with Peace National Network), David Dellinger (Mobilization for Survival), Norma Becker (WRL), Jennifer Davis (executive director, American Committee on Africa), Margaret Scott Olmstead (founding director, WILPF), Bishop Antonio Ramos (Inter-religious Task Force on Central America), the Reverend Robert Moore (executive director, Coalition for Nuclear Disarmament), Connie Hogarth (executive board, SANE). "Jesse Jackson: Study War No More," presidential campaign brochure, 1984, SANE Papers, Series G, Box 77, SCPC.

18. Jesse Jackson to Rainbow Coalition supporters, December 13–14, 1985, SANE Papers, Series G, Box 77, SCPC.

19. Henry, "Toward a Multiracial Democracy," 16–23.

20. Micah Zenko, "The 2012 Nuclear Security Summit: Obama's Work in Progress," *Council on Foreign Relations*, March 27, 2012, http://blogs.cfr.org/zenko/2012/03/27/the-2012-nuclear-security-summit-obamas-work-in-progress/.

21. Anne E. Kornblut, "Clinton Demurs on Obama's Nuclear Stance," *Washington Post*, August 3, 2007, http://www.washingtonpost.com/wp-dyn/content/article/2007/08/02/AR2007080202288.html; "Obama: Use of Nuclear Weapons 'Not on the Table,'" August 2, 2007, http://www.msnbc.com/ msn.com/id/20093852/.

22. Jeff Zeleny, "Obama to Urge Elimination of Nuclear Weapons," *New York Times*, October 2, 2007, http://www.nytimes.com/2007/10/02/us/politics/02obama.html.

23. Alexander Mooney, "Obama Says Time to Rid World of Nuclear Weapons," *CNN.com*, July 16, 2008, http://www.cnn.com/2008/POLITICS/07/16/obama.speech/.

24. Cirincione served as a nonproliferation advisor to the Obama campaign. Chris Schneidmiller, "Obama Moving on Nuclear Arms Control Pledges, Expert Says," *Global*

Security Newswire, February 17, 2009, http://www.nti.org/gsn/article/obama-moving-on
-nuclear-arms-control-pledges-expert-says/.

25. "Two Nuclear Appointments," *Tri-Valley CAREs Citizen's Watch*, January 2009,
pp. 1–2.

26. "Two Nuclear Appointments," *Tri-Valley CAREs Citizen's Watch*, January 2009,
pp. 1–2.; Mark Thompson, "Obama's Nuclear War," *Time*, January 26, 2009, http://www
.time.com/time/nation/article/0,8599,187 3887,00.html.

27. Barack Obama, "Inaugural Address," January 20, 2009, reprinted in *Washington
Post*, January 21, 2009, p. A22.

28. Thompson, "Obama's Nuclear War"; Suzzanne Bohan, "Obama Kills Controversial
Nuclear Program in Budget Proposal," *Contra Costa Times*, March 5, 2009, http://www.
contracostatimes.com/fdcp?123739 6983362.

29. Tim Reid, "President Obama Seeks Russia Deal to Slash Nuclear Weapons," *The
Times*, February 4, 2009, http://www.timesonline.co.uk/tol/news/world/us_and_americas/
article5654836.ece.

30. Schneidmiller, "Obama Moving on Nuclear Arms Control Pledges, Expert Says."

31. Richard Wolffe, *Revival: The Struggle for Survival Inside the Obama White House*
(New York: Crown, 2010), 212.

32. "Obama Prague Speech on Nuclear Weapons, Full Text," *Huffington Post*, May 6, 2009,
http://www.huffingtonpost.com/2009/04/05/obama-prague-speech-on-nu_n_183219.html.

33. "Obama Prague Speech on Nuclear Weapons, Full Text."

34. Daryl G. Kimball, "Arms Control Association Praises Obama's Commitment to a
Nuclear Weapons Free World," *Arms Control Association*, April 5, 2009, http://www.arms
control.org/pressroom/ObamaPragueSpeech.

35. Kimball, "Arms Control Association Praises Obama's Commitment to a Nuclear
Weapons Free World."

36. Wolffe, *Revival*, 38.

37. Wolffe, *Revival*, 40–45.

38. Melissa Harris-Perry, "Barack Obama and Martin Luther King, Jr.," *The Nation*,
January 18, 2010, http://www.alternet/org/story/145237/; Michael Eric Dyson, "On Dr. King,
Jesse Jackson, Al Sharpton, and Barack Obama," *Big Think*, http://www.bigthink.com/
ideas/862; http://www.youtube.com/watch?v=-pkkdjngBuo.

39. Wittner, *Toward Nuclear Abolition*, 481; David E. Sanger and Peter Baker, "Obama
Limits When U.S. Would Use Nuclear Arms," *New York Times*, April 5, 2010, http://www
.nytimes.com/2010/04/06/world/06arms.html?pagewanted=all.

40. Nuclear Posture Review Report, Department of Defense, April 2010, http://www
.defense.gov/npr/docs/2010%20Nuclear%20Posture%20Review%20Report.pdf.

41. Peter D. Feaver, Obama's Nuclear Modesty, *New York Times*, April 9, 2010, http://www
.nytimes.com/2010/04/09/opinion/09feaver.html?pagewanted=all; Scott Sagan, "After the
Nuclear Posture Review: Obama's Disarming Influence," *Bulletin of Atomic Scientists*, April
19, 2011, http://www.thebulletin.org/print/web-edition/features/after-the-nuclear-posture
-review-obamas-disarming-influence.

42. Feaver, "Obama's Nuclear Modesty"; Sagan, "After the Nuclear Posture Review."

43. Joseph Cirincione, "Some Nuclear Sunshine," *Yes!*, May 4, 2010, http://www.yesmagazine.org/peace-justice/some-nuclear-sunshine.

44. Sagan, "After the Nuclear Posture Review."

45. Joseph Cirincione, "Will Obama End the Nuclear Era?" *Daily Beast*, April 12, 2010, http://www.thedailybeast.com/articles/2010/04/12/will-obama-end-the-nuclear-era.html.

46. Cirincione, "Will Obama End the Nuclear Era?"; Alexandra Brell, "Obama's Vision Has Turned into Concrete Victories," *The Hill*, April 15, 2010, http://thehill.com/blogs/congress-blog/politics/92407-obamas-vision-has-turned-into-concrete-victories; Mary Beth Sheridan, "Obama Secures 47-Nation Pact at Nuclear Summit," *Washington Post*, April 14, 2010, http://www.washingtonpost.com/wp-dyn/content/article/2010/04/13/AR2010041300427.html; Darlene Superville, "US Helped Czech Republic Remove Nuclear Material," *Seattle Times*, April 5, 2013, http://seattletimes.com/html/politics/2020716628_apususnuclearsecurity.html; "Myanmar Says It's Ready to Sign Nuclear Agreement," *CBS News*, November 21, 2012, http://www.cbsnews.com/8301-505245_162-57553105/myanmar-says-its-ready-to-sign-nuclear-agreement/; Kelsey Davenport, "Myanmar Signs Agreement with IAEA," *Arms Control Today* (October 2013), http://www.armscontrol.org/act/2013_10/Myanmar-Signs-Agreement-With-IAEA; Jeff Mason and Fredrik Dahl, "U.S. to Help in 'Elimination' of Sensitive Japanese Nuclear Stockpile," *Reuters*, March 24, 2014, http://www.reuters.com/article/2014/03/24/us-nuclear-usa-japan-idUSBREA2N0IK20140324.

47. Sheridan, "Obama Secures 47-Nation Pact at Nuclear Summit."

48. Charles J. Hanley, "Analysis: Nuclear Summit Signals New Mindset," *Associated Press*, April 14, 2010, http://www.wlfi.com/dpps/news/national/south/analysis-nuclear-summit-signals-new-mindset-jgr_3314263.

49. Steve Clemons, "Obama's Nuclear Wizardry and the Iran Factor," *Politico*, April 13, 2010, http://www.politico.com/news/stories/0410/35691.html.

50. Cirincione, "Will Obama End the Nuclear Era?"

51. David Ignatius, "Obama's Policy Process More Orderly than Bush's," *Washington Post*, April 14, 2010, http://azstarnet.com/news/opinion/article_f3394656-494d-5de9-86c4-f4e619d31694.html.

52. Wolffe, *Revival*, 256–57.

53. Wolffe, *Revival*, 258–60.

54. As director of research for American University's Nuclear Studies, I travel annually to Hiroshima and Nagasaki. On August 6, 2010, in Hiroshima, I was given a stack of thank-you letters from Japanese citizens to deliver to President Obama.

55. Thank-you letters from Japanese citizens to President Obama.

56. Noritaka Egusa, "Nuclear Weapons Can Be Eliminated: Hiroshima, Nagasaki Mayors Call for Obama's 'World Without Nuclear Weapons,'" *Hiroshima Peace Media Center*, May 8, 2009, http://www.hiroshimapeacemedia.jp/mediacenter/article.php?story=20090507132132807_en. On June 24, 1982, at the second UN Special Session on Disarmament, then Hiroshima mayor Takeshi Araki proposed a new program to promote the solidarity of cities toward

eliminating nuclear weapons. As mayors around the world supported Araki's proposal, they formed Mayors for Peace. As of July 2012, Mayors for Peace has 5,296 cities in 153 countries and regions. http://www.mayorsforpeace.org.

57. Justin McCurry, "John Roos Is First US Representative to Attend Hiroshima Memorial Ceremony in Japan," *The Guardian*, August 6, 2010, http://www.guardian.co .uk/world/2010/aug/06/john-roos-us-attends-hiroshima-japan; Martin Fackler, "At Hiroshima Ceremony, a First for a U.S. Envoy," *New York Times*, August 6, 2010, http://www .nytimes.com/2010/08/07/world/asia/07japan.html; Joshua Rhett Miller, "Son of Pilot Who Dropped A-Bomb Opposes Plan to Send U.S. Delegation to Hiroshima Ceremony," *FoxNews.com*, August 4, 2010, http://www.foxnews.com/politics/2010/08/04/tibbets-son -disapproves-plan-send-delegation-hiroshima-ceremony/.

58. "U.S. Conducts 1st Subcritical Nuclear Test Under Obama," *Kyodo News*, October 13, 2010, http://mdn.mainichi.jp/mdnnews/news/20101013p2g00m0dm072000c.html.

59. "Japan Alarmed at U.S. Subcritical Test," Asahi Shimbun, October 10, 2015, http:// www.asahi.com/english/TKY201010140308.htm; "U.S. Conducts 1st Subcritical Nuclear Test Under Obama"; Yumi Kanazaki, "U.S. Responds to Letter of Protest from Hiroshima Against Subcritical Nuclear Test," *Hiroshima Peace Media Center*, January 14, 2011, http:// www.hiroshimapeacemedia.jp/mediacenter/article.php?story=2011011411095432_en.

60. "Nagasaki, Hiroshima Criticize U.S. for Subcritical Nuclear Test," *Kyodo News*, October 13, 2010, http://www.japantoday.com/category/national/view/nagasaki-hiroshima -criticize-us-for-subcritical-nuclear-test.

61. "Hiroshima Mayor Hits U.S. Subcritical Nuke Test," *Kyodo News*, October 14, 2010, http://search.japantimes.co.jp/printnn20101014a3.html.

62. "Japan Alarmed at U.S. Subcritical Test."

63. Robert Draper, *Do Not Ask What Good Can Do: Inside the U.S. House of Representatives* (New York: Free Press, 2012), xv–xix.

64. Chris Frates, "McConnell Tells the Alley How He'd Run the Senate Next Year," *National Journal*, July 9, 2012, http://influencealley.nationaljournal.com/2012/07/mcconnell -tells-the-alley-how.php.

65. Carol E. Lee and Glenn Thrush, "Barack Obama Vows to Work with GOP After 'Shellacking,'" *Politico*, November 3, 2010, http://www.politico.com/news/stories/1110/44657.html.

66. David E. Sanger, "Obama Nuclear Agenda Only Gets Harder After Treaty," *New York Times*, December 21, 2010, http://www.nytimes.com/2010/12/22/us/politics/22assess .html.

67. Peter Baker, "Obama's Gamble on Arms Pact Pays Off," *New York Times*, December 22, 2010, http://www.nytimes.com/2010/12/23/world/23start.html?_r=1&pagewanted=all; Mikhail Gorbachev, "The Senate's Next Task: Ratifying the Nuclear Test Ban Treaty, *New York Times*, December 28, 2010, http://www.nytimes.com/2010/12/29/opinion/29gorbachev .html; Sanger, "Obama Nuclear Agenda Only Gets Harder After Treaty."

68. Baker, "Obama's Gamble on Arms Pact Pays Off."

69. Baker, "Obama's Gamble on Arms Pact Pays Off"; Sanger, "Obama Nuclear Agenda Only Gets Harder After Treaty."

70. Yumi Kanazaki, "Hiroshima Responds to U.S. Ratification of New START Treaty," *Hiroshima Peace Media Center*, December 24, 2010, http://www.hiroshimapeacemedia.jp/mediacenter/article.php?story=20101224141458104_en.

71. M. J. Lee, "U.S. Defuses Biggest Nuke," *Politico*, October 25, 2011, http://dyn.politico.com/printstory.cfm?uuid=DD9DA181-ABC9-4DD1-81E0-C2F773F781EC.

72. Daryl G. Kimball, "Obama's Prague Agenda Two Years On," *Arms Control Now*, April 4, 2011, http://armscontrolnow.org/2011/04/04/obamas-prague-agenda-two-years-on/.

73. Sagan, "After the Nuclear Posture Review: Obama's Disarming Influence."

74. "The Nuclear 'Implementation Study,'" *New York Times*, March 11, 2012, http://www.nytimes.com/2012/03/12/opinion/the-nuclear-implementation-study.html.

75. "Nuclear 'Implementation Study'"; "The Bloated Nuclear Weapons Budget," *New York Times*, October 10, 2011, http://www.nytimes.com/2011/10/30/opinion/sunday/the-bloated-nuclear-weapons-budget.html.

76. "Possible Nuclear Weapons Cuts Worry Republican Lawmakers," *iWatch News*, March 5, 2012, http://www.iwatchnews.org/2012/03/05/8313/possible-nuclear-weapons-cuts-worry-republican-lawmakers; "AP Sources: Obama Edges Toward Decision on Plan That Could Mean Large New Cuts in Nuclear Arms," *Washington Post*, July 3, 2012, http://www.washingtonpost.com/world/national-security/obama-edging-...stantial-new-cuts-in-nuclear-arms/2012/07/03/gJQAD4CwJW_print.html; "Nuclear 'Implementation Study'"; Robert Burns, "US Weighing Steep Nuclear Arms Cuts," *Associated Press*, February 14, 2012, http://www.boston.com/new/nation/washington/articles/2012/02/14/ap_newsbreak_us_weighing_steep_nuclear_arms_cuts/; Adam Weinstein, "Obama May Ditch Most US Nukes," *Mother Jones*, February 17, 2012, http://www.motherjones.com/politics/2012/02/nuclear-weapons-reduction-obama; Schneidmiller, "Obama Moving on Nuclear Arms Control Pledges, Expert Says." Obama announced shortly after taking the oath of office that his plan was to reduce the number of nuclear weapons to one thousand.

77. "Possible Nuclear Weapons Cuts Worry Republican Lawmakers"; Weinstein, "Obama May Ditch Most US Nukes."

78. Zenko, "The 2012 Nuclear Security Summit"; Dan Froomkin, "Barack Obama's Broken Nuclear Promises Undermine Success," *Huffington Post*, March 28, 2012, http://www.huffingtonpost.com/2012/03/27/barack-obama-nuclear-policy_n_1383081.html; Major Garrett, "What Obama's Nuclear Security Summit Means for Iran and North Korea," *Atlantic*, March 2012, http://www.theatlantic.com/international/print/2012/03/what-obamas-nuclear-security-summit-means-for-iran-and-north-korea/255026/; "Obama's Remarks at Hankuk University, South Korea, March 2012," *Council on Foreign Relations*, March 26, 2012, http://www.cfr.org/south-korea/obamas-remarks-hankuk-university-south-korea-march-2012/p27733; Aamar Madhani, "Obama: U.S. and Russia Should Further Reduce Nuke Stockpiles," *USA Today*, March 26, 2012, http://content.usatoday.com/communities/theoval/post/2012/03/obama-us-and-russia-should-further-reduce-nuke-stockpile/1#.T3MX45j-KJU.

79. Jeffrey Goldberg, "Obama to Iran and Israel: 'As President of the United States, I Don't Bluff,'" *Atlantic*, March 2, 2012, http://www.theatlantic.com/international/archive/

2012/03/obama-to-iran-and-israel-as-president-of-the-united-states-i-dont-bluff/253875/; Froomkin, "Barack Obama's Broken Nuclear Promises Undermine Success"; Jo Becker and Scott Shane, "Secret 'Kill List' Proves a Test of Obama's Principles and Will," *New York Times*, May 29, 2012, http://www.nytimes.com/2012/05/29/world/obamas-leader ship-in-war-on-al-quaeda.html; Benjamin Hart, "Jeremy Scahill Says Obama Strikes in Yemen Constitute Murder," *Huffington Post*, June 3, 2012, http://www.huffingtonpost .com/2012/06/02/jeremy-scahill-says-drone-strikes-murders_n_1565441.html; Robert Burns, "Panetta Asks Israel for Patience on Iran," *Associated Press*, August 1, 2012, http://abc-news.go.com/International/wireStory/panetta-us-force-option-iran-nukes-16902791#. UBqA8I7-KJU.

80. Julian Borger, "Obama Accused of Nuclear U-Turn as Guided Weapons Plan Emerges," *The Guardian*, April 21, 2013, http://www.theguardian.com/world/2013/apr/21/ obama-accused-nuclear-guided-weapons-plan; "The GOP Is Wrong to Say Obama Cut Nuclear Weapons Budget," *Washington Post*, August 31, 2012, http://articles.washing tonpost.com/2012-08-31/opinions/35490294_1_nuclear-weapons-nuclear-warheads -and-bombs-nuclear-stockpile; Dana Priest, "The B61 Bomb: A Case Study in Costs and Needs," *Washington Post*, September 16, 2012, http://articles.washingtonpost.com/2012 -09-16/world/35496610_1_b61s-nuclear-weapons-nuclear-strategists; "Throwing Money at Nukes," *New York Times*, May 26, 2013, http://www.nytimes.com/2013/05/27/opinion/ throwing-money-at-nukes.html?_r=0.

81. Dana Priest, "Aging U.S. Nuclear Arsenal Slated for Costly and Long-Delayed Modernization," *Washington Post*, September 15, 2012, http://articles.washingtonpost. com/2012-09-15/world/35497119_1_nuclear-stockpile-nuclear-weapons-nuclear-facilities; Jeff Tollefson, "U.S. Nuclear Warheads Set to Get a Facelift," *Scientific American*, May 7, 2013, http://www.scientificamerican.com/article.cfm?id=us-nuclear-warheads-set-to-get -a-facelift; Joseph Cirincione, "Exploding Budgets," *Time*, October 10, 2012, http://nation .time.com/2012/10/10/exploding-budgets/; David E. Hoffman, "Hey, Big Spender," *Foreign Policy*, October 22, 2012, http://www.foreignpolicy.com/articles/2012/10/22/hey_big _spender#sthash.z7F4FRBy.dpbs; Jon Wolfsthal, "The US Trillion Dollar Nuclear Triad," Center for Nonproliferation Studies, January 7, 2014, http://www.nonproliferation.org/ us-trillion-dollar-nuclear -triad/.

82. Erika Fichelberger and Dana Liebelson, "How Obama Learned to Love the Bomb," *Mother Jones*, April 23, 2013, http://www.motherjones.com/politics/2013/04/obama-bud-get-nuclear-nonproliferation-stockpile%20; R. Jeffrey Smith, "Obama Proposes Shifting Funds from Nuclear Nonproliferation to Nuclear Weapons," *Center for Public Integrity*, April 9, 2013, http://www.publicintegrity.org/2013/04/09/12467/obama-proposes-shifting -funds-nuclear-nonproliferation-nuclear-weapons; "Hiroshima, Nagasaki Warn Obama on Plutonium Tests," *Japan Times*, August 21, 2013, http://www.japantimes.co.jp/news/ 2013/08/21/national/hiroshima-nagasaki-warn-obama-on-plutonium-tests/.

83. Joseph Cirincione, "Susan Rice on Nuclear Weapons," *Huffington Post*, June 5, 2013, http://www.huffingtonpost.com/joe-cirincione/susan-rice-on-nuclear-wea_b_3390019.html.

84. Scott Wilson, "Obama, in Berlin, Calls for U.S., Russia to Cut Nuclear Warheads," *Washington Post,* June 19, 2003, http://articles.washingtonpost.com/2013-06-19/world/40054173 _1_brandenburg-gate-president-obama-berlin-wall; "Obama Echoes JFK Speech—The One on Nukes," *USA Today*, June 21, 2013, http://www.usatoday.com/story/theoval/2013/06/19/ obama-kennedy-berlin-nuclear-weapons-american-university/2437599/; "US Envoy Caroline Kennedy Visits Nagasaki," *Washington Post*, December 9, 2013, http://www.washingtonpost .com/world/asia_pacific/us-envoy-caroline-kennedy-visits-nagasaki/2013/12/09/870b3d14-61 3f-11e3-a7b4-4a75ebc432ab_story.html.

85. Elizabeth Palmer, "Iran Committed to Deal with the U.S., Foreign Minister Says," *CBS News*, December 16, 2013, http://www.cbsnews.com/news/iran-committed-to-deal-with -the-us-foreign-minister-says/; David Ignatius, "Iran Committed to Making a Deal," *Washington Post*, December 16, 2013, http://www.washingtonpost.com/opinions/david-ignatius -iran-committed-to-making-a-deal/2013/12/15/0261a632-65c4-11e3-a0b9-249bbb34602c_ story.html; David Kenner, "The President Who Went Nuclear," *Foreign Policy*, December 1, 2013, http://www.foreignpolicy.com/articles/2013/12/01/obama_nuclear_weapons_middle _east#sthash.undP5at7.dpbs; William Branigin, "Last of Syria's Chemical Weapons Handed Over for Destruction, International Body Says," *Washington Post*, June 23, 2014, http:// www.washingtonpost.com/world/middle_east/agency-last-of-syri...ruction/2014/06/ 23/4eb9a138-fad9-11e3-8176-f2c941cf35f1_story.html.

86. Kenner, "President Who Went Nuclear"; Sandra I. Erwin, "A Test for U.S. Nuclear Weapons: Can They Beat the Sequester?" *National Defense*, November 24, 2013, http:// www.nationaldefensemagazine.org/blog/Lists/Posts/Post.aspx?ID=1347; Benjamin Loehrke, "When the Nuclear Budget Binge Ended," *Ploughshares Fund*, February 14, 2012, http:// ploughshares.org/blog/2012-02-14/when-nuclear-budget-binge-ended; Michael Crowley, "A Unifying Theme for Obama's Foreign Policy," *Time*, September 23, 2013, http://swampland .time.com/2013/09/23/barack-obama-and-the-wmd-threat/; Ryan Grim and Joshua Hersh, "Iran Sanctions Bill from Senators Bob Menendez and Mark Kirk Could Endanger U.S. Negotiations," *Huffington Post*, December 19, 2013, http://www.huffingtonpost.com/2013/12/19/ iran-sanctions-bill_n_4472439.html; Tim Lockette, "Rogers Amendment Pushes Back at Obama's Nuke Cuts," *Anniston Star*, July 23, 2013, http://annistonstar.com/view/full_ story/23198989/article-Rogers-amendment-pushes-back-at-Obama-nuke-cuts; Douglas P. Guarino, "Compromise Bill Limits Restrictions on Nuclear Arms Control Efforts," *National Journal*, December 12, 2013, http://www.nationaljournal.com/global-security-newswire/ compromise-bill-limits-restrictions-on-nuclear-arms-control-efforts-20131212.

87. Ta-Nehisi Paul Coates, "Is Obama Black Enough?" *Time*, February 1, 2007, http:// www.time.com/time/nation/article/0,8599,1584736,00.html; Alex Spillius, "Barack Obama Accused of Not Doing Enough for Black People," *The Telegraph*, December 22, 2009, http:// www.telegraph.co.uk/news/worldnews/barackobama/6868202/Barack-Obama-accused-of -not-doing-enough-for-black-people.html; Maureen O'Donnell, "Panel Criticizes Obama's Handling of Black Agenda," *Chicago Sun Times*, March 21, 2010, http://www.suntimes.com/ news/politics/obama/2114506,CST-NWS-black21.article; "Smiley and Sharpton Spar over

Black Agenda, Obama," *Black America*, February 25, 2010, http://www.blackamericaweb .com/?q=articles/news/moving_america_news/16617/2; Don Terry, "A Delicate Balancing Act for the Black Agenda," *New York Times*, March 18, 2010, http://www.nytimes.com/2010/ 03/19/us/19cncagenda.html?pagewanted=all; Chris Hedges, "The Obama Deception: Why Cornel West Went Ballistic," *TruthDig*, May 16, 2011, http://www.truthdig.com/report/ item/the_obama_deception_why_cornel_west_went_ballistic_20110516/.

88. Anthony Coley, "An Open Letter to Tavis Smiley," *CNN.com*, March 19 2010, http:// articles.cnn.com/2010-03-19/opinion/coley.obama.tavis.smiley_1_african-american- african-americans-accountable?_s=PM:OPINION; Katherine Fung, "Al Sharpton, Me- lissa Harris-Perry Clash with Cornel West," *Huffington Post*, February 8, 2012, http://www .huffingtonpost.com/2012/02/08/al-sharpton-melissa-harris-perry-cornel-west_n_1263522 .html; Zerlina Maxwell, "Al Sharpton Defends Melissa Harris-Perry from Cornel West's 'Arrogant' and 'Disingenuous' Attacks," *The Grio*, February 8, 2012, http://thegrio.com/ 2012/02/08/al-sharpton-defends-melissa-harris-perry-from-cornel-west/;Harris-Perry,"Barack Obama and Martin Luther King, Jr."

89. Malcolm X speaking in Cairo, July 1964, http://www.columbia.edu/cu/ccbh/mxp.

Bibliography

Manuscript Sources

African Americans in the Military Records, Proquest

American Committee on Africa Records, Proquest

American Friends Services Committee Records, Swarthmore College Peace Collection (SCPC)

American Interracial Peace Committee Records, SCPC

American Peace Crusade Records, SCPC

American Women for Peace Records, SCPC

Athletes United for Peace Records, SCPC

Bayard Rustin Papers, Library of Congress (LOC) and Proquest

Bertha McNeill Papers, SCPC

Blacks Against Nukes Records, SCPC

Brotherhood of Sleeping Car Porters Records, Proquest

Chicago Peace Council Records, SCPC

Claude A. Barnett Papers, Proquest

Coalition for a Nuclear Free Harbor Records, SCPC

Coalition for a Nuclear Test Ban Records, SCPC

Coalition for Non-Nuclear World Records, SCPC

Coalition for Nuclear Disarmament Records, SCPC

Committee for a Sane Nuclear Policy Records, SCPC

Committee for Non-Violent Action Records, SCPC

Desmond Tutu Papers, SCPC

Erna Prather Harris Papers, SCPC

Fellowship of Reconciliation (United States) Records, SCPC

Great Peace March Records, SCPC

Hiroshima Peace Center Records, SCPC

Hiroshima Peace Pilgrimage Records, SCPC

Hiroshima Peace Society Records, SCPC

Hiroshima-Nagasaki Commemorations Records, SCPC

Homer A. Jack Papers, SCPC

Illinois Nuclear Weapons Freeze Campaign Records, SCPC

James Haughton Papers, SCRBC
Mary Church Terrell Papers, SCPC
Mary McLeod Bethune Papers, Proquest
National Association for the Advancement of Colored People Records, LOC
National Association of Colored Women's Clubs Records, Proquest
National Association of Atomic Veterans Records, SCPC
National Campaign for No-First-Use of Nuclear Weapons Records, SCPC
National Committee for Radiation Victims Records, SCPC
National Committee on Atomic Information Records, LOC
Nelson Mandela Papers, SCPC
Nuclear Weapons Freeze Campaign Records, SCPC
Peace Information Center Records, SCPC
Performing Artists for Nuclear Disarmament Records, SCPC
Revolutionary Action Movement Papers, Proquest
Riverside Church Disarmament Records, SCPC
Stephen Biko Papers, SCPC
Southern Christian Leadership Conference Records, Proquest
War Resisters League Records, SCPC
Women Strike for Peace Records, SCPC
Women's International League for Peace and Freedom (United States) Records, SCPC

Federal Bureau of Investigation Files

American Friends Service Committee
Black Panther Party
Clergy and Laity Concerned About
    Vietnam
Coretta Scott King
Harry S. Truman
Henry Wallace
John F. Kennedy, Jr.

Malcolm X
Marian Anderson
Martin Luther King, Jr.
NAACP
Paul Robeson Sr.
Pearl Buck
Roy Wilkins
Stokely Carmichael

Newspapers and Periodicals

Amsterdam News
Atlanta Daily World
Augusta Chronicle
Baltimore Afro-American
Bulletin of Atomic Scientists
California Eagle
Chicago Defender
Chicago Globe
Chicago Tribune

The Crisis
Detroit Free Press
Ebony
Essence
Fellowship
Jet
Liberation
Life
Los Angeles Sentinel

Los Angeles Times

National Guardian

New York Herald Tribune

New York Times

Norfolk Journal and Guide

Philadelphia Tribune

Pittsburgh Courier

Revolutionary Worker

San Francisco Chronicle

Time

USA Today

Village Voice

Washington Afro-American

Washington Post

WRL News

Books

Acheson, Dean. *The Korean War*. New York: Norton, 1971.

Alfred, Helen, ed. *Toward a Socialist America: A Symposium of Essays*. New York: Peace Publications, 1958.

Alperovitz, Gar. *Atomic Diplomacy, Hiroshima and Potsdam: The Use of the Atomic Bomb and the American Confrontation with Soviet Power*. New York: Penguin Books, 1965.

———. *The Decision to Use the Atomic Bomb*. New York: Vintage Books, 1995.

Anderson, Carol. *Eyes Off the Prize: The United Nations and the African American Struggle for Human Rights, 1944–1955*. Cambridge: Cambridge University Press, 2003.

Anderson, Jervis. *Bayard Rustin: Troubles I've Seen*. New York: HarperCollins, 1997.

Aptheker, Herbert, ed. *The Correspondence of W.E.B. Du Bois: Volume II Selections, 1944–1963*. Amherst: University of Massachusetts Press, 1978.

———, ed. *Newspaper Columns by W.E.B. Du Bois, Volume 2, 1945–1961*. White Plains: Kraus-Thomson, 1986.

———, ed. *Pamphlets and Leaflets by W.E.B. Du Bois*. White Plains: Kraus-Thomson, 1986.

———, ed. *Writings by W.E.B. Du Bois in Non-Periodical Literature Edited by Others*. Millwood: Kraus-Thomson, 1982.

Asada, Sadao. "The Mushroom Cloud and National Psyches: Japanese and American Perceptions of the Atomic-Bomb Decision, 1945–1995," in *Living with the Bomb: American and Japanese Cultural Conflicts in the Nuclear Age*, ed. Laura Hein and Mark Selden. New York: Sharpe, 1997.

Ayres, Alex, ed. *The Wisdom of Martin Luther King, Jr.* New York: Meridian, 1993.

Balaji, Murali. *Professor and the Pupil: The Politics and Friendship of W.E.B. Du Bois and Paul Robeson*. New York: Nation Books, 2007.

Baldwin, James. *The Fire Next Time*. New York: Vintage Books, 1962.

Bennett, Scott H. *Radical Pacifism: The War Resisters League and Gandhian Nonviolence in America, 1915–1963*. Syracuse: Syracuse University Press, 2003.

Bidwai, Praful. *New Nukes: India, Pakistan and Global Nuclear Disarmament*. New York: Olive Branch Press, 2000.

Bird, Kai, and Lawrence Lifschultz. *Hiroshima's Shadow: Writings on the Denial of History and the Smithsonian Controversy*. Stony Creek: Pamphleteer's Press, 1998.

Bird, Kai, and Martin J. Sherwin. *American Prometheus: The Triumph and Tragedy of J. Robert Oppenheimer*. New York: Vintage Books, 2005.

Blackwell, Joyce. *No Peace Without Freedom: Race and the Women's International League for Peace and Freedom, 1915–1975*. Carbondale: Southern Illinois University Press, 2004.

Blum, John Morton. *V Was for Victory: Politics and American Culture During World War II*. New York: Harcourt Brace Jovanovich, 1976.

Borstelmann, Thomas. *The Cold War and the Color Line: American Race Relations in the Global Arena*. Cambridge: Harvard University Press, 2001.

Boulton, David, ed. *Voices from the Crowd: Against the H-Bomb*. Philadelphia: Dufour Editions, 1964.

Boyd, Herb, ed. *Race and Resistance: African Americans in the 21st Century*. Cambridge: South End Press, 2002.

Boyer, Paul. *By the Bomb's Early Light: American Thought and Culture at the Dawn of the Atomic Age*. New York: Pantheon Books, 1985.

———. *Fallout: A Historian Reflects on America's Half-Century Encounter with Nuclear Weapons*. Columbus: Ohio State University Press, 1998.

Branch, Taylor. *Pillar of Fire: America in the King Years 1963–65*. New York: Simon & Schuster, 1998.

Broderick, Francis L. *W.E.B. Du Bois: Negro Leader in a Time of Crisis*. Stanford: Stanford University Press, 1959.

Brooks, Charlotte. "In the Twilight Zone Between Black and White: Japanese American Resettlement and Community in Chicago, 1942–1945," in *Blacks and Asians: Crossings, Conflict, and Commonality*, ed. Hazel M. McFerson. Durham: Carolina Academic Press, 2006.

Brooks, Jennifer E. *Defining the Peace: World War II Veterans, Race, and the Remaking of Southern Political Tradition*. Chapel Hill: University of North Carolina Press, 2004.

Burner, David. *Making Peace with the 60s*. Princeton: Princeton University Press, 1996.

Carson, Clayborne, ed. *The Papers of Martin Luther King, Jr. Volume IV: Symbol of the Movement January 1957–December 1958*. Berkeley: Uvniversity of California Press, 2000.

———, ed. *The Papers of Martin Luther King, Jr. Volume V: Threshold of a New Decade January 1959–December 1960*. Berkeley: University of California Press, 2005.

Carter, April. "The Sahara Protest Team," in *Liberation Without Violence: A Third Party Approach*, ed. A. Paul Hare and Herbert H. Blumberg. Totowa: Rowman & Littlefield, 1977.

Castledine, Jacqueline. *Cold War Progressives: Women's Interracial Organizing for Peace and Freedom*. Urbana: University of Illinois Press, 2012.

———. "Quieting the Chorus: Progressive Women's Race and Peace Politics in Post War New York," in *Anticommunism and the African American Freedom Movement*, ed. Robbie Lieberman and Clarence Lang. New York: Palgrave Macmillan, 2009.

Chase, James. *Acheson: The Secretary of State Who Created the American World*. New York: Simon & Schuster, 1998.

Clarke, John Henrik, ed. *Marcus Garvey and the Vision of Africa*. New York: Vintage Books, 1974.

Cleaver, Kathleen, and George Katsiaficas, eds. *Liberation, Imagination, and the Black Panther Party*. New York: Routledge, 2001.

Crane, Conrad C. *American Airpower Strategy in Korea 1950–1953*. Lawrence: University of Kansas Press, 2000.

Cruse, Harold. *The Crisis of the Negro Intellectual*. New York: Morrow, 1967.

Daizaburo, Yui. "Between Pearl Harbor and Hiroshima/Nagasaki: Nationalism and Memory in Japan and the United States," in *Living with the Bomb: American and Japanese Cultural Conflicts in the Nuclear Age*, ed. Laura Hein and Mark Selden. New York: Sharpe, 1997.

Daughtry, Herbert D., Sr. *No Monopoly on Suffering: Blacks and Jews in Crown Heights (and Elsewhere)*. Trenton: Africa World Press, 1997.

DeBenedetti, Charles. *An American Ordeal: The Antiwar Movement of the Vietnam Era*. Syracuse: Syracuse University Press, 1990.

D'Emilio, John. *Lost Prophet: The Life and Times of Bayard Rustin*. New York: Free Press, 2003.

Dittmer, John. *Local People: The Struggles for Civil Rights in Mississippi*. Urbana: University of Illinois, 1995.

Douglass, James W. *JFK and the Unspeakable: Why He Died and Why It Matters*. New York: Touchstone, 2008.

Dower, John W. *Cultures of War*. New York: Norton, 2010.

———. *Embracing Defeat: Japan in the Wake of World War II*. New York: Norton, 1999.

———. "Triumphal and Tragic Narratives of the War in Asia," in *Living with the Bomb: American and Japanese Cultural Conflicts in the Nuclear Age*, ed. Laura Hein and Mark Selden. New York: Sharpe, 1997.

———. *War Without Mercy: Race and Power in the Pacific War*. New York: Pantheon Books, 1986.

Draper, Robert. *Do Not Ask What Good Can Do: Inside the U.S. House of Representatives*. New York: Free Press, 2012.

Du Bois, W.E.B. *The Autobiography of W.E.B. Du Bois: A Soliloquy on Viewing My Life from the Last Decade of Its First Century*. New York: International Publishers, 1968.

———. *In Battle for Peace*. Millwood: Kraus-Thomson, 1976.

———. "The Negro and Socialism," in *Toward a Socialist America: A Symposium of Essays*, ed. Helen Alfred. New York: Peace Publications, 1958.

Duberman, Martin Bauml. *Paul Robeson*. New York: Knopf, 1988.

Dudziak, Mary L. *Cold War, Civil Rights: Race and the Image of American Democracy*. Princeton: Princeton University Press, 2000.

Dumbrell, John. *The Carter Presidency: A Re-Evaluation*. Manchester: Manchester University Press, 1993.

Dyson, Michael Eric. *I May Not Get There with You: The True Martin Luther King, Jr.* New York: Free Press, 2000.

Farber, David, ed. *The Sixties: From Memory to History*. Chapel Hill: University of North Carolina Press, 1994.

Foner, Philip S., ed. *Paul Robeson Speaks: Writings, Speeches, and Interviews, 1918–1974*. New York: Brunner/Mazel, 1978.

———, ed. *W.E.B. Du Bois Speaks: Speeches and Addresses 1920–1963*. New York: Pathfinder Press, 1970.

Foster, Catherine. *Women for All Seasons: The Story of the Women's International League for Peace and Freedom*. Athens: University of Georgia Press, 1989.

Fradkin, Philip L. *Fallout: An American Nuclear Tragedy*. Tucson: University of Arizona Press, 1989.

Franklin, John Hope, and Alfred A. Moss Jr. *From Slavery to Freedom: A History of African Americans*. New York: McGraw-Hill, 1994.

Fried, Richard M. *Nightmare in Red: The McCarthy Era in Perspective*. New York: Oxford University Press, 1990.

Fujino, Diane C. *Heartbeat of Struggle: The Revolutionary Life of Yuri Kochiyama*. Minneapolis: University of Minnesota Press, 2005.

Gaines, Kevin K. *American Africans in Ghana: Black Expatriates and the Civil Rights Era*. Chapel Hill: University of North Carolina Press, 2006.

Gallicchio, Marc. *The African American Encounter with Japan and China: Black Internationalism in Asia, 1895–1945*. Chapel Hill: University of North Carolina Press, 2000.

Garrow, David J. *Bearing the Cross: Martin Luther King, Jr., and the Southern Christian Leadership Conference*. New York: HarperCollins, 1986.

Gerson, Joseph. *Empire and the Bomb: How the US Uses Nuclear Weapons to Dominate the World*. London: Pluto Press, 2007.

Gilmore, Glenda. *Defying Dixie: The Radical Roots of Civil Rights, 1919–1950*. New York: Norton, 2008.

Gitlin, Todd. *The Sixties: Years of Hope, Days of Rage*. New York: Bantam Books, 1987.

Gore, Dayo F. *Radicalism at the Crossroads: African American Women Activists in the Cold War*. New York: New York University Press, 2011.

Green, Michael Cullen. *Black Yanks in the Pacific: Race in the Making of American Military Empire After World War II*. Ithaca: Cornell University Press, 2010.

Hall, Simon. *Peace and Freedom: The Civil Rights Movement and Antiwar Movements in the 1960s*. Philadelphia: University of Pennsylvania Press, 2005.

Hansberry, Lorraine. *To Be Young, Gifted, and Black: Lorraine Hansberry in Her Own Words*. Englewood Cliffs: Prentice-Hall, 1969.

Hare, Paul, and Herbert H. Blumberg, eds. *Liberation Without Violence: A Third Party Approach*. Totowa: Rowman & Littlefield, 1977.

Harris, Joseph E. *African-American Reactions to War in Ethiopia, 1936–1941*. Baton Rouge: Louisiana State University Press, 1994.

Harris, William J., ed. *The LeRoi Jones/Amiri Baraka Reader*. New York: Thunder's Mouth Press, 1999.

Hasegawa, Tsuyoshi. *Racing the Enemy: Stalin, Truman, and the Surrender of Japan*. Cambridge: Harvard University Press, 2005.

Hastings, Max. *The Korean War*. New York: Simon & Schuster, 1987.

Height, Dorothy. *Open Wide the Freedom Gates: A Memoir*. New York: Public Affairs, 2003.

Hein, Laura, and Mark Selden, ed. *Living with the Bomb: American and Japanese Cultural Conflicts in the Nuclear Age*. New York: Sharpe, 1997.

Hendershot, Cyndy. *Paranoia, the Bomb, and 1950s Science Fiction Films*. Bowling Green: Bowling Green University Press, 1999.

Henry, Charles P., ed. *Ralph J. Bunche: Selected Speeches and Writings*. Ann Arbor: University of Michigan Press, 1995.

———. "Toward a Multiracial Democracy: The Jackson and Obama Contributions," in *The Obama Phenomenon: Toward a Multiracial Democracy*, ed. Charles P. Henry, Robert L. Allen, and Robert Chrisman. Urbana: University of Illinois Press, 2011.

Henry, Charles P., Robert L. Allen, and Robert Chrisman, eds. *The Obama Phenomenon: Toward a Multiracial Democracy*. Urbana: University of Illinois Press, 2011.

Hersey, John. *Hiroshima*. New York: Bantam Books, 1946.

Hillard, David. *Huey: Spirit of the Panther*. New York: Thunder's Mouth Press, 2006.

Hirsch, Susan E., and Lewis A. Erenberg, eds. *The War in American Culture: Society and Consciousness During World War II*. Chicago: University of Chicago Press, 1996.

Honey, Maureen, ed. *Bitter Fruit: African American Women in World War II*. Columbia: University of Missouri Press, 1999.

Horne, Gerald. *Black and Red: W.E.B. Du Bois and the Afro-American Response to the Cold War, 1944–1963*. Albany: State University of New York Press, 1986.

———. *Black Liberation/Red Scare: Ben Davis and the Communist Party*. Newark: University of Delaware Press, 1994.

———. *Communist Front? The Civil Rights Congress, 1946–1956*. London: Associated University Presses, 1988.

———. *Race Woman: The Lives of Shirley Graham Du Bois*. New York: New York University Press, 2000.

Isaacs, Harold R. *The New World of Negro Americans*. New York: Viking Press, 1963.

Jackson, Thomas F. *From Civil Rights to Human Rights: Martin Luther King, Jr., and the Struggle for Economic Justice*. Philadelphia: University of Pennsylvania Press, 2007.

Jones, Bartlett C. *Flawed Triumphs: Andy Young at the United Nations*. Lanham: University Press of America, 1996.

Jones, Charles E., ed. *The Black Panther Party Reconsidered*. Baltimore: Black Classic Press, 1998.

Jones, Charles E., and Michael L. Clemons. "Global Solidarity: The Black Panther Party in the International Arena," in *Liberation, Imagination, and the Black Panther Party*, ed. Kathleen Cleaver and George Katsiaficas. New York: Routledge, 2001.

Juguo, Zhang. *W.E.B. Du Bois: The Quest for the Abolition of the Color Line*. New York: Routledge, 2001.

Kaplan, Carla, ed. *Zora Neale Hurston: A Life in Letters*. New York: Doubleday, 2002.

Karabell, Zachary. *The Last Campaign: How Harry Truman Won the 1948 Election*. New York: Vintage Books, 2000.

Katz, Milton S. *Ban the Bomb: A History of Sane, the Committee for a Sane Nuclear Policy, 1957–1985*. New York: Greenwood Press, 1986.

Kearney, Reginald. *African American Views of the Japanese: Solidarity or Sedition?* Albany: State University of New York Press, 1998.

Kelley, Robin D.G. *Hammer and Hoe: Alabama Communists During the Great Depression*. Chapel Hill: University of North Carolina Press, 1990.

Kelley, Robin D.G., and Sidney J. Lemelle, eds. *Imagining Home: Class, Culture, and Nationalism in the African Diaspora*. New York: Verso, 1994.

King, Martin Luther, Jr. *Strength to Love*. Philadelphia: Fortress Press, 1963.

———. *Where Do We Go from Here: Chaos or Community?* New York: Harper & Row, 1967.

King, Mel. *Chain of Change: Struggles for Black Community Development*. Boston: South End Press, 1981.

Klehr, Harvey. *Heyday in American Communism*. New York: Basic Books, 1984.

Kochiyama, Yuri. *Passing It On*. Los Angeles: UCLA Asian American Studies Center Press, 2004.

Kozol, Jonathan. *Savage Inequalities: Children in America's Schools*. New York: Harper Perennial, 1991.

Kurashige, Scott. *The Shifting Grounds of Race: Black and Japanese Americans in the Making of Multiethnic Los Angeles*. Princeton: Princeton University Press, 2008.

Levinsohn, Florence Hamlish. *Harold Washington: A Political Biography*. Chicago: Chicago Review Press, 1983.

Lewis, David Levering. *King: A Critical Biography*. New York: Praeger, 1970.

———. *W.E.B. Du Bois: The Fight for Equality and the American Century, 1919–1963*. New York: Holt, 2000.

Lieberman, Robbie. "'Another Side of the Story': African American Intellectuals Speak Out for Peace and Freedom During the Early Cold War Years," in *Anticommunism and the African American Freedom Movement*, ed. Robbie Lieberman and Clarence Lang. New York: Palgrave Macmillan, 2009.

———. *The Strangest Dream: Communism, Anticommunism, and the U.S. Peace Movement, 1945–1963*. Syracuse: Syracuse University Press, 2000.

Lieberman, Robbie, and Clarence Lang, eds. *Anticommunism and the African American Freedom Movement*. New York: Palgrave Macmillan, 2009.

Lifton, Robert Jay, and Greg Mitchell. *Hiroshima in America: Fifty Years of Denial*. New York: Putnam's, 1995.

Lokos, Lionel. *House Divided: The Life and Legacy of Martin Luther King*. New Rochelle: Arlington House, 1968.

Lynn, Susan. *Progressive Women in Conservative Times: Racial Justice, Peace, and Feminism, 1945–1960s.* New Brunswick: Rutgers University Press, 1992.

Marable, Manning. *Black Liberation in Conservative America.* Boston: South End Press, 1997.

———. *How Capitalism Underdeveloped Black America.* Cambridge: South End Press, 2000.

———. *Living Black History: How Reimagining the African-American Past Can Remake America's Racial Future.* New York: Basic Civitas Books, 2006.

———. *Malcolm X: A Life of Reinvention.* New York: Viking Press, 2011.

———. *Race, Reform, and Rebellion: The Second Reconstruction in America, 1945–1982.* Jackson: University Press of Mississippi, 1984.

———. *W.E.B. Du Bois: Black Radical Democrat.* Boston: Twayne, 1986.

Marable, Manning, and Myrlie Evers-Williams, eds. *The Autobiography of Medgar Evers: A Hero's Life and Legacy Revealed Through His Writings, Letters, and Speeches.* New York: Basic Civitas Books, 2005.

Markle, Gerald E., and Frances B. McCrea. *Minutes to Midnight: Nuclear Weapons Protest in America.* Newbury Park: Sage, 1989.

McCluskey, Audrey Thomas, and Elaine M. Smith, eds. *Mary McLeod Bethune: Building a Better World, Essays and Selected Documents.* Bloomington: Indiana University Press, 1999.

McFerson, Hazel M. *Blacks and Asians: Crossings, Conflict, and Commonality.* Durham: Carolina Academic Press, 2006.

McGuire, Phillip. *Taps for a Jim Crow Army: Letters from Black Soldiers in World War II.* Santa Barbara: ABC-Clio, 1983.

McKnight, Gerald D. *The Last Crusade: Martin Luther King, Jr., the FBI, and the Poor People's Campaign.* Boulder: Westview Press, 1998.

McMillen, Neil R., ed. *Remaking Dixie: The Impact of World War II on the American South.* Jackson: University Press of Mississippi, 1997.

Meier, August, and Elliot Rudwick. *CORE: A Study in the Civil Rights Movement, 1942–1968.* Urbana: University of Illinois Press, 1975.

Meriwether, James H. *Proudly We Can Be Africans: Black Americans and Africa, 1935–1961.* Chapel Hill: University of North Carolina, 2002.

Miller, Merle. *Plain Speaking: An Oral Biography of Harry S. Truman.* Berkeley: Berkeley Medallion, 1974.

Miller, Richard E. *The Messman Chronicles: African Americans in the U.S. Navy, 1932–1943.* Annapolis: Naval Institute Press, 2004.

Miller, Richard L. *Under the Cloud: The Decades of Nuclear Testing.* New York: Free Press, 1986.

Milne, June, ed. *Kwame Nkrumah, The Conakry Years: His Life and Letters.* London: Panaf, 1990.

Moore, Christopher Paul. *Fighting for America: Black Soldiers—The Unsung Heroes of World War II.* New York: Ballantine Books, 2005.

Morehouse, Maggi M. *Fighting in the Jim Crow Army: Black Men and Women Remembering World War II.* Lanham: Rowman & Littlefield, 2000.

Morris, Aldon D. *The Origins of the Civil Rights Movement: Black Communities Organizing for Change.* New York: Free Press, 1984.

Morrison, Toni, ed. *To Die for the People: The Writings of Huey P. Newton.* New York: Writers and Readers Publishing, 1995.

Mullen, Bill V. *Popular Fronts: Chicago and African-American Cultural Politics, 1935–1946.* Urbana: University of Illinois Press, 1999.

Mullen, Bill V., and James Smethurst, eds. *Left of the Color Line: Race, Radicalism, and Twentieth-Century Literature in the United States.* Chapel Hill: University of North Carolina Press, 2003.

Naeve, Virginia, ed. *Friends of the Hibakusha.* Denver: Alan Swallow, 1964.

Naison, Mark. *Communists in Harlem During the Great Depression.* Urbana: University of Illinois Press, 1983.

Nunez, Ralph da Costa. *A Shelter Is Not a Home...or Is It? Lessons from Family Homelessness in New York City.* New York: White Tiger Press, 2004.

Obama, Barack. *The Audacity of Hope: Thoughts on Reclaiming the American Dream.* New York: Crown, 2006.

———. *Dreams of My Father.* New York: Three Rivers Press, 1995.

Ottley, Roi. *New World A-Coming: Inside Black America.* Boston: Houghton Mifflin, 1943.

Paterson, Thomas G., ed. *Cold War Critics: Alternatives to American Foreign Policy in the Truman Years.* Chicago: Quadrangle Books, 1971.

Phillips, Kevin. *The Politics of Rich and Poor: Wealth and the American Electorate in the Reagan Aftermath.* New York: Random House, 1990.

Pierpaoli, Paul G., Jr. *Truman and Korea: The Political Culture of the Early Cold War.* Columbia: University of Missouri Press, 1999.

Plummer, Brenda Gayle. *Rising Wind: Black Americans and U.S. Foreign Affairs, 1935–1960.* Chapel Hill: University of North Carolina Press, 1996.

———. *In Search of Power: African Americans in the Era of Decolonization, 1956–1974.* Cambridge: Cambridge University Press, 2013.

———, ed. *Window on Freedom: Race, Civil Rights, and Foreign Affairs 1945–1988.* Chapel Hill: University of North Carolina Press, 2003.

Poen, Monte M., ed. *Strictly Personal and Confidential: The Letters Harry Truman Never Mailed.* Boston: Little, Brown, 1982.

Powell, Adam Clayton, Jr. *Adam by Adam: The Autobiography of Adam Clayton Powell, Jr.* New York: Dial Press, 1971.

Rampersad, Arnold. *The Life of Langston Hughes, Volume II: 1941–1967, I Dream a World.* Oxford: Oxford University Press, 2002.

Ransby, Barbara. *Eslanda: The Large and Unconventional Life of Mrs. Paul Robeson.* New Haven: Yale University Press, 2013.

Robeson, Paul. *Here I Stand.* Boston: Beacon Press Books, 1958.

Rustin, Bayard. *Down the Line: The Collected Writings of Bayard Rustin*. Chicago: Quadrangle Books, 1971.

Sales, William W., Jr. *From Civil Rights to Black Liberation: Malcolm X and the Organization of Afro-American Unity*. Boston: South End Press, 1994.

Schapsmeier, Edward L., and Frederick H. Schapsmeier. *Prophet in Politics: Henry A. Wallace and the War Years, 1940–1965*. Ames: Iowa State University Press, 1970.

Schell, Jonathan. *The Fate of the Earth*. New York: Knopf, 1982.

Scott, William R. *The Sons of Sheba's Race*. Bloomington: Indiana University Press, 1993.

Shawki, Ahmed. *Black Liberation and Socialism*. Chicago: Haymarket Books, 2006.

Sidel, Ruth. *Keeping Women and Children Last: America's War on the Poor*. New York: Penguin Books, 1996.

Simmons, Charles A. *The African American Press: A History of News Coverage During National Crisis, with Special Reference to Four Black Newspapers, 1827–1965*. Jefferson: McFarland, 1998.

Simmons, Charles E. "Don't Dump on Us: The Environmental Justice Movement," in *Race and Resistance: African Americans in the 21st Century*, ed. Herb Boyd. Cambridge: South End Press, 2002.

Sitkoff, Harvard. "African American Militancy in the World War II South: Another Perspective," in *Remaking Dixie: The Impact of World War II on the American South*, ed. Neil R. McMillen. Jackson: University Press of Mississippi, 1997.

———. *A New Deal for Blacks: The Emergence of Civil Rights as a National Issue, Volume I: The Depression Decade*. New York: Oxford University Press, 1978.

Small, Melvin, and William D. Hoover, eds. *Give Peace a Chance: Exploring the Vietnam Antiwar Movement*. Syracuse: Syracuse University Press, 1992.

Solomon, Mark. "Black Critics of Colonialism and the Cold War," in *Cold War Critics: Alternatives to American Foreign Policy in the Truman Years*, ed. Thomas G. Paterson. Chicago: Quadrangle Books, 1971.

Stouffer, Samuel A. *The American Soldier: Adjustment During Army Life, Volume 1*. Princeton: Princeton University Press, 1949.

Stueck, William. *The Korean War: An International History*. Princeton: Princeton University Press, 1995.

Sutherland, Bill, and Matt Meyer. *Guns and Gandhi in Africa: Pan African Insights on Nonviolence, Armed Struggle and Liberation in Africa*. Trenton: Africa World Press, 2000.

Swerdlow, Amy. *Women Strike for Peace: Traditional Motherhood and Radical Politics in the 1960s*. Chicago: University of Chicago Press, 1993.

Takaki, Ronald. *Hiroshima: Why America Dropped the Atomic Bomb*. Boston: Little, Brown, 1995.

Taylor, Richard. *Against the Bomb: The British Peace Movement 1958–1965*. Oxford: Clarendon Press, 1988.

Torr, James D., ed. *Ronald Reagan*. San Diego: Greenhaven Press, 2001.

Tracy, James. *Direct Action: Radical Pacifism from the Union Eight to the Chicago Seven*. Chicago: University of Chicago Press, 1996.

Tyson, Timothy B. *Radio Free Dixie: Robert F. Williams and the Roots of Black Power*. Chapel Hill: University of North Carolina Press, 1999.

Vivian, Octavia. *Coretta: The Story of Coretta Scott King*. Minneapolis: Fortress Press, 2006.

Von Eschen, Penny M. *Race Against Empire: Black Americans and Anticolonialism, 1937–1957*. Ithaca: Cornell University Press, 1997.

———. *Satchmo Blows Up the World: Jazz Ambassadors Play the Cold War*. Cambridge: Harvard University Press, 2004.

Walker, J. Samuel. *Prompt and Utter Destruction: Truman and the Use of Atomic Bombs Against Japan*. Chapel Hill: University of North Carolina Press, 1997.

Walters, Ronald W. *South Africa and the Bomb: Responsibility and Deterrence*. Lexington: Lexington Books, 1987.

Warren, Wini. *Black Women Scientists in the United States*. Bloomington: Indiana University Press, 1999.

Washington, James M., ed. *A Testament of Hope: The Essential Writings and Speeches of Martin Luther King, Jr*. New York: HarperCollins, 1986.

Washington, Mary Helen. "Alice Childress, Lorraine Hansberry, and Claudia Jones: Black Women Write the Popular Front," in *Left of the Color Line: Race, Radicalism, and Twentieth-Century Literature in the United States*, ed. Bill V. Mullen and James Smethurst. Chapel Hill: University of North Carolina Press, 2003.

Weisbrot, Robert. *Freedom Bound: A History of America's Civil Rights Movement*. New York: Penguin Books, 1990.

Westad, Odd Arne. *The Global Cold War: Third World Interventions and the Making of Our Times*. Cambridge: Cambridge University Press, 2005.

White, Graham, and John Maze. *Henry A. Wallace: His Search for a New World Order*. Chapel Hill: University of North Carolina Press, 1995.

White, Walter. *A Man Called White: The Autobiography of Walter White*. New York: Viking Press, 1948.

Wittner, Lawrence S. *Cold War America: From Hiroshima to Watergate*. New York: Praeger, 1974.

———. *One World or None: A History of the World Nuclear Disarmament Movement Through 1953*. Stanford: Stanford University Press, 1993.

———. *Rebels Against War: The American Peace Movement, 1933–1983*. Philadelphia: Temple University Press, 1984.

———. *Resisting the Bomb: A History of the World Nuclear Disarmament Movement, 1954–1970*. Stanford: Stanford University Press, 1997.

———. *Toward Nuclear Abolition: A History of the World Nuclear Disarmament Movement, 1971 to the Present*. Stanford: Stanford University Press, 2003.

Wolffe, Richard. *Revival: The Struggle for Survival Inside the Obama White House*. New York: Crown, 2010.

Woods, Jeff. *Black Struggle, Red Scare: Segregation and Anti-Communism in the South, 1948–1968*. Baton Rouge: Louisiana State University Press, 2004.

Woodward, Bob: *Obama's Wars*. New York: Simon & Schuster, 2010.

Wynn, Neil A. *The Afro-American and the Second World War*. New York: Holmes and Meier, 1993.

X, Malcolm. *The Autobiography of Malcolm X*. New York: Ballantine Books, 1964.

Zinn, Howard. *A People's History of the United States: 1942–Present*. New York: Harper Perennial, 1995.

———. "Reagan's Economic Policies Favored the Rich," in *Ronald Reagan*, ed. James D. Torr. San Diego: Greenhaven Press, 2001.

Articles

Allen, Ernest, Jr. "When Japan Was 'Champion of the Darker Races': Satokata Takahashi and the Flowering of Black Messianic Nationalism." *Black Scholar* 24 (1994): 23–46.

Allman, Jean. "Nuclear Imperialism and the Pan-African Struggle for Peace and Freedom: Ghana, 1959–1962." *Souls* 10, no. 2 (2008): 83–102.

Anderson, Carol. "From Hope to Disillusion: African Americans, the United Nations, and the Struggle for Human Rights, 1944–1947." *Diplomatic History* 20, no. 4 (1996): 531–63.

———. "International Conscience, the Cold War, and Apartheid: The NAACP's Alliance with the Reverend Michael Scott for South West Africa's Liberation,1946–1951. *Journal of World History* 19, no. 3 (September 2008): 297–325.

Andrain, Charles F. "The Pan-African Movement: The Search for Organizations and Community." *Phylon* 23, no. 1 (1962): 5–17.

Berg, Manfred. "Black Civil Rights and Liberal Anticommunism: The NAACP in the Early Cold War." *Journal of American History* 94 (June 2007): 75–96.

Blackwell-Johnson, Joyce. "African American Activists in the Women's International League for Peace and Freedom, 1920s–1950s." *Peace and Change* 23, no. 4 (1998): 466–82.

Borstelmann, Thomas. "Jim Crow's Coming Out: Race Relations and American Foreign Policy in the Truman Years." *Presidential Studies Quarterly* 29, no. 3 (1999): 549–67.

Carter, Steven R. "Colonialism and Culture in Lorraine Hansberry's Les Blancs." *MELUS* 15, no. 1, Ethnic Women Writers V (Spring 1988): 27–46.

———. "Commitment Amid Complexity: Lorraine Hansberry's Life in Action." *MELUS* 7, no. 3, Ethnic Women Writers I (Autumn 1980): 39–53.

Darby, Henry E., and Margaret N. Rowley. "King on Vietnam and Beyond." *Phylon* 47, no. 1 (1986): 43–50.

Drake, St. Clair. "Black Studies and Global Perspectives: An Essay." *Journal of Negro Education* 53, no. 3 (1984): 226–42.

Draper, Theodore. "American Communism Revisited." *New York Review of Books* 32 (May 9, 1985): 32–37.

———. "The Popular Front Revisited." *New York Review of Books* 32 (May 30, 1985): 44–50.

Du Bois, W.E.B. "A Chronicle of Race Relations." *Phylon* 3, no. 2 (1942): 206–20.

Dudziak, Mary L. "Desegregation as a Cold War Imperative." *Stanford Law Review* 41, no. 1 (1988): 61–120.

Fairclough, Adam. "Martin Luther King, Jr. and the War in Vietnam." *Phylon* 45, no. 1 (1984): 19–39.

Falk, Florence. "Performing Artists for Nuclear Disarmament." *Performing Arts Journal* 6, no. 2 (1982): 110–11.

Farrell, James J. "Thomas Merton and the Religion of the Bomb." *Religion and American Culture* 5, no. 1 (1995): 77–98.

Finch, Roy. "The New Peace Movement–Part I." *Dissent* 15 (Winter 1963): 87–95.

———. "The New Peace Movement–Part II." *Dissent* 10 (Spring 1963): 139–48.

Friedman, Andrea. "The Strange Career of Annie Lee Moss: Rethinking Race, Gender, and McCarthysim." *Journal of American History* 94, no. 2 (2007): 445–68.

Gloster, Hugh M. "Hiroshima in Retrospect." *Phylon* 17, no. 3 (1956): 271–78.

Hellwig, David J. "Afro-American Reactions to the Japanese and the Anti-Japanese Movement, 1906–1924." *Phylon* 38, no. 1 (1977): 93–104.

Higuchi, Toshihiro. "An Environmental Origin of Antinuclear Activism in Japan, 1954–1963: The Government, the Grassroots Movement, and the Politics of Risk." *Peace and Change* 33, no. 3 (2008): 333–67.

Hogan, Nancy. "Shielded from Liability." *American Bar Association Journal* 80 (May 1994): 56–60.

Klotman, Phillis R. "Langston Hughes's Jess B. Semple and the Blues." *Phylon* 36, no. 1 (1975): 68–77.

Little, Monroe. "Remembering Hiroshima: Cultural Politics, World War II and American Consciousness." *Western Journal of Black Studies* 21, no. 1 (1997): 34–41.

Loud, Oliver Schule. "Atomic Energy—for Better or for Worse, Part II." *Phylon* 9, no. 2 (1948): 115–24.

Lucas, Helen Laville, and Scott Lucas. "The American Way: Edith Sampson, the NAACP, and African American Identity in the Cold War." *Diplomatic History* 20, no. 4 (1996): 565–90.

McKay, George. "Just a Closer Walk with Thee: New Orleans-Style Jazz and the Campaign for Nuclear Disarmament in 1950s Britain." *Popular Music* 22, no. 3 (2003): 261–81.

Meriwether, James H. "'Worth a Lot of Negro Votes': Black Voters, Africa, and the 1960 Presidential Campaign," *Journal of American History*, vol. 95, no. 3 (December 2008): 737–63.

Morgan, H. Wayne. "History and the Presidency: Harry S. Truman." *Phylon* 19, no. 2 (1958): 162–70.

Obama, Barack. "Breaking the War Mentality." *Sundial* (March 10, 1983): 2–5.

Okihiro, Gary Y., and Julie Sly. "The Press, Japanese Americans, and the Concentration Camps." *Phylon* 44, no. 1 (1983): 66–83.

Parker, Jason C. "Cold War II: The Eisenhower Administration, the Bandung Conference, and the Reperiodization of the Postwar Era." *Diplomatic History* 30, no. 5 (2006): 867–92.

———. "'Made-in-America Revolutions'? The 'Black University' and the American Role in the Decolonization of the Black Atlantic." *Journal of American History* 96, no. 3 (December 2009): 727–50.

Powell, Adam Clayton, Jr. "Is This a 'White Man's War'?" *Common Sense* 10, no. 4 (April 1942): 111–12.

Reed, Merl E. "The FBI, MOWM, and CORE, 1941–1946." *Journal of Black Studies* 21, no. 4 (1991): 465–79.

Roark, James L. "American Black Leaders: The Response to Colonialism and the Cold War, 1943–1953." *African Historical Studies* 4, no. 2 (1971): 253–70.

Sawyer, Mary R. "The Fraternal Council of Negro Churches, 1934–1964." *Church History* 59 (1990): 51–61.

Scott, William R. "Black Nationalism and the Italo-Ethiopian Conflict, 1934–1936." *Journal of Negro History* 63, no. 2 (1978): 118–34.

Stone, Oliver, and Peter Kuznick. "Barack's Betrayal." *New Statesman* (April 11, 2011): 40–41.

Sundquist, Eric F. "Who Was Langston Hughes?" *Commentary* 102, no. 6 (1996): 55–59.

Wilkerson, Margaret B. "The Sighted Eyes and Feeling Heart of Lorraine Hansberry." *Black American Literature Forum* 17, no. 1, Black Theatre Issue (Spring 1983): 8–13.

Electronic Sources

"AP Sources: Obama Edges Toward Decision on Plan That Could Mean Large New Cuts in Nuclear Arms." *Washington Post*, July 3, 2012. http://www.washingtonpost.com/world/national-security/Obama-edging-...stantial-new-cuts-in-nuclear-arms/2012/07/03/gJQAD4CwJW_print.html.

Baker, Peter. "Obama's Gamble on Arms Pact Pays Off." *New York Times*, December 22, 2010. http://www.nytimes.com/2010/12/23/world/23start.html?r=1&pagewanted=all.

Bechtel, Marilyn. "On the 60th Anniversary of Hiroshima and Nagasaki." *People's Weekly World*, July 28, 2005. http://www.pww.org/article/view/7477/1/280/.

Becker, Jo, and Scott Shane. "Secret 'Kill List' Proves a Test of Obama's Principles and Will." *New York Times*, May 29, 2012. http://www.nytimes.com/2012/05/29/world/obamas-leadership-in-war-on-al-quaeda.html.

Bell, Alexandra. "Obama's Vision Has Turned into Concrete Victories." *The Hill*, April 15, 2010. http://www.thehill.com/blogs/congress-blog/politics/92407-obamas-vision-has-turned-into-concrete-victories.

"The Bloated Nuclear Weapons Budget." *New York Times*, October 10, 2011. http://www.nytimes.com/2011/10/30/opinion/sunday/the-bloated-nuclear-weapons-budget.html.

Bohan, Suzanne. "Obama Kills Controversial Nuclear Program in Budget Proposal." *Contra Costa Times*, March 5, 2009. http://www.contracostatimes.com/fdcp?1237396983362.

Borger, Julian. "Obama Accused of Nuclear U-Turn as Guided Weapons Plan Emerges." *The Guardian*, April 21, 2013. http://www.theguardian.com/world/2013/apr/21/obama-accused-nuclear-guided-weapons-plan.

Branigin, William. "Last of Syria's Chemical Weapons Handed Over for Destruction, International Boby Says." *Washington Post*, June 23, 2014. http://www.washingtonpost.com/world/middle_east/agency-last-of-syri...ruction/2014/06/23/4eb9a138-fad9-11e3-8176-f2c941cf35f1_story.html.

Broad, William J., and David E. Sanger. "Obama's Youth Shaped His Nuclear Free Vision." *New York Times*, July 5, 2009. http://www.nytimes.com/2009/07/05/world/05nuclear.html?pagewanted=all.

Burns, Robert. "Panetta Asks Israel for Patience on Iran." *Associated Press*, August 1, 2012. http://www.abcnews.com/Internional/wireStory/panetta-us-force-option-iran-nukes-16902791#.UBqA817-KJU.

———. "US Weighing Steep Nuclear Arms Cuts." *Associated Press*, February 14, 2012. http://www.boston.com/new/nation/washington/articles/2012/02/14/ap_newsbreak_us_weighing_steep_nuclear_arms_cuts.

Cirincione, Joseph. "Exploding Budgets." *Time*, October 10, 2012. http://nation.time.com/2012/10/10/exploding-budgets/.

———. "Some Nuclear Sunshine." *Yes!*, May 4, 2010. http://www.Yesmagazine.org/peace-justice/some-nuclear-sunshine.

———. "Susan Rice on Nuclear Weapons." *Huffington Post*, June 5, 2013. http://www.huffingtonpost.com/joe-cirincione/susan-rice-on-nuclear-wea_b_3390019.html.

———. "Will Obama End the Nuclear Era?" *Daily Beast*, April 12, 2010. http://www.thedailybeast.com/articles/2010/04/12/will-obama-end-the-nuclear-era.html.

Clemons, Steve. "Obama's Nuclear Wizardry and the Iran Factor." *Politico*, April 13, 2010. http://www.politico.com/news/stories/0410/35691.html.

Coates, Ta-Nehisi Paul. "Is Obama Black Enough?" *Time*, February 1, 2007. http://www.time.com/time/nation/article/0,8599,1584736,00.html.

Coley, Anthony. "An Open Letter to Tavis Smiley." *CNN.com*, March 19, 2010. http://articles.cnn.com/2010-03-19/opinion/coley.obama.tavis.smiley_1_african-American-african-americans-accountable?_s=PM;OPINION.

Crowley, Michael. "A Unifying Theme for Obama's Foreign Policy." *Time*, September 23, 2013. http://swampland.time.com/2013/09/23/barack-obama-and-the-wmd-threat/.

Daley, Tad. "How Reagan Brought the World to the Brink of Nuclear Destruction." *Alternet*, February 7, 2011. http://www.alternet.org/module/printversion/149821.

Davenport, Kelsey. "Myanmar Signs Agreement with IAEA." *Arms Control Today*, October 2013. http://www.armscontrol.org/act/2013_10/Myanmar-Signs-Agreement-With-IAEA.

Dyson, Michael Eric. "On Dr. King, Jesse Jackson, Al Sharpton, and Barack Obama." *Big Think*. http://www.bigthink.com/ideas/862.

Egusa, Noritaka. "Nuclear Weapons Can Be Eliminated: Hiroshima, Nagasaki Mayors Call for Obama's 'World Without Nuclear Weapons.'" Hiroshima Peace Center, May 8, 2009. http://www.hiroshimapeacemedia.jp/mediacenter/article.php?story=20090507132132807_en.

Epstein, William. "Uncertain Prospects for UNSSOD III." *Peace* 4, no. 3 (June–July 1988): 14. http://archive.peacemagazine.org/v04n3p14.htm.

Erwin, Sandra I. "A Test for U.S. Nuclear Weapons: Can They Beat the Sequester?" *National Defense*, November 24, 2013. http://www.nationaldefensemagazine.org/blog/Lists/Posts/Post.aspx?ID=1347.

Fackler, Martin. "At Hiroshima Ceremony, a First for a U.S. Envoy." *New York Times*, August 6, 2010. http://www.nytimes.com/2010/08/07/world/asia/07japan.html.

Feaver, Peter D. "Obama's Nuclear Modesty." *New York Times*, April 9, 2010. http://www.nytimes.com/2010/04/09/opinion/09feaver.html?pagewanted=all.

Fichelberger, Erika, and Dana Liebelson. "How Obama Learned to Love the Bomb." *Mother Jones*, April 23, 2013. http://www.motherjones.com/politics/2013/04/obama-budget-nuclear-nonproliferation-stockpile%20.

Frates, Chris. "McConnell Tells the Alley How He'd Run the Senate Next Year." *Nation Journal*, July 9, 2012. http://influencealley.nationaljournal.com/2012/07/Mcconnell-tells-the-alley-how.php.

Froomkin, Dan. "Barack Obama's Broken Nuclear Promises Undermine Success." *Huffington Post*, March 28, 2012. http://www.huffingtonpost.com/2012/03/27Barack-obama-nuclear-policy_n_1383081.html.

Fung, Katherine. "Al Sharpton, Melissa Harris-Perry Clash With Cornel West." *Huffington Post*, February 8, 2012. http://www.huffingtonpost.com/2012/02/08/al-sharpton-melissa-harris-perry-cornel-west_n_1263522.html.

Garrett, Major. "What Obama's Nuclear Security Summit Means for Iran and North Korea." *The Atlantic*, March 2012. http://www.theatlantic.com/international/print/2012/03/what-obamas-nuclear-security-summit-means-for-iran-and-north korea/255026/.

Gershman, Carl. "The World According to Andrew Young." *Commentary*, August 1978. http://www.commentarymagazine.com/article/the-world-according-to-andrew-young/.

Goldberg, Jeffrey. "Obama to Iran and Israel: 'As President of the United States, I Don't Bluff.'" *The Atlantic*, March 2, 2012. http://www.theatlantic.com/International/archive/2012/03/Obama-to-iran-and-israel-as-president-of-the-united-states-i-dont-bluff-/253875/.

"The GOP Is Wrong to Say Obama Cut Nuclear Weapons Budget." *Washington Post*, August 31, 2012. http://articles.washingtonpost.com/2012-08-31/opinions/35490294_1_nuclear-weapons-nuclear-warheads-and-bombs-nuclear-stockpile.

Gorbachev, Mikhail. "The Senate's Next Task: Ratifying the Nuclear Test Ban Treaty." *New York Times*, December 28, 2010. http://www.nytimes.com/2010/12/29/opinion/29gorbachev.html.

Grim, Ryan, and Joshua Hersh. "Iran Sanctions Bill from Senators Bob Menendez and Mark Kirk Could Endanger U.S. Negotiations." *Huffington Post*, December 19, 2013. http://www.huffingtonpost.com/2013/12/19/iran-sanctions-bill_n_4472439.html.

Guarino, Douglas P. "Compromise Bill Limits Restrictions on Nuclear Arms Control Efforts." *National Journal*, December 12, 2013. http://www.nationaljournal.com/global-security-newswire/compromise-bill-limits-restrictions-on-nuclear-arms-control-efforts-20131212.

Hanley, Charles J. "Analysis: Nuclear Summit Signals New Mindset." *Associated Press*, April 14, 2010. http://www.wlfi.com/dpps/news/nationa/south/analysis-nuclear-Summit-signals-new-mindset-jgr_3314263.

Harris-Perry, Melissa. "Barack Obama and Martin Luther King, Jr." *The Nation*, January 18, 2010. http://www.alternet/org/story/145237/.

Hart, Benjamin. "Jeremy Scahill Says Obama Strikes in Yemen Constitute Murder." *Huffington Post*, June 3, 2012. http://www.huffingtonpost.com/2012/06/02/Jeremy-scahill-says-drone-strikes-murders_n_1565441.html.

Hedges, Chris. "The Obama Deception: Why Cornel West Went Ballistic." *Truthdig*, May 16, 2011. http://www.truthdig/com/report/item/the_obama_deception_why_Cornel_west_went_ballistic_20110516/.

"Hiroshima Mayor Hits U.S. Subcritical Nuke Test." *Kyodo News*, October 14, 2010. http://search.japantimes.co.jp/printnn20101014a3.html.

"Hiroshima, Nagasaki Warn Obama on Plutonium Tests," *Japan Times*, August 21, 2013. http://www.japantimes.co.jp/news/2013/08/21/national/hiroshima-nagasaki-warn-obama-on-plutonium-tests/.

Hoffman, David E. "Hey, Big Spender." *Foreign Policy*, October 22, 2012. http://www.foreignpolicy.com/articles/2012/10/22/hey_big_spender#sthash.z7F4FRBy.dpbs.

Ignatius, David. "Iran Committed to Making a Deal." *Washington Post*, December 16, 2013. http://www.washingtonpost.com/opinions/david-ignatius-iran-committed-to-making-a-deal/2013/12/15/0261a632-65c4-11e3-a0b9-249bbb34602c_story.html.

———. "Obama's Policy Process More Orderly Than Bush's." *Washington Post*, April 14, 2010. http://www.azstarnet.com/news/opinion/article_f3394656-494d-5de9-86c4-f4e619d31694.html.

In Our Hands. United States: New Star Video. VHS. 2002.

"Japan Alarmed at U.S. Subcritical Test." *Asahi Shimbun*, October 14, 2010. http://www.asahi.com/english/TKY201010140308.htm.

Kanazaki, Yumi. "Hiroshima Responds to U.S. Ratification of New START Treaty." Hiroshima Peace Media Center, December 24, 2010. http://www.hiroshimapeacemedia.jp/Mediacenter/article/php?story=20101224141458104_en.

———. "U.S. Responds to Letter of Protest from Hiroshima Against Subcritical Nuclear Test." Hiroshima Peace Media Center, January 14, 2011. http://www.Hiroshimapeacemedia.jp/mediacenter/article.php?story=2011011411095432_en.

Katz, William Loren. "Harry Belafonte Reaffirms a Proud Tradition." *Black World Today*, January 26, 2006. http://www.tbwt.org/index.php ?option=content&task=view&id=656&Itemid=41.

Kenner, David. "The President Who Went Nuclear." *Foreign Policy*, December 1, 2013. http://www.foreignpolicy.com/articles/2013/12/01/obama_nuclear_weapons_middle_east#sthash.undP5at7.dpbs.

Kimball, Daryl. "Arms Control Association Praises Obama's Commitment to a Nuclear Weapons Free World." *Arms Control Association*, April 5, 2009. http://www.Arms control.org/pressroom/ObamaPragueSpeech.

———. "Obama's Prague Agenda Two Years On." *Arms Control Now*, April 4, 2011. http://armscontrolnow.org/2011/04/04/obamas-prague-agenda-two-years-on/.

Kornblut, Anne E. "Clinton Demurs on Obama's Nuclear Stance." *Washington Post*, August 3, 2007. http://www.washingtonpost.com.wp-dyn/content/article/2007/08/02/AR2007080202288.html.

Kreisler, Harry, "Legislating for the People: Conversation with Ronald V. Dellums." February 10, 2000. http://globetrotter.berkeley.edu/people/Dellums/dellums-cono.html.

Kuznick, Peter. "The Decision to Risk the Future: Harry Truman, the Atomic Bomb, and the Apocalyptic Narrative." *Japan Focus*, July 30, 2007. http://www.japanfocus.org/products/details/2479.

Lee, Carol E., and Glenn Thrush. "Barack Obama Vows to Work with GOP After 'Shellacking.'" *Politico*, November 3, 2010. http://www.politico.com/news/stories/1110/44657.html.

Lee, M. J. "U.S. Defuses Biggest Nuke." *Politico*, October 25, 2011. http://www.politico.com/printstory.cfm?uuid=DD9DA181-ABC9-4DD1-81E0-C2F773F781EC.

Lockette, Tim. "Rogers Amendment Pushes Back at Obama's Nuke Cuts." *Anniston Star*, July 23, 2013. http://annistonstar.com/view/full_story/23198989/article-Rogers-amendment-pushes-back-at-Obama-nuke-cuts.

Loehrke, Benjamin. "When the Nuclear Budget Binge Ended." *Ploughshares Fund*, February 14, 2012. http://ploughshares.org/blog/2012-02-14/when-nuclear-budget-binge-ended.

Madhani, Aamar. "Obama: U.S. and Russia Should Further Reduce Nuke Stockpiles." *USA Today*, March 26, 2012. http://content.usatoday.com/communities/theoval/post/2012/03/Obama-us-russia-should-further-reduce-nuke-stockpile/1#.T3MX45j-KJU.

"Malcolm X Speaking in Cairo." July 1964. http://www.columbia.edu/cu/ccbh/mxp.

Mason, Jeff, and Fredrik Dahl. "U.S. to Help in 'Elimination' of Sensitive Japanese Nuclear Stockpile." *Reuters*, March 24, 2014. http://www.reuters.com/article/2014/03/24/us-nuclear-usa-japan-idUSBREA2NOIK20140324.

Maxwell, Zerlina. "Al Sharpton Defends Melissa Harris-Perry from Cornel West's 'Arrogant' and 'Disingenuous' Attacks." *The Grio*, February 8, 2012. http://www.thegrio.com/2012/02/08/al-sharpton-defends-melissa-harris-perry-from-cornel-west/.

McCurry, Justin. "John Roos Is First US Representative to Attend Hiroshima Memorial Ceremony in Japan." *The Guardian*, August 6, 2010. http://www.guardian.co.uk/World/2010/aug/06/john-roos-us-attends-hiroshima-japan.

Miller, Joshua Rhett. "Son of Pilot Who Dropped A-Bomb Opposes Plan to Send U.S. Delegation to Hiroshima Ceremony." *FoxNews.com*, August 4, 2010. http://www .Foxnews.com/politics/2010/08/04/tibbets-son-disapproves-plan-send-delegation -Hiroshima-ceremony/.

Mooney, Alexander. "Obama Says Time to Rid World of Nuclear Weapons." *CNN.com*, July 16, 2008. http://www.cnn.com/2008/POLITICS/07/16/obama.speech/.

"Myanmar Says It's Ready to Sign Nuclear Agreement." *CBS News*, November 21, 2012. http://www.cbsnews.com/8301-505245_162-57553105/myanmar-says-its-ready -to-sign-nuclear-agreement/.

"Nagasaki, Hiroshima Criticize U.S. for Subcritical Nuclear Test." *Kyodo News*, October 13, 2010. http://www.japantoday.com/category/national/view/nagasaki-hiroshima -criticizes-us-for-subcritical-nuclear-test.

"The Nuclear 'Implementation Study.'" *New York Times*, March 11, 2012. http://www .nytimes.com/20102/03/12/opinion/the-nuclear-implementation-study.html.

Nuclear Posture Review Report. Department of Defense, April 2010. http://www.defense. Gov/npr/docs/2010%20Nuclear%20Posture%20Review%20Report.pdf.

"Obama Echoes JFK Speech—The One on Nukes." *USA Today*, June 21, 2013. http://www .usatoday.com/story/theoval/2013/06/19/obama-kennedy-berlin-nuclear-weapons -american-university/2437599/.

"Obama Prague Speech on Nuclear Weapons, Full Text." *Huffington Post*, May 6, 2009. http://www.huffingtonpost.com/2009/04/05/obama-prague-speech-on-nu_n_183 219.html.

"Obama Remarks at Hankuk University, South Korea, March 2012." *Council on Foreign Relations*, March 26, 2012. http://www.cfr.org/south-korea/obamas-remarks-hankuk -university-south-korea-march-2012/p27733.

"Obama: Use of Nuclear Weapons 'Not on the Table.'" *MSNBC.com*, August 2, 2007. http:// www.msnbc.com/.

O'Donnell, Maureen. "Panel Criticizes Obama's Handling of Black Agenda." *Chicago Sun Times*, March 21, 2010. http://www.suntimes.com/news/politics/obama/2114506,CST -NWS-black21.article.

Palmer, Elizabeth. "Iran Committed to Deal with the U.S., Foreign Minister Says." *CBS News*, December 16, 2013. http://www.cbsnews.com/news/iran-committed-to-deal -with-the-us-foreign-minister-says/.

"Possible Nuclear Weapons Cuts Worry Republican Lawmakers." *iWatch News*, March 5, 2012. http://www.iwatchnews.org/ 2012/03/05/8313/possible-nuclear-weapons -cuts-worry-republican-lawmakers.

Priest, Dana. "Aging U.S. Nuclear Arsenal Slated for Costly and Long-Delayed Moderniza-tion." *Washington Post*, September 15, 2012. http://articles. washingtonpost.com/2012- 09-15/world/35497119_1_nuclear-stockpile-nuclear-weapons-nuclear-facilities.

———. "The B61 Bomb: A Case in Study in Costs and Needs." *Washington Post*, September 16, 2012. http://articles.washingtonpost.com/2012-09-16/world/ 35496610_1_b61s-nuclear-weapons-nuclear-strategists.

Reid, Tim. "President Obama Seeks Russia Deal to Slash Nuclear Weapons." *The Times*, February 4, 2009. http://www.timesonline.co.uk/tol/news/world/us_and_americas/Article5654836.ece.

Robinson, Greg. "Paul Robeson and Japanese Americans." *Nichi Bei Times* (San Francisco), March 13, 2008. http://www.blackpast.org/?q=perspectives/paul-robeson-and-japanese-americans-1942-1949.

Rudner, Bob. "A Long Way to Go to Be Ignored: The Last Atomic Veterans." *WISE News Communique*, March 15, 1996. http://www.10.antenna.nl/wise/ 448/4444.html.

Rustin, Bayard. "In Apprehension How Like a God!" 1948. http://pamphlets.quaker.org/wpl1948a.html.

Sagan, Scott. "After the Nuclear Posture Review: Obama's Disarming Influence." *Bulletin of Atomic Scientists*, April 19, 2011. http://www.thebulletin.org/print/web-edition/features/after-the-nuclear-posture-review-obamas-disarming-influence.

Sanger, David. "Obama Nuclear Agenda Only Gets Harder After Treaty." *New York Times*, December 21, 2010. http://www.nytimes.com/2010/12/22/us/politics/22assess.html.

Sanger, David, and Peter Baker. "Obama Limits When U.S. Would Use Nuclear Arms." *New York Times*, April 5, 2010. http://www.nytimes.com/2010/04/06/world/06arms.html?pagewanted=all.

Schneidmiller, Chris. "Obama Moving on Nuclear Arms Control Pledges, Expert Says. *Global Security Newswire*, February 17, 2009. http://www.nti.org/gsn/article/Obama-moving-on-nuclear-arms-control-pledges-expert-says/.

Scott-Heron, Gil. *From South Africa to South Carolina*. CD. Re-released April 7, 1998. Original release 1976.

Sheridan, Mary Beth. "Obama Secures 47-Nation Pact at Nuclear Summit." *Washington Post*, April 14, 2010. http://www.washingtonpost.com/wp-dyn/content/article/2010/04/13/AR2010041300427.html.

"Smiley and Sharpton Spar over Black Agenda, Obama." *Black America*, February 25, 2010. http://www.blackamericaweb.com/?q=articles/news/moving_america_news/16617/.

Smith, R. Jeffrey. "Obama Proposes Shifting Funds from Nuclear Nonproliferation to Nuclear Weapons." Center for Public Integrity, April 9, 2013. http://www.publicintegrity.org/2013/04/09/12467/obama-proposes-shifting-funds-nuclear-nonproliferation-nuclear-weapons.

"South Carolina Debate: Why Would Dr. King Endorse You?" http://www.youtube.com /watch?v=-pkkdjngBuo.

Spillius, Alex. "Barack Obama Accused of Not Doing Enough for Black People." *The Telegraph*, December 22, 2009. http://www.telegraph.co.uk/news/worldnews/Barackobama/6868202/Barack-Obama-accused-of-not-doing-enough-for-black-people.html.

Superville, Darlene. "US Helped Czech Republic Remove Nuclear Material." *Seattle Times*, April 5, 2013. http://seattletimes.com/html/politics/2020716628_ apususnuclearsecurity.html.

Terry, Don. "A Delicate Balancing Act for the Black Agenda." *New York Times*, March 18, 2010. http://www.nytimes.com/2010/03/19/us/19cncagenda.html?pagewanted=all.

Thompson, Mark. "Obama's Nuclear War." *Time*, January 26, 2009. http://www.time.Com/
    time/nation/article/0,8599,187,3887,00.html.

"Throwing Money at Nukes." *New York Times*, May 26, 2013. http://www.nytimes.com/
    2013/05/27/opinion/throwing-money-at-nukes.html?_r=0.

Tollefson, Jeff. "U.S. Nuclear Warheads Set to Get a Facelift." *Scientific American*, May 7,
    2013. http://www.scientificamerican.com/article.cfm?id=us-nuclear-warheads
    -set-to-get-a-facelift.

Truman, Harry S. "Address Before a Joint Session of Congress." March 12, 1947. http://
    www.yale.edu/lawweb/avalon/trudoc.htm.

"U.S. Conducts 1st Subcritical Nuclear Test Under Obama." *Kyodo News*, October 13, 2010.
    http://mdn.mainichi.jp/mdnnews/news/20101013p2g00m0dm072000c.html.

"US Envoy Caroline Kennedy Visits Nagasaki." *Washington Post*, December 9, 2013. http://
    www.washingtonpost.com/world/asia_pacific/us-envoy-caroline-kennedy-visits
    -nagasaki/2013/12/09/870b3d14-613f-11e3-a7b4-4a75ebc432ab_story.html.

Weinstein, Adam. "Obama May Ditch Most US Nukes." *Mother Jones*, February 17, 2012.
    http://www.motherjones.com/politics/2012/02/nucleard-weapons-reduction-obama.

Willis, Jack, Saul Landau, and Penny Bernstein. *Paul Jacobs and the Nuclear Gang*. United
    States: Cinema Guild. DVD. 1978.

Wilson, Scott. "Obama, in Berlin, Calls for U.S., Russia to Cut Nuclear Warheads."
    Washington Post, June 19, 2003. http://articles.washingtonpost.com/2013-06-19/
    world/40054173_1_brandenburg-gate-president-obama-berlin-wall.

Wittner, Lawrence S. "The Forgotten Alliance of African Nationalists and Western Paci-
    fists." March 19, 2007. http://www.zmag.org/znet/viewArticle/1798.

Wolfsthal, Jon. "The US Trillion Dollar Nuclear Triad." James Martin Center for Nonprolif-
    eration Studies, January 7, 2014. http://www.nonproliferation.org/us-trillion-dollar
    -nuclear -triad/.

Zeleny, Jeff. "Obama to Urge Elimination of Nuclear Weapons." *New York Times*, October
    2, 2007. http://www.nytimes.com/2007/10/02/us/politics/02obama.html.

Zenko, Micah. "The 2012 Nuclear Security Summit: Obama's Work in Progress." *Coun-
    cil on Foreign Relations*, March 27, 2012. http://blogs.cfr.org/zenko/2012/ 03/27/
    the-2012-nuclear-security-summit-obamas-work-in-progress/.

Interview
Johnson, Greg. Interviewed by author. December 30, 2013. Silver Spring, Md.

Index

Stanford Nuclear Age Series

(*Stanford Nuclear Age Series continues on next page*)

The Fate of the Earth and The Abolition
Jonathan Schell With a
New Introduction by the Author
2000

The Struggle Against the Bomb:
Volume Two, Resisting the Bomb,
A History of the World Nuclear
Disarmament Movement, 1954–1970
By Lawrence S. Wittner
1997

James B. Conant:
Harvard to Hiroshima and the
Making of the Nuclear Age
By James G. Hershberg
1993

The Struggle Against the Bomb:
Volume One, One World or None, A History
of the World Nuclear Disarmament
Movement Through 1953
By Lawrence S. Wittner
1993

A Preponderance of Power:
National Security, the Truman
Administration, and the Cold War
By Melvyn P. Leffler
1992

The Wizards of Armageddon
By Fred Kaplan New Foreword
by Martin J. Sherwin
1983, reissued 1991

Robert Oppenheimer:
Letters and Recollections
Edited by Alice Kimball Smith
and Charles Weiner,
New Foreword by Martin J. Sherwin
1980, reissued 1995

The Advisors: Oppenheimer,
Teller, and the Superbomb
Herbert F. York, with a New Preface and
Epilogue Historical Essay by Hans A. Bethe
1976, reissued 1989

The Voice of the Dolphins and Other Stories
By Leo Szilard
1961, expanded in 1991 with an
introduction by Barton J. Bernstein

Atomic Energy for Military Purposes
By Henry D. Smyth Preface by Philip Morrison
1945, reissued with New Foreword, 1989